Reaching *for the* Skies

IVAN·RENDALL
Reaching
for the
Skies

BBC
BOOKS

TITLE-PAGE
The Lockheed SR-71 Blackbird:
the fastest production aircraft in the world

HALF-TITLE
Learning to ride the wind:
Otto Lilienthal, pioneer glider pilot

Published by BBC Books
a division of BBC Enterprises Limited
Woodlands, 80 Wood Lane, London W12 0TT

First published 1988

© CBS Inc., John Gau and Ivan Rendall 1988

ISBN 0 563 20680 2

Set in 11 on 14pt Monophoto Plantin Light
and printed and bound in England by Butler & Tanner Limited
Frome and London
Colour separations by Technik Limited, Berkhamsted
Jacket printed by Belmont Press, Northampton

CONTENTS

INTRODUCTION

As a piece of applied science the aeroplane has a place alongside the wheel, gunpowder, the printing press and the steam engine as one of the great levers of change in world history. The effect of aircraft on the way we live has been profound: they have shrunk the world, mingling previously isolated cultures, they have added a new and menacing dimension to warfare, spawned new technologies, created new economic zones and given us a toehold in Space.

The speed of the technical advances which have wrought those developments is startling: a single lifetime is all that separates us from a generation for whom aeroplanes were little more than a centuries-old dream. Interviewing pioneer aviators for the television series *Reaching for the Skies*, we heard a number of variations on the story: 'I met Louis Blériot, the first man to fly across the Channel in 1909, and John Young, the first Shuttle pilot in 1981.'

The impetus behind the scale and pace of the progress in aviation has been people – people of ingenuity, people with stark, physical courage, people who persisted with their ideas, often in the face of failure and ridicule, people of vision. Benjamin Franklin, the American statesman and scientist famous for his experiments with kites as lightning-conductors, watched Professor Jacques Charles launch his first hydrogen balloon in Paris in 1783. 'What use is it?' asked a scornful onlooker. Franklin's response went straight to the heart of scientific experiment: 'What use is a new-born babe?'

Vision coupled with a scientific mind and an ability to tinker and experiment are the very stuff of the pioneers of aviation. An English baronet, Sir George Cayley, had just such a mind. As a young man he grappled with the problems of heavier-than-air flight and by 1799 he had mastered the principles. He embodied his ideas in a drawing of a glider which he inscribed on a silver disc for posterity. Then he set about testing his theories with experiments. By 1809 he had built the world's first model glider and wrote up his work in a series of seminal articles. Today he is acknowledged as the father of the science of aeronautics but his work caused barely a ripple in established scientific circles at the time.

The world had to wait a century before Orville and Wilbur Wright combined a glider with an internal com-

OPPOSITE: The Grumman X-29: the latest in America's X Series of experimental aircraft which are constantly increasing our understanding of the art and science of flight

THE FATHER OF AERONAUTICS

In 1809 Sir George Cayley wrote that the problem of heavier-than-air flight was 'confined within these limits – to make a surface support a given weight by the application of power to the resistance of air'. What he lacked was the power. In 1853, aged 80, he built a glider which carried a man on a short flight.

RIGHT: Sir George Cayley
OPPOSITE: One side of the disc bears his idea for a glider; the other the forces of lift, drag and thrust
BELOW: A replica of Cayley's model glider: it had a movable tailplane and an adjustable weight to change its centre of gravity

bustion engine to usher in the aviation age. Like Cayley they were methodical and scientific in their approach but they had, too, the raw courage needed to put their work to the test and make the first powered and manned flights. A young American engineer, Ken Kellett, reconstructed one of their gliders (page 50) and flew a replica of their famous Flyer for *Reaching for the Skies*. One of the few people to have experienced anything like the Wrights, it was their 'bravery' which struck him. He is a trained pilot; they were testing the ungainly machine for the first time while still learning to fly themselves.

Engine power has always been at the heart of progress in aviation. Less than thirty years after the Wright Brothers' flights a young RAF officer, Frank Whittle, realised that piston engines would reach the limit of their ability to power aircraft ever faster, higher and further, and with ever bigger loads. A new power source would be needed and in 1930 he patented the gas turbine, or jet, engine. He told us how the established interests of the aircraft industry were sceptical of a young man whose ideas would make their products obsolete, but he persisted on his own and produced the power which opened up a second age in aviation – the Jet Age.

Each hurdle in the story of aviation has been overcome by a mixture of inquisitiveness, persistence, ingenuity and courage. After the war, the next great hurdle was to fly faster than sound. In an interview for the programme 'The Quest for Speed', the British test pilot Capt. Eric 'Winkle' Brown likened the challenge to a combination of splitting the atom for the scientist while climbing Mount Everest

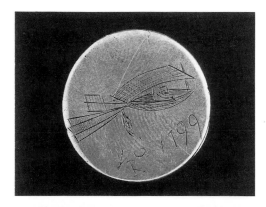

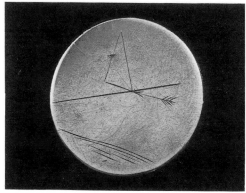

The X-29 (see p. 6) has been built to explore forward-swept wings, an idea which originated nearly half a century ago but which has had to wait until stronger materials than metal alloys had been developed. In America Lockheed has undertaken many high-technology projects, some of them secret. Its SR-71 Blackbird strategic reconnaissance aircraft (title-page picture) flies for hours at a time at over three times the speed of sound on the verge of space. The intricate web of technologies which enable it to do so were developed specially for the purpose by a team of engineers and pilots led by a legendary figure in aircraft design, Kelly Johnson. Lockheed's Ben Rich told us: 'If you can think of it, we can do it, but the question is can we afford it?'

If the human qualities needed for pioneering aviation have not changed, what has changed is the cost. When the Shuttle flew in 1981, it had taken the financial muscle of the world's richest economy combined with the technical expertise of thousands of people in hundreds of companies in the world's most technically advanced country to build it. Yet even as the Shuttle was being built, an aeronautical engineer in California, Burt Rutan, was pioneering small lightweight aircraft with new shapes and new materials which could be built by enthusiasts at home. They were lighter, more efficient and above all cheaper. In 1986 his brother Dick, with copilot Jeanna Yeager, flew an experimental aircraft based on that work, Voyager, round the world on a single tank of fuel. They returned to much acclaim and enthusiasm. But there were echoes of 1783. 'What good is it?' asked the sceptics. Benjamin Franklin should have been at Edwards Air Force Base to tell them.

for the pilot. It was a step into the unknown every bit as great as Christopher Columbus setting out across a flat Earth and sailing ever westwards. The man who did it for the first time, General Charles 'Chuck' Yeager, was fatalistic about the risks. He told us: 'It didn't make any difference to me whether the X-1 blew into a million pieces or not because I couldn't do anything about that, so you put it out of your mind.' Within days of the fiftieth anniversary of the Wright Brothers' flights, 'Chuck' Yeager flew at two and a half times the speed of sound. Less than a decade later Man was in Space.

Pioneering in aviation is a continuous process though the goals change. The simple pursuit of more speed, height, range and size has given way to research into new materials, new technologies and new ways to solve old problems.

CHAPTER·ONE

LIGHTER THAN AIR

Paris was unusually restless on 27 August 1783. It was a rainy day yet there was a sense of occasion in the city: thousands of curious citizens were making their way to the Champ-de-Mars where Professor Jacques Charles, of the Academy of Sciences, was preparing to conduct an experiment.

By late afternoon the park was packed. For those who had paid in advance there was an enclosure, but thousands of eager latecomers had to scramble for whatever vantage points were left on high ground and rooftops. At 5 o'clock a canon fired; Professor Charles and his team stood back; a silken globe, twelve feet in diameter, rose above the awestruck crowd, getting smaller and smaller the higher it flew, until it disappeared into the clouds. It was the first-ever free flight of a hydrogen balloon. It landed eleven miles away near the village of Gonesse. The villagers – less sophisticated folk than the Parisians – thought it was a dragon and hacked it to death.

The end of The Globe after its 45-minute flight

Within a month Parisians were treated to an even greater spectacle. King Louis XVI and Queen Marie Antoinette assembled with their Court at Versailles to watch Joseph and Jacques Montgolfier give a demonstration of a hot-air balloon. It was three times the size of Professor Charles's and underneath it there hung a cage containing a sheep, a duck and a cockerel. Shrouded in evil-smelling smoke, the balloon lifted off and was carried away on the breeze. It landed eight miles away in the Vaucresson Forest where the animals escaped. The King presented the Montgolfiers with the Order of St Michel.

It was clearly only a matter of time before a man would fly in a balloon. The King decided that criminals should be used for the experiment but a young nobleman, François Pilâtre de Rozier, protested – to be the first man to fly was a great honour not a punishment. He volunteered but the King demurred, so he enlisted the support of the Marquis d'Arlandes, who succeeded in changing the King's mind. But such favours had a price: d'Arlandes wanted to share the honour of flying in the balloon; by October the pair were experimenting with the Montgolfiers, using a tethered balloon.

On 21 November 1783 they were ready. This time the venue was a royal palace in the Bois de Boulogne. There had been no publicity but the Paris grapevine ensured that thousands turned out to watch. The Montgolfiers super-vised the final preparations: a last-minute repair to the canopy, stoking the fires in the launching box, and checking the restraining ropes as the canopy billowed upwards. De Rozier and d'Arlandes climbed aboard, one on either side of the gallery to balance it. A wire basket, filled with burning straw, was attached underneath; the fabric tightened. When it was full of hot air, the ropes were released and the great blue and gold balloon rose majestically above a sea of upturned faces. The pilots doffed their hats to the silent, mesmerised crowd.

In minutes they were high above the city and looking down on a sight never seen before – Paris laid out like a map. It was breathtaking. D'Arlandes put more straw on the fire and they rose to around 1500 feet, where all Paris could see them. They looked serene but on board there was something of an emergency: the fabric had caught fire. Fortunately they were able to put it out. After 25 minutes aloft they let the fire die and began a gentle descent, landing just over five miles from the palace.

Public interest was now enormous. Two weeks later, on 1 December, over 400,000 people turned out at the Tuileries to watch Professor Charles, accompanied by Noel Robert (a craftsman who had developed a way of coating silk with rubber to make balloons), make the first manned flight in a hydrogen-filled balloon. On that first flight they covered 27 miles. They carried sand as ballast, which they dropped over the side to lighten the balloon and make it rise; a vent at the top released gas, making it descend. Charles had a barometer to

*Professor Charles sold tickets for his manned flight to offset
the huge cost of filling his balloon with hydrogen; interest
was so great that many tried to avoid payment*

measure air pressure from which he could calculate height. When they landed, Charles went up again solo and, without the weight of Robert, shot up to 10,000 feet, only coming down because of pain in his ears due to the loss of pressure.

In the space of two weeks Paris had seen two spectacular flights – and with them the dawning of a new age. In scientific circles the debate over the value of balloons and manned flight continued unabated. A new vocabulary evolved: ballooning became known as aerostation, balloons became aerostats, and balloonists, grasping at the dream of travel by air, became aeronauts. It soon became clear that gas-filled balloons were more practical, and the essential features of Charles's design have remained broadly unchanged for over two centuries; many details which he thought of could be found in the gigantic helium balloons which flew into the stratosphere in the 1950s.

PIONEERS OF THE
BALLOON AGE
The death of de Rozier cast a
shadow over ballooning for a
time. But, undeterred,
Blanchard turned
professional, making the first
balloon flight in America; he
died of a heart attack after a
flight in 1809. Professor
Charles never flew again, and
after Joseph Montgolfier had
flown once, both brothers
retired. Dr John Jeffries
returned to the US to practise
medicine in Boston where he
died in 1819.

The first manned flight

Death of de Rozier

François Pilâtre de Rozier

Blanchard and Jeffries set out over the Channel

Jean Pierre Blanchard

Dr John Jeffries

But the problem which has always faced balloonists remains – how to control the craft. A fair degree of control of ascent and descent existed, but there was no means of steering; pilots were at the mercy of the winds. Many solutions were inspired by devices for steering ships – oars, rudders, sails – but they all failed. They were all part of the dream to travel far and wide in balloons, a dream which had to be put to the test. The English Channel was the obvious challenge, and within a year the race to be the first across was on.

In October 1784 James Sadler became the first Englishman to fly, using a hot-air balloon based on the Montgolfier pattern. By the end of the year he was in Dover planning to fly to France. At the same time Pilâtre de Rozier was busily making plans to fly to England. Then another team arrived in Dover – Jean Pierre Blanchard and Dr John Jeffries.

Blanchard came from Normandy. He was poor and made it into ballooning the hard way, by technical knowledge, sheer guts and, lacking a sponsor, self-promotion – he put on displays for cash and sold accounts of his exploits. For that, and because he unerringly sought the limelight, he was shunned in French ballooning circles and moved to England. There he met Jeffries, an 'American' doctor who had settled in London after supporting Britain in the American War of Independence. For a seat in the gondola he agreed to pay Blanchard's expenses. Their balloon was hydrogen-filled and the gondola was boat-shaped, with oars and a hand-driven propeller. It was packed with provisions and scientific instruments: brandy and biscuits, cork life-jackets, a barometer, flotation bladders in case they landed in the sea, even a letter to Benjamin Franklin in Paris from his father in England.

On 7 January 1785 the weather looked right. At one o'clock, in front of a huge crowd, they lifted off from the white cliffs and drifted out to sea. Near Calais, a sharp-eyed lookout saw the black speck in the sky and soon the French cliffs were crowded with spectators. In the thinner air, however, the relative pressure of gas inside the balloon was higher and it began to swell. Blanchard let out some hydrogen; too much – suddenly they were descending towards the choppy sea. Provisions, instruments and a lot more besides went over the side. The rate of descent slowed, but it was not the voyage of scientific discovery Jeffries had hoped, more like a roller-coaster ride, getting closer to the sea all the time. About fifteen miles out they were down to their undergarments and cork life-jackets, waiting to hit the water. But as they approached the French coast, the balloon miraculously started to rise again; frozen stiff but triumphant, they crossed the coast near Cap Blanc-Nez.

Over land they started to drop again, towards a forest; out went the life-jackets and, as a last resort, the flotation bladders thoughtfully filled with what Jeffries estimated was six pounds of urine. They levelled out along a tree-line and Jeffries grabbed at branches while Blanchard vented gas. Naked, shivering, but still clutching the first-ever airmail letter, the elated pair were soon on the ground surrounded by enthusiastic spectators who carried them off to a heroes' welcome. The King awarded Blanchard a pension for life.

Blanchard and Jeffries' somewhat lucky flight stole the limelight from the father of manned ballooning, Pilâtre de Rozier. He still intended to make a crossing for the glory of France, using a hybrid balloon, a combination of two technologies: hydrogen in one balloon for buoyancy and hot air in another to give control over ascent and descent. It was a lethal combination. On 15 June, with a companion, Roumain, he lifted off from Calais and swiftly rose to 5000 feet. The wind started blowing them back over France. Spectators saw de Rozier vent gas, presumably to check swelling of the hydrogen balloon. A spark, from the fire or from static electricity, ignited the gas and in an instant the whole thing was a fiery ball. As it plummeted to earth de Rozier shouted to the crowd through a megaphone, but his words were lost and both men were killed by the impact. François Pilâtre de Rozier, who had been on the first-ever manned flight, became the first man to die in a flying machine.

It was 1903 before heavier-than-air machines made their first, faltering flights; balloonists had the sky to themselves for over a century. There were four categories of aeronaut: there were showmen, like Blanchard, who flew for spectacle and for profit; there were soldiers – as early as 1794, at the Battle of Fleurus, balloons were used to spy on the enemy; there were travellers who made flights of hundreds of miles over mountains and seas, exploring the Earth from a new perspective. Lastly, there were scientists who reached out into the skies, flying at altitudes higher than Mount Everest before the Wright Brothers were born. Unlocking the secrets of the Earth's atmosphere is probably the aeronauts' greatest contribution to aviation.

Dr Jeffries was one of the first to see the scientific possibilities. In 1784, before he flew the Channel, he saw that balloons could provide 'a full investigation of the nature and properties of the atmosphere which surrounds us and into which we have hitherto been unable to rise'. Before crossing the Channel together, he and Blanchard made a purely scientific flight to 9000 feet over London, carefully noting the drop in temperature from 51°F at ground level to 29°F.

Flights of a real scientific significance were not frequent. They needed the right people, the right mixture of courage and scientific curiosity, the right backing, the right technology and a certain amount of luck. In 1804 a Frenchman, Joseph Gay-Lussac, set a height record of 23,000 feet on a flight to see if the Earth's magnetic field varied with altitude. Four years later his record was broken by two Italian meteorologists, Pascal Andreoli and Carlo Brioschi, who took a

BRITAIN'S PROFESSIONAL AERONAUT
Charles Green (*seated right*) gave joy rides and demonstrations to finance his interest. In 1836, with Robert Holland (*seated centre*) and Monck Mason (*standing between them*), he made one of the epic balloon journeys of all time. Taking off from London on 7 November, they crossed the Channel at dusk and 18 hours later, after dining on meats and coffee heated by a quick-lime stove, they landed 480 miles away at Weilburg in modern Germany to great acclaim. Charles Green wanted to cross the Atlantic by balloon but he failed to find backers. He made his 500th and last flight in 1852.

Royal Gardens, VAUXHALL.

THE MOST INTERESTING
AND
Grand Night
OF THE SEASON.

The Proprietors have now the pleasure of performing the grateful duty of announcing a

SUPERB
GALA

In honor of the Anniversary of the Natal Day of His Majesty, the Royal Patron of Vauxhall Gardens ; which auspicious event, of course, calls forth the united talent and industry of this large Establishment in all its departments, and the Public may feel assured that the most ample justice will be done on this occasion, and that our Sovereign's Birth Day will be celebrated in every way worthy the event, as well as to mark the gratitude of the Proprietors for the distinguished Patronage conferred upon them by their Majesties.

This INTERESTING FETE will take place on

MONDAY, 22d Aug.

And the event will be marked by the grandest Illuminations---the most superb Decorations---additional Entertainments---a double Display of Fire Works by both the Artists---besides the usual routine of Amusements, which have so much delighted the Visitors the whole Season.

In consequence of the unmixed gratification and astonishment evinced at the Intrepid and Grand Ascent, last Monday, and the constant inquiries for a repetition of the treat, the Proprietors have no alternative, upon such a night as the present, but to afford the Visitors every novelty and gratification within their power. Regardless, therefore, of the great expense naturally attendant on such a Voyage, the Proprietors have again engaged

MR. GREEN,
WHO WILL, ON THIS OCCASION, MAKE ANOTHER

NIGHT ASCENT
IN HIS MAGNIFICENT
BALLOON!
PRECISELY AT TEN O'CLOCK,

When the same facilities afforded on the former Night will be given to the Visitors to inspect this wonderful Machine; and Mr. GREEN will, as before, ascend from the Gardens in the midst of the Company. Any Lady or Gentleman wishing to occupy the vacant Seat, may know the Terms by applying at the Gardens.

Neither the limits of a Bill nor of an Advertisement will permit the various Entertainments to be enumerated ; suffice it to say, that an uninterrupted succession of Amusements will take place, from the time the Doors open, and the Gardens will be illuminated at an early Hour.

DOORS OPEN AT HALF-PAST SEVEN. ADMISSION, 4s.

☞ The Gardens are open Four Nights every Week, viz. on Mondays, Wednesdays, Thursdays, and Fridays.

Balne, Printer, 38, Gracechurch-Street.

hot-air balloon to 25,000 feet. In 1850 two more Frenchmen, Jean Barral and Jacques Bixio, flew to 23,000 feet where they discovered that the clouds contained ice crystals.

The next major scientific flights were made by two Englishmen, Henry Coxwell, an experienced balloonist, and James Glaisher, a meteorologist and Fellow of the Royal Society. Glaisher made his first balloon flight at the age of 53; he had many years' experience making observations from the ground and his curiosity about the workings of the atmosphere tempted him to ascend into it and find out more. He persuaded the British Association to back the project and Henry Coxwell to supervise building a massive 90,000-cubic-foot balloon to be filled with coal gas. Their intention was to fly up to 'five miles' (around 26,000 feet). Glaisher's primary objective was to study the rate at which temperature and humidity reduced with height, but he was also interested in air currents, solar radiation, magnetism and the 'electrical condition' of the atmosphere, and in the formation of different types of clouds. To get as much data as possible out of the flight he spared no effort in planning for it. His instruments – barometer, wet- and dry-bulb thermometers, hygrometers – were arranged in a pattern which enabled him to establish a routine for his observations. He set them up in a confined space on the ground and practised making observations quickly so that he would not waste time on the flight.

Coxwell decided to start from the Midlands to minimise the possibility of drifting out to sea. The gas they needed was similar to the coal gas used to light the streets, but had to be much lighter. He picked Wolverhampton where the manager of the local gas company was willing to set aside a gasometer and distil the gas specially for them. Their first flight was on 17 July 1862. They quickly rose through several layers of cloud and Glaisher started his routine of observations. At 15,500 feet they prepared to put on extra clothing against the colder air above. Then Glaisher noted that the temperature, instead of continuing to fall as expected, began to rise. It remained warm up to 19,000 feet, then dropped dramatically. They had discovered a warm air current coming in from the west, an aerial Gulf Stream, which warmed Britain in winter.

They made another flight in August, then on 5 September they set off on their most remarkable flight. The take-off was in still, rather overcast conditions, but at 7000 feet they emerged into brilliant blue sky, cold air pierced by warm sun, all above a silent, woolly cloudscape. Within six minutes they were at 15,000 feet and Glaisher threw a homing pigeon over the side. It spread its wings, then fell 'like a piece of paper'. At 20,000 feet another pigeon went over the side, then another from 25,000 feet. The last one flapped its wings in the thin air, then dropped like a stone. Coxwell unloaded sand ballast and they passed through the old altitude record of 25,000 feet just ten minutes after take-off.

Glaisher noted that Coxwell was panting hard for breath, which he attributed to all the exertion of handling the balloon. Then, peering at his barometer, he realised that his sight was beginning to fail and he began to lose the use of his arms and legs. He continued to observe, but as they passed through 29,000 feet he passed out. The line to the gas-release valve was tangled in the rigging and Coxwell, who recognised that his own senses were also beginning to fail, climbed out of the gondola to untangle it. His hands were black from the cold and useless, so he gripped the line in his teeth and pulled. The valve opened, gas escaped, and they began to descend rapidly. Both men recovered; Glaisher poured brandy on Coxwell's hands. They dumped more ballast to slow the descent and at 23,000 feet Glaisher began making observations again. His wet-bulb thermometer was encrusted in ice but he was able to record the warm airstream again and experimented with another pigeon.

They landed safely in a large field outside Ludlow and had to walk seven miles into town. When the details of their record-breaking flight were reported they became national heroes. Glaisher did not fly again, content to work on the data he had amassed and to correspond with other scientists on his thoughts about the atmosphere. His flights had broken records but they also set a standard for atmospheric exploration. In addition to discovering the warm air current and much more besides, he found that temperature did not decrease uniformly with height and that humidity reduced to virtually nothing above 25,000 feet.

While James Glaisher was making flights of scientific discovery in Britain, an American balloonist, Thaddeus C. Lowe, was demonstrating the military potential of balloons in the American Civil War. Many senior officers were doubtful of their value: they were unpredictable machines, in unfavourable winds they might even finish up grounded behind the enemy's lines. Until Lowe developed portable gas generators, they had to be filled at the nearest gas-main and towed, inflated, across country to the battle, soaking up manpower. To be effective they needed expert handling, and though Lowe's reports on the movements of the Confederate Army were said to have saved the Union Army at the Battle of Fair Oaks in June 1862, when the war was over his Balloon Corps was disbanded.

In the Franco–Prussian War of 1870, when the Prussians surrounded Paris, balloonists set to work inside the besieged capital, and before the city fell in 1871 they made a total of 66 flights over the heads of the Prussian Army, carrying 110 people and over two million letters. One of those pilots was France's leading aeronaut, Gaston Tissandier. After the war he was approached by two French scientists, Joseph Croce-Spinelli and Theodore Sivel, to make a high-altitude flight, ostensibly in the name of science while incidentally taking the altitude record back from the British. On 15 April 1875 they lifted off in high spirits in

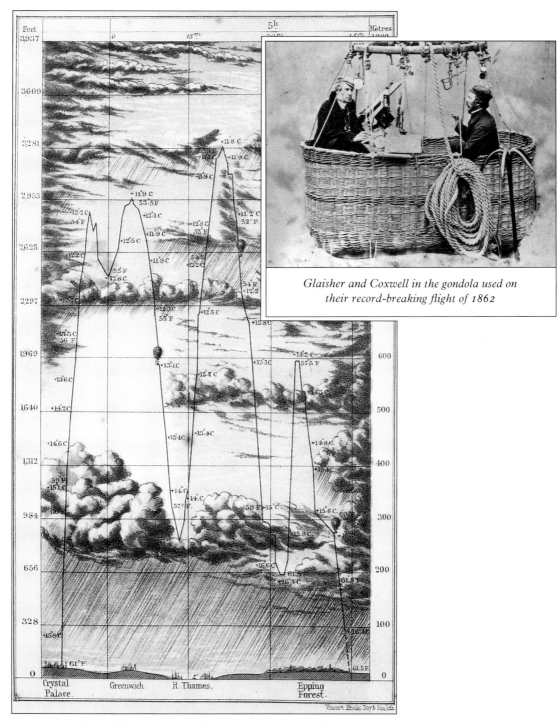

Glaisher and Coxwell in the gondola used on
their record-breaking flight of 1862

On 21 July 1863 Coxwell flew over London to make
these detailed observations of the atmosphere and the weather

a balloon optimistically called 'Le Zénith'. They carried oxygen and all took occasional sucks from the bottle. It was not enough. Above 25,000 feet they all passed out. Spinelli came too at one point, but instead of descending he dumped ballast before passing out again. A strong current forced Le Zénith down. Tissandier regained consciousness and found his two companions cold and stiff. He crash-landed without delay, but both were dead. In death they were bigger heroes than in life.

Tissandier was undaunted by the experience and before long he turned his attention to the problem which had plagued aeronauts for a century – how to steer a balloon. The idea of a dirigible, literally a 'steerable', had been around since 1784 when a French military engineer designed a giant oval balloon with propellers, and a crew of 80 to turn them by muscle-power. It was never built, but the design had tantalised aeronauts ever since. In 1852 Henri Giffard, another Frenchman, built a steam-powered dirigible. In three hours it covered seventeen miles but, though it was steerable, it did not have enough power to fly against the wind. Tissandier used an electric motor; on 8 October 1883 he made two flights with his brother, but it was clearly underpowered.

But just around the corner was an invention which would ultimately revolutionise transport of all kinds – the internal-combustion engine. In August 1888 Dr Karl Wolfert, a Berlin clergyman, fitted a 2-hp Daimler engine to a small balloon and made a brief flight. He persevered, and by 1897 he was ready

During the Siege of Paris the Interior Minister, Léon Gambetta, flew 55 miles in an improvised
balloon made out of a variety of fabrics to rejoin the government in Tours

Rounding the Eiffel Tower

UN NAUFRAGE AÉRIEN
dirigeable » de M. de Santos-Dumont

Disaster at the Trocadéro

ALBERT SANTOS-DUMONT
Between 1901 and 1903
Santos-Dumont made a series
of spectacular flights over
Paris in his steerable balloons,
becoming in the process a hero
to rank with Pilâtre de Rozier
over a century before.

The 1903 model

to give a public demonstration of a new dirigible. On the evening of 14 June, before a huge crowd at Berlin's Tempelhof, he started the engine, apparently unconcerned at the flames which shot out of the exhausts. He flew to 3000 feet above a city packed with spectators. Suddenly the craft exploded. In a matter of seconds 28,000 cubic feet of gas went up in a great fireball, showering the streets below with the charred remains of Dr Wolfert, his engineer and their airship.

Despite this inauspicious début the idea of an 'airship' as an ocean liner of the skies was an immensely powerful one, and in the next thirty years it came tantalisingly close to success. In the process the idea consumed a great deal of money, talent and human life. Wealthy men offered prizes to encourage designers and pilots. A financier, Henri Deutsch de la Muerth, put up 100,000 francs for a flight of seven miles from St-Cloud round the Eiffel Tower in under 30 minutes. Albert Santos-Dumont, a Brazilian living in France, took up the challenge. He built a series of airships and in 1901, in his fifth design, he made an attempt to win the prize. Instead, he crashed into the Trocadéro Restaurant and had to be rescued by the fire brigade. In October he tried again but was just outside the time. By popular demand he was awarded the prize for his sheer guts and divided the money between his workers and the poor of Paris.

Santos-Dumont's airships were non-rigid – elongated balloons with a balcony underneath for the engine and the pilot. In 1903 two more Frenchmen, Pierre and Paul Lebaudy, produced a semi-rigid airship with a keel. The Lebaudy 1 was much stronger and, carrying a more powerful engine, it could travel at 25 mph. On 12 November they made a flight of 37 miles, landing at the Champs-de-Mars.

The British were again slow to follow up French innovation. It was not until 1907 that Nulli Secundus, the first British airship, flew. When it did it was hardly a technical innovation: non-rigid, underpowered, a 122-foot sausage made out of gold-beater's skin, with straps over the envelope to support a platform for the crew. At first it was a secret Army project, but when it was ready, such was the popular demand, on 5 October it was displayed over the packed streets of London. It landed at the Crystal Palace and was tied down for the night. In the morning its skin was sodden with rain and it was dismantled, never to fly again.

Britain and France persevered. By 1910 a French semi-rigid airship, the Clement-Bayard, flew 244 miles from Paris to London in six hours; the same year an Englishman, E. T. Willows, flew from England to France. But such flights were soon eclipsed by the rapid progress made in Germany since the death of Wolfert through the vision and dedicated efforts of one man, whose name was to become synonymous with airships – Count Ferdinand von Zeppelin.

By the turn of the century Germany was a powerful industrial country with a technically advanced navy and army looking for a place on the world stage.

Von Zeppelin was a distinguished cavalry officer and his interest in dirigibles was first and foremost military. The French Army's 'La France' of 1884 had alarmed him, foreshadowing a day when hostile airships would attack a defenceless Fatherland. When he retired from the Army, he became determined to equip Germany with a battle fleet of airships capable of making long-range reconnaissance flights or carrying bombs. He was 60 years old, technically untrained, yet despite official rebuffs and with no government backing, he dug deep into his own fortune to fulfil his dream.

From the outset his ideas were functional. He realised that, to be effective, military airships would have to be more than unwieldy powered balloons only able to operate in ideal conditions. They would need a crew to fly them and to fight; they would need to be armed; they would need range; and they would have to be sturdy enough to operate in bad weather. To achieve that they would also need to be big, but neither size nor the technical complexity of the undertaking daunted him. He decided on a rigid structure, a vast cathedral-sized lattice-work of lightweight girders surrounding huge, individual gas 'cells', each one the size of a balloon.

In 1900 his first airship, Luftschiff–Zeppelin (LZ) 1, was ready. When it emerged from its huge floating hangar on Lake Constance on the evening of 2 July, the crowd along the shore gasped in amazement. It was by far the biggest airship ever built: 420 feet long, with a capacity of 400,000 cubic feet. After a short prayer the Count and his crew of four climbed aboard. Though it was an airship, the scene was unmistakably nautical: the captain shouted orders to the crew, lines were let go fore and aft, and the great bulk moved slowly away from the quayside. There the comparison ended: the handlers at the bow were quicker off the mark than those at the stern and the nose rose steeply. They climbed to 1200 feet. There was a movable weight amidships for trimming the craft; Count Zeppelin ordered it wound forward immediately. The nose came down, but the weight locked in the forward position and LZ–1 headed for the surface of the Lake. To avoid a crash, the Count reversed the engines and narrowly avoided disaster. After an erratic 20-minute flight they made a softish landing four miles away from the hangar. The flight highlighted more problems than it solved. Clearly they needed better control, but it was from such pioneering efforts that progress was made.

LZ–2 was not ready until 1906 and it was broken up on the ground by strong winds. Undaunted, the Count dug into his fortune again and started on LZ–3 the same year, incorporating all the lessons he had learned about construction and handling. This time he got it right, and on its first flight LZ–3 stayed up for over two hours. Before long he made a flight of over 200 miles; the King and Queen of Württemburg and the Crown Prince of Germany went for joy rides;

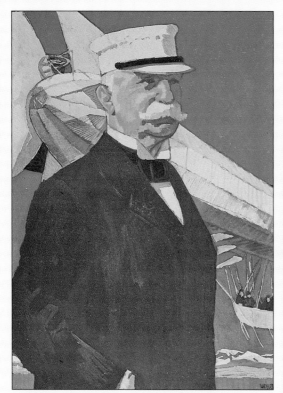

Count Ferdinand von Zeppelin – the originator

Hugo Eckener – the man who made things happen

MASTER AIRSHIP BUILDERS

In 40 years the Zeppelin company built 130 airships for use in peace and war. The most successful by far was LZ-127, the Graf Zeppelin; the most notorious was LZ-129, the Hindenberg.

The 775-foot Graf Zeppelin under construction

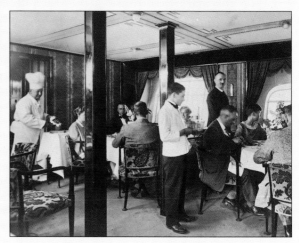

A snapshot of lunch served on the Graf over Siberia

The Graf off Franz Josef Land in 1931; she flew over a million miles and crossed the Atlantic 144 times

The 803-foot Hindenberg under construction in 1936

In 1936 the fare to America was just over £100

and the government began to show an interest. It voted 400,000 marks to build LZ–4, with a promise to buy both airships for just over two million marks if LZ–4 could make a 24-hour flight.

The 70-year-old patriot seemed about to reap his reward when disaster struck. On 4 August 1908 LZ–4 took off from Lake Constance for an endurance run which would seal the deal with the government. An engine fault forced the Count to stop near Echterdingen. While waiting for repairs to be completed, a gust of wind tore it from its moorings. It snagged on nearby trees which tore open a gas cell; a spark of static electricity set the hydrogen alight, and in seconds the whole craft was a blazing inferno and two crew members were dead.

It was a devastating blow. The Count had mortgaged his property to build LZ–4 and a single spark had destroyed it all in seconds. It should have spelled the end of the airship: flying surrounded by hydrogen was clearly dangerous. In fact it was just the beginning of a new chapter in the story. What followed came to be known as 'The Miracle of Echterdingen'. German national pride had been stung; a national hero dispossessed. A fiercely nationalistic people responded from their hearts: money and gifts in kind flooded into the Zeppelin offices and within a day the cost of a new airship had been raised. Even the German government joined the patriotic fervour and purchased LZ–3 for the army. Count Zeppelin was back in business and his dream of military airships was under way.

In 1909 he started work on another dream, German commercial airships spanning the world. He built six and formed the world's first airline, DELAG. Between 1910 and 1913 it carried over 30,000 passengers between German cities and on pleasure flights without loss of life, though three of the airships were lost in crashes.

At the outbreak of war in 1914 the longer range and greater payload of 'Zeppelins' seemed to rival winged aircraft as the means to wage war in the air. DELAG's remaining fleet was requisitioned and plans laid for attacks on Britain. At first both sides used airships for maritime reconnaissance, especially over the North Sea. The British non-rigid airships were inferior, lacking the range of the Zeppelins, but for a time they all did valuable, if rather routine work. Then in January 1915 the Kaiser authorised air attacks on Britain, principally in response to the Royal Navy's blockade of Germany. On the 19th Yarmouth was attacked: two people were killed and property was damaged. In May seven people were killed in the first raid on London. Then on 6 June LZ–37 set out over Belgium to bomb London. It was spotted by Flt-Lt R. Warneford of the Royal Naval Air Service flying a Morane fighter. He dropped six small bombs on LZ–37 and within minutes it was falling on fire over Ghent.

It was the first time that the vulnerability of airships had been demonstrated in war. They were huge, slow targets and highly combustible. But one loss was not conclusive and Germany built more airships. Britain improved her defences: anti-aircraft guns were installed and defensive fighters were stationed in southern England. The Zeppelins struck at night; the gunners used searchlights; fighter pilots learned to fly in the dark. Both sides had their successes and failures but the climax came on 2 September 1916, when sixteen German airships set out to bomb London. SL–11 was caught by Lt W. Leefe-Robinson over Cuffley; he was armed with new incendiary ammunition and the airship was soon falling in flames, in full view of Londoners and the remaining German crews, who turned for home without attacking.

It was a turning-point. By the end of 1916 another five airships had been shot down and the defences had the upper hand. Zeppelin raids continued sporadically until the end of the war but they were less and less effective and more costly and the role of strategic bomber was taken over by winged aircraft.

The technology of rigid airships had advanced a great deal during the war, but aeroplanes had progressed even further. Von Zeppelin died in 1917 and by the end of the war the airship's military value was seen to be nil, and Germany was prevented under the terms of the Armistice from building any more for herself. Although DELAG reopened for business in 1919 it was closed by the Allied Control Commission. If airships were to have a future it would depend on the victorious Allies.

The story might have ended there, but as thoughts turned to commercial aviation it seemed that airships might yet have a role, and that Britain might realise the Count's dream of passenger-carrying airships circling the globe. In June 1919 two British officers, John Alcock and Arthur Whitten Brown, were the first to cross the ocean by air. Barely three weeks later, on 2 July, the British rigid airship R–34, with a crew of 30, set out from East Fortune in Scotland. It arrived in New York on the 6th and returned to its base in England on the 13th, having covered 6330 miles. To some people the arguments were conclusive: airships took longer, but aeroplanes had shorter ranges and they were noisy and draughty. Airships combined the luxury of an ocean liner with a little more speed and they could operate directly between the great population centres of the world, inland or on the coast. In 1919 the airship appeared to have a bright future.

In the 1920s Britain, France and the United States had airship programmes. A strong undercurrent of national rivalry developed, in which size and luxury became the hallmarks. With one or two exceptions, they all ended in disaster. In 1921 Britain completed the R–38, at 2.5 million cubic feet the largest airship ever built. But for economic reasons the government postponed further airship operations and sold it to the US Navy. While undergoing tests over the Humber on 24 August it broke up, killing 49 crew members. France had acquired LZ–114 as war reparations. The French Navy renamed it Dixmude and flew it with

Lt R. A. J. Warneford's victory over LZ-37 on 6 June 1915. To save weight, the crew did not carry parachutes; 10 of the 11 on board were killed

great success for a time, including a record flight of 118 hours in 1923. In December the same year, returning from a flight over the Sahara, it exploded during a storm over the Mediterranean with the loss of all 50 men on board. France cancelled the rest of its programme.

In the same year the US Navy launched the 'Shenandoah', which had been built in conjunction with the Zeppelin company. It was filled with the newly-discovered inert gas, helium, making it much safer. The Navy planned to fly it

Britain built 200 non-rigid airships to patrol coastal shipping,
particularly the North Sea

to the North Pole and, working up for that goal, it made several successful flights across the US. However, in September 1925, on a publicity tour of State Fairs, it flew into a violent storm over Ohio and broke in half in mid-air. The nose section flew off on its own with part of the crew, who with great skill landed it. The remainder fell to earth in several sections. Twenty-nine of the 43 crew survived, mainly because it did not catch fire, but it showed that even with non-flammable gas airships were vulnerable.

In 1925 the Treaty of Locarno lifted the restrictions on Germany building airships. Zeppelin's disciples were undaunted by the disasters that had occurred elsewhere; they were just waiting for an opportunity to show the world that Germans were the masters of airship design and operation. Foremost amongst them was Hugo Eckener. Cast from the same mould as the Count, for him airships symbolised a proud and resourceful Germany, part of a technical and national renaissance after the crushing defeat in the Great War.

Money was in short supply in Germany. The government could not fund the enterprise, so Eckener took his case to the German people and, invoking the 'Miracle of Echterdingen', raised two million marks. It was not enough but he started building anyway, and as the first German airship since the war progressed, so the government came up with the money to finish it.

With Eckener was the man who had been at Zeppelin's side from the early days – Ludwig Dürr. Eckener provided the drive and the charisma for the enterprise while Dürr brought the technical expertise accumulated in 25 years designing airships. The result of their efforts when it was completed in October 1928 was remarkable: 775 feet long, with a discreet gondola providing room for a luxury lounge, individual cabins, a bar and exquisitely equipped kitchens; it had taken Germany just three years to get back in front. Zeppelin's daughter named the giant after her father: 'Graf Zeppelin'. The inaugural flight carried twenty passengers and 40 crew to New York. It was another turning-point: thousands turned out to see the marvel, Eckener was given a ticker-tape parade and went back to Germany a national hero. It was the beginning of a ten-year career in which the Graf was the only really successful passenger-carrying airship ever built.

Eckener's goal was regular, commercial airship services round the world, but Germany was financially weak and he could not get the support he needed. What he did understand was the popular fascination with airships and he set out to use it to generate the support he needed. He made widely publicised flights, taking politicians and opinion-formers to the Mediterranean on the Graf; in a little over three days they saw the Alps, Greece, the Dead Sea and the Pyramids. In 1929 he persuaded the US newspaper tycoon, William Randolph Hearst, to sponsor a flight round the world. Hearst was not that interested in airships but he knew what would sell newspapers. The journey became the biggest story of its day: from New York across the Atlantic to Europe, over the wastes of Siberia to Japan, across the Pacific to San Francisco, and back to New York. Hearst newspapers carried one of the epic aerial journeys of all time. After a trip to the Arctic in 1931, the dream of commercial airships began to take shape, and over the next five years the Graf made regular flights to South America, the only non-stop, long-range air services of the time.

For Britain airships were a means of binding the Empire together. In 1924 the government inaugurated the Imperial Airship Scheme: two monster airships, R–100 and R–101, and an Imperial Airship Base at Cardington in Bedfordshire from which they would range through the Empire. The Labour government wanted to build them at the publicly-owned Royal Airship Works at Cardington; others favoured private capital. In the end there was a compromise: R–101 was built at Cardington, R–100 by Vickers at Howden. Inevitably they became political symbols: R–100 was a 'capitalist' and R–101 a 'socialist' airship.

In 1929, as Graf Zeppelin circled the globe, it was clear that R–101 was not living up to expectations: costs had mounted, she was far too heavy, her lifting capacity was only just over half the sixty tons intended; she was also leaky. R–100 on the other hand was in fine form: it exceeded its anticipated lifting capacity and performed well in tests during the early part of 1930, on one flight exceeding 80 mph.

Politics now re-entered the arena. Lord Thomson, the Secretary of State for Air, was determined to fly to India in R–101 in October 1930 and be back in time for the Imperial Conference in London in the middle of the month. He was deeply committed to the airship programme and to the 'socialist' airship and even adopted the title Lord Thomson of Cardington, the name of the Imperial Airship Base. He insisted that R–101 be ready. At Cardington they used drastic means: they cut the airship in half and inserted a complete new section to increase lift, making it 777 feet long, just two feet longer than the Graf Zeppelin. They took out the heavy powered-steering system; they loosened the nets which held the gas cells in place, so that more hydrogen could be pumped in.

On 30 July R–100 made a stunningly successful inaugural flight to Montreal, carrying 44 passengers in sublime luxury. It took 79 hours to get there and 57 to return. Back at Cardington efforts were redoubled and R–101 came out of its huge shed on 1 October. With scant regard for a proper programme of tests, on the evening of 4 October the biggest airship in the world, 5.5 million cubic feet of hydrogen, dumped water ballast and lifted off on her maiden voyage to India with Lord Thomson and other distinguished passengers. She was clearly overweight and unstable but they set off through the night, flying low over London. It was a stormy night and the giant airship was junketed around the sky by winds; gas cells vented precious hydrogen as the gas surged around inside. At 2 am over Beauvais in northern France a particularly strong gust forced her down. The crew managed to level out using engines and elevators, then the wind caught them again over high ground to the south of the town. The great airship slid gently into the side of the hill, then, dragged along by the wind, bounced back into the air again. Fifty feet up, her back broke and she landed hard. In the inferno which followed Lord Thomson and 47 others out of the 54 on board died.

It was aviation's *Titanic*. Britain and France and their Empires went into conspicuous mourning. The dead were brought back to Cardington to be buried in a mass grave and every part of the ceremonial funeral procession by horse-drawn wagons, train and ship was painstakingly covered by newsreels and news-papers. At Westminster Abbey the Great, the Good and the Prince of Wales mourned the dead and marked the passing of Britain's airship programme. R–100 was scrapped.

In the United States the airship was seen in military terms. The great champion was Admiral William E. Moffett. He fought hard in Washington, and in 1926 Congress authorised expenditure on a five-year plan to build long-range maritime reconnaissance airships for the Navy. The 'Akron' and the 'Macon'

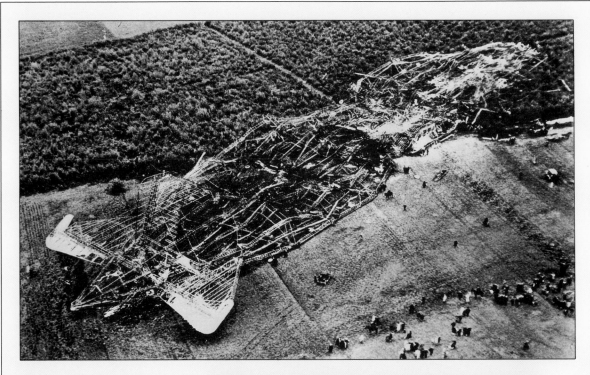

THE END OF THE DREAM

More airships came to disastrous, often fiery ends than survived to be scrapped; only a few fare-paying passengers were killed and miraculously there were survivors of even the worst disasters.

ABOVE: All that was left of the R-101 after 5 million cubic feet of hydrogen went up in flames on 5 October 1930
RIGHT: The funeral procession was two miles long and lined by 500,000 people
OPPOSITE TOP: The end of the Hindenberg
OPPOSITE BELOW: Even in death airships were a public spectacle. Sightseers flocked to see the wreck of America's Shenandoah; part of its fabric was turned into raincoats called 'Shenandoah Slickers'

carried their own fighters for defence. (They were hooked underneath and would be dropped, fly off, fight off the enemy and carry out their observations, then return and hook up to the airship again.) The airships took five years to build and were operated only briefly before Akron crashed in the Atlantic in 1933 and Macon off California in 1935. (The only large airship operated by the US Navy without crashing was the 'Los Angeles', built by the Zeppelin company to replace the R-38. It was retired in 1932.)

With hindsight it seems extraordinary that after so many disasters, especially the R-101 crash, Germany *started* building the biggest airship ever, the 'Hindenberg', in the same year. Once again the indefatigable Hugo Eckener got the project under way, and once again politics and national symbolism played a leading part in finishing it. In 1933 Germany was in political turmoil and money for the giant had all but dried up. Then Hitler came to power. He had no particular interest in airships as military machines, but he and his Propaganda Minister, Joseph Goebbels, like Hearst in 1929, saw that the true value of airships lay in their power to attract attention. Millions of marks were suddenly available and when Hindenberg emerged from its hangar in March 1936 it was smothered in swastikas.

It was nearly the size of the *Queen Mary*, the largest ocean liner of the day, and wherever it flew heads turned upwards. Its first job was to drop leaflets all over Germany in support of Hitler's policy of remilitarising the Rhineland, and its huge bulk became a familiar sight at Nazi Party rallies. It was hydrogen-filled though Eckener had hoped to get helium from the US (there was a law forbidding export of the gas). Designed for the North Atlantic, it was soon a familiar sight over New York City too, making ten round trips in 1925, the only means of travelling from Europe to America by air direct. Vast as it was, it still carried only 50 passengers and needed a crew of 60, but in luxury it surpassed even the 'Graf'. It seemed that Germany after all could master airships in a way which eluded other nations. Two more, even bigger, were under construction: the LZ-30 with passenger accommodation for 100, and LZ-131 with room for 150.

In May 1937 the Hindenberg set off for New York on its first trip of the year. There were warnings of a terrorist bomb on board but a search revealed nothing. The rest is history. As it was docking at Lakehurst, NJ, spectators saw a glow developing at the stern. Within seconds the Hindenberg was blazing and falling to the ground. Miraculously most of those on board did survive, but 36 died and film cameras had recorded not only the inferno and the wreck but the burns of the survivors too. This time it was the end. The US government banned flights to the US. The Graf Zeppelin went to a museum. The era of the airship was at an end.

Only just. LZ-130 was ready and the indomitable Eckener had one last

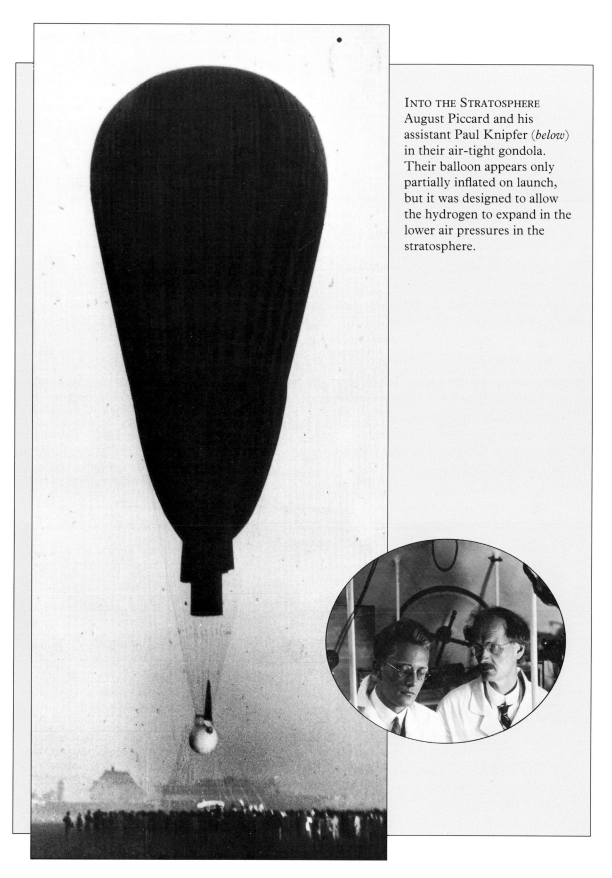

INTO THE STRATOSPHERE
August Piccard and his
assistant Paul Knipfer (*below*)
in their air-tight gondola.
Their balloon appears only
partially inflated on launch,
but it was designed to allow
the hydrogen to expand in the
lower air pressures in the
stratosphere.

attempt at persuading the US to supply helium. Then Hitler invaded Austria and spoilt his chances for ever. In its last days the rigid airship made a brief appearance in exactly the role Count Zeppelin had originally conceived for it – military reconnaissance. LZ–130 made a number of electronic surveillance flights over the North Sea just before the start of the Second World War, trying to fathom out the secrets of British radar. Soon, however, airships were more valuable for their metal and LZ–130 and the Graf were cut up for scrap. (Since the war small airships have been built for joy-riding and as flying billboards, and more recently the US Navy has shown a renewed interest in them for maritime reconnaissance.)

For 37 years mere balloons had been eclipsed, but just as airships were passing from the scene, high-flying balloons made a comeback in their role of exploring the atmosphere. In 1901 Arthur Berson, a German meteorologist, set a new altitude record of 35,000 feet in a hydrogen-filled balloon. Taking oxygen to breathe, he reached the outer limit of the troposphere, that part of the atmosphere which contains water vapour and where temperature falls with increasing height. His data, taken with Glaisher's and more from experiments with unmanned balloons, suggested that above that level there was a new, and cloudless, band of the Earth's atmosphere – the stratosphere – where there was no humidity and temperature did not fall.

Berson's record stood for 26 years. Then in 1927 a US Army captain, Hawthorn Gray, took up the challenge of flying into the stratosphere. The only way to get there was by balloon and in May he took off in an open gondola and reached 42,470 feet, seeing for the first time the cold and cloudless upper atmosphere with its deep blue sky and constant brilliant sunshine. On the way down he travelled so fast he was forced to bail out using a parachute.

Later the same year he set off again and reached 44,300 feet. Once again he was in an open gondola, breathing oxygen and wearing an electrically-heated flying suit. He recorded observations in his log and reported by radio to a chase aircraft far below. Suddenly all communication stopped. The following day a boy found the gondola hanging in a tree near Sparta, Tennessee. Gray's body was still inside. Whether he died from lack of oxygen or whether his lungs collapsed in the lower air pressure was never determined. What was clear was that, though temperature remained constant in the stratosphere, pressure continued to fall, and to survive in it aeronauts would need a sealed, pressurised gondola.

It took only two years for balloonists to devise the means to reach into the stratosphere, forcing it to yield up more of its secrets. In May 1931 a Swiss physicist, Auguste Piccard, and his assistant Paul Knipfer became the first men to fly into the stratosphere and return safely. They took off from Augsburg in

The aeronaut's dream of crossing the Atlantic by balloon was finally realised in August 1978. America's Max Anderson, Ben Abruzzo and Larry Newman near the end of their 6-day flight from Maine to France in Double Eagle II

Cmdr Malcolm Ross (right) *and Lee Lewis, in suits which they tested for astronauts on a 30-hour flight to over 80,000 feet*

Germany, in an ingenious pressurised gondola designed by Piccard. It was a sealed aluminium sphere with one side painted black to absorb the sun's rays, the other white to reflect them. Using an electric motor to rotate the gondola he hoped to control the temperature inside by turning it towards or away from the direct rays of the sun.

Piccard was interested in cosmic rays, phenomena which had fascinated scientists for years; he believed that they might provide energy. The flight did not help much with his research but they did fly to 51,770 feet, a new record. The electric motor froze up with the black side facing the sun and they sweated inside, and the gas-release line would not work. They drifted helplessly, waiting for nightfall when the gas would contract in the colder air. After a slow and dark descent they landed on a glacier high up in the Alps. Next day they scrambled down the mountain. Piccard made further ascents and gathered valuable information about cosmic rays, pushing his own record up to 57,000 feet in 1934.

It was no longer a world record. In 1933 a mini space race developed between the Soviet Union and the United States. Both sent manned, pressurised capsules high into the stratosphere. In September Georgi Prokofiev, Konstantin Godunov and Ernst Bernbaum in the Russian balloon 'Stratostat USSR' set a new record of 58,700 feet. Two months later the US balloon 'A Century of Progress', flown by Lt Thomas Settle and Major Charles Fordney, went to 61,000 feet. In January 1934 the Russians responded with a flight to 72,000 feet which ended in disaster: the gondola broke free from the balloon and fell to earth killing the occupants. In July three Americans, William Kepner, Albert Stevens and Orvil Anderson, nearly suffered the same fate: the gondola broke free from their balloon 'Explorer' and began plummeting to earth. They were in contact by radio and Kepner gave a running commentary on their descent until all three bailed out and landed safely by parachute. In November 1935 America won the race when Anderson and Stevens in 'Explorer II' reached 72,000 feet, nearly fourteen miles up. National pride played a part but the secrets of the atmosphere were the objective, and long-term experiments included observations on fruit flies after a journey into low pressures, and collecting air samples at high altitude that contained tiny spores which were then germinated on the ground.

Stratospheric ballooning was brought to a halt by the Second World War but in the 1950s it was revived again in the USA. Between 1956 and 1961 US Navy and Air Force aeronauts pushed the record up steadily. Their purpose was not only to find out about the stratosphere but to prepare the way for man to fly into space. In 1957 Major David Simons, a USAF doctor, spent 43 hours in a tiny pressurised capsule flying above 101,000 feet, for the first time making physiological observations of himself in prolonged exposure to such heights. In 1959 Navy aeronauts looked at Venus from 81,000 feet. In 1960 Capt. Joe W. Kittenger made a parachute drop from 102,800 feet, free-falling to 17,500 feet. The last balloon flight to those altitudes was in May 1961. Navy Commanders Malcolm Ross and Victor Prather flew to 113,740 feet, setting a record for balloons which stands to the present day. They were testing suits for Mercury astronauts. They valved off too much helium and made a hair-raising descent into the Gulf of Mexico. Sadly Prather was drowned while being rescued by a helicopter.

Aeronauts had the upper reaches of the atmosphere to themselves for 180 years. Aircraft had always lagged behind; their wings needed air to create lift. Then in the late 1950s the tranquility of the stratosphere was being regularly shattered by jet and rocket-powered aircraft from the United States and the Soviet Union. On 6 April 1961, just before aeronauts Ross and Prather set their record, the first cosmonaut, Yuri Gagarin had flown right through the stratosphere in a matter of seconds, followed on 5 May by the first US astronaut, Alan Shepherd.

A 1910 French Deperdussin monoplane

CHAPTER·TWO

THE PIONEERS

On 2 May 1903 the Aero Club de France held one of its glittering evenings. Henri Deutsch de la Muerth was there; so was the veteran balloonist, Gaston Tissandier. They went to hear a lecture by Octave Chanute, an American pioneer of the infant art of gliding. His talk started with a tribute to the experiments of Otto Lilienthal, the German glider pilot who had died in a crash in 1896. After covering his own work in America, he moved on in some detail to the research of a virtually unknown pair of brothers, Orville and Wilbur Wright. They had been experimenting with gliders since 1900 at Kitty Hawk, a lonely spot on the Atlantic coast of North Carolina. According to Chanute, their persistence was beginning to pay off. He spoke of flights as long as 600 feet.

The Aero Club's membership was generally more interested in ballooning and airships, but a small number had an interest in gliding. Foremost amongst these was Ernest Archdeacon, an expatriate Irish lawyer. Chanute's lecture troubled him; he had heard rumours about the Wright Brothers and clearly they were progressing. His worry was political, not aeronautical: if they succeeded, then Paris would suffer the indignity of seeing Americans first conquer the air in heavier-than-air machines. He approached the Club's Technical Committee on Aerial Locomotion and suggested that it encourage gliding by urgently sponsoring competitions with prizes. He opened the subscription with a personal donation of 3000 francs, then commissioned a glider to be built along the lines of the Wrights' 1902 glider, which had been illustrated in Chanute's lecture.

Archdeacon and a fellow enthusiast, Captain Ferber of the French Army, were largely alone in their anxiety. No competitions were held and most Club members remained confident that Paris, the birthplace of manned flight, would remain the world's centre of developments in aeronautics, and moreover that airships, not gliders, held the key to aerial navigation. This view, shared by most aeronautical savants, was firmly endorsed later that year when, on 12 November, the Lebaudy Brothers flew their semi-rigid airship, Lebaudy 1, a record 37 miles.

That very same evening, over 3000 miles away in his wooden shed among the

Otto Lilienthal flying his biplane glider near Berlin in 1895, the year before his death

sand-dunes at Kitty Hawk, Orville Wright took out his diary to record the events of his own, less remarkable day. Mr Chanute had been to see how they were progressing and had left that morning by sailboat for the mainland. He and Wilbur had spent most of the day at 'Big Hill', flying their glider from a wooden track which they had devised to launch it. Nobody paid much attention; it was their fourth season at Kitty Hawk and the local fishermen were used to seeing them skimming over the dunes. But that autumn they had another aircraft in the shed. It looked very similar to the glider, except for the engine mounted on the lower wing, which drove two propellers.

On the morning of 17 December 1903, with the help of five local men, they set the new machine up on the track. At 10.30 they were ready: the wind was blowing at just over 20 mph, they started the engine and Orville lay on the lower wing. He let go the restraining rope and the aircraft started to move forward. Before reaching the end of the track he was airborne. He found the controls difficult to operate, and after an erratic flight lasting just twelve seconds he landed on the sand. They carried the aircraft back to the track and made some minor repairs. It was Wilbur's turn next and he went a little further in much the same roller-coaster way, then Orville had another go with the same results. With their gliding experience behind them they learned quickly, and when Wilbur made the last flight of the day he stayed up for nearly a minute and covered 284 yards. They had made the first-ever powered, controlled and manned flights in a flying machine.

The first person to know was their father: to mark the occasion they sent him a telegram with the bare details of the flights and telling him they would be home for Christmas. Orville and Wilbur Wright were born into the large, loving, if rather strict, family of Bishop Milton Wright, of the United Brethren Church. He was a devout, though enlightened man, and his wife Susan was a stimulating and resourceful mother. She encouraged their natural inquisitiveness and they grew up with enquiring minds alongside a solid and unquestioning belief in God; the hallmark of all aspects of their lives was Truth.

Wilbur was born in 1867 and Orville in 1871, yet they behaved like twins. Their lives were entwined: neither married and as adults they continued to live in the family home; they were inseparable. Neither had a distinguished school career, but the Bishop had an extensive library and Wilbur, especially, read voraciously on subjects which interested him. Orville read too but he was inclined to experiment with problems. In 1889, while still at school, he built a printing press and published a local newspaper, *The West Side News*. The following year he and Wilbur joined forces and turned it into a daily which Wilbur edited and Orville printed. In 1892 they set up another business together, selling and servicing bicycles. They became expert lightweight engineers and soon started manufacturing their own 'Wright Specials'.

The bicycle business prospered and became just the springboard they needed to support another joint interest – the problem of mechanical flight. They were aware of the various attempts to build flying machines in the nineteenth century, but it was probably an article in *McClure's Magazine* about Otto Lilienthal, 'The Flying Man', which first aroused their serious interest. In May 1899 Wilbur wrote to the Secretary of the Smithsonian Institution, America's premier scientific body, who sent a reading list which included Sir George Cayley's seminal articles of 1809–10 on aerodynamics, 'Aerial Navigation', and Octave Chanute's 'Progress in Flying Machines' of 1894. They read these and anything else they could find, including Lilienthal, and gradually drew together the threads of nearly a century of theoretical work on winged flight.

Aviation began to dominate their lives: they started a correspondence with Chanute; they went out on to the prairies around Dayton to observe the flight of birds, absorbing not only general impressions but also the minute details. At home they had animated debates about their thoughts and observations.

In October Percy S. Pilcher, an English glider pilot and the natural heir to Lilienthal, was killed in a crash. Like his mentor, Pilcher hung from the wings of his glider, using his own weight to control lateral equilibrium: if the wings moved out of the horizontal he swung in the opposite direction. He and Lilienthal were searching for a way to control their gliders without fully understanding the forces which were acting on them. It took the instincts of a tight-rope walker

THE KITTY HAWK YEARS

Each autumn between 1900 and 1903 the Wright Brothers spent at Kitty Hawk, NC, trying out a new flying machine.

The first was a tethered kite-glider with wing-warping and a front elevator which they controlled with lines from the ground; in 1901 they were back with a larger, free-flying machine. Over the winter they used a small wind-tunnel for basic research and came back with their third glider in which they made hundreds of flights in 1902.

They spent weeks on end living in their shed among the sand dunes

The No.1 kite-glider had a 17-foot wingspan; it was chiefly flown unmanned though they made a few piloted flights on it

The No.2 glider had a 22-foot wingspan and the wing-warping was operated by the pilot's feet

The No.3 glider was stretched to 32 feet with a vertical rudder as well as the wing-warping and front elevator

combined with the mind of a scientist and they learnt a great deal, but when they died much of their knowledge was lost with them.

The Wrights read about Pilcher and set about finding a safer and more precise way of experimenting. They built a biplane kite with a five-foot wingspan and attached lines to the corners of the wings, so that they could be twisted in flight to simulate the actions of the birds. From the safety of the ground they discovered that they could deliberately upset the equilibrium of the kite, making it turn, then by reversing the direction of the twist, regain it. They called the process 'wing-warping'. The next stage was to build a much larger kite, which could still be controlled from the ground but, once tested, could support a pilot. For that they needed strong and consistent winds which could not be found around Dayton. Once again their approach to solving the problem was systematic: Wilbur wrote to the Weather Bureau for details of wind strengths from all over America and the trail led them to Kitty Hawk.

In the autumn of 1900 they went to have a look. It was perfect: a steady wind blew in from the Atlantic over miles and miles of uninhabited sand; the local fishermen and the family who kept the post office were solid people, almost like a family away from home. For the next three years Orville and Wilbur made an annual pilgrimage to Kitty Hawk, each time building on the experience of the previous years. Four years of intensive theoretical and practical work with gliders culminated in 1903, when they added an engine and propellers. The four flights of 17 December marked the birth of powered and controlled flight in aeroplanes.

Their scientific approach and their understanding of the importance of controlling lateral balance by using wing-warping ultimately led to the conquest of the air by aeroplanes, but recognition of their achievement did not come quickly or easily, partly due to their way of dealing with their success. They did not rush to tell the rest of the world what they had done. It was not their way; family came first, hence the telegram to their father. Their main concern that week was not publicity but getting home to Dayton for the traditional family Christmas. Reporters came to the house to ask for photographs of the 'Flyer' but they refused; they gave some local press interviews, but when the articles appeared they were so appalled at the wild inaccuracies that they stopped talking to the press. On 5 January 1904, to clarify the position, they issued a simple, rather terse statement of what they had done, but not how they had done it. They were businessmen; they had invested their own money and a lot of effort in their machine; they realised they had the key to the aeroplane and they intended to profit from it. On 14 January Wilbur consulted a patent attorney and filed a patent for their wing-warping system.

Their statement came too late to stop garbled accounts of their flights reaching Europe. Generally they made little impact, but for Archdeacon and Ferber they were a shock. If the reports were true the Americans were far ahead. To spur on his countrymen Archdeacon hurriedly unveiled the glider he had commissioned after Chanute's lecture and put it on display at the Aero Club in Paris.

On 4 February there was a dinner at the Aero Club. In a passionate and chauvinistic speech Victor Tatin, a respected member, expressed outrage at the mere thought that the conquest of the air might have been achieved outside France and counselled scepticism about the Wrights' claims without evidence. Archdeacon spoke next; he reminded the audience that he had warned them about the Wrights and urged them to press ahead with gliding experiments.

By April his own glider was ready for tests. There were many similarities with the Wright 1902 glider, but the crucial difference was that it had no wing-warping system, nor any other means of maintaining lateral equilibrium. A volunteer pilot, Gabriel Voisin, made several flights in it at Berck-sur-Mer, the longest only about 60 feet. It was not much of an advance on Lilienthal, and Archdeacon was honest enough to admit that they had a long way to catch up with the Wrights, but he predicted that they would do it quickly. It was a year before he was ready again, and the new glider was a failure.

In the meantime the Wrights had been busy: they applied for patents in France and Germany as well as the US; their French patent was granted on 1 July and published on 1 September. During April and May they built a completely new aircraft based on the 'Flyer', and started flying again, without publicity, at Huffman Prairie near Dayton. On 20 September, watched by a few curious locals, Wilbur used the wing-warping system to fly in a complete circle for the first time. He made no announcement, it was simply part of perfecting his machine. On 9 November he flew four circles, staying up for a little over five minutes and covering nearly $2\frac{3}{4}$ miles. Over the next year, and largely in secret, they improved their design still further, and on 5 October 1905 Wilbur made the longest flight ever – over 25 miles in 39 minutes. The new aircraft, the Flyer III, was the world's first practical powered aircraft.

The Wrights saw the potential in aircraft to carry out military observation, and once they felt ready to sell machines they wrote to the US and British governments. Initially they were turned down flat in disbelief, but before long military officers arrived in Dayton in search of more information. The Wrights were courteous but gave no demonstrations and the officers saw little for their pains; the aircraft stayed firmly locked up in their sheds. The Wrights wanted a firm order before they revealed their secrets. They were honest men and they expected their stated achievements to be accepted as fact; they saw no need to give demonstrations to disbelievers. Instead they became prolific letter-writers, opening up correspondence with the French and German governments too, but no takers emerged. Confident that they were far ahead of the field and that

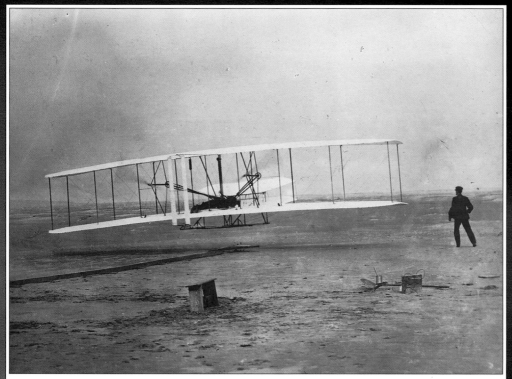

The first controlled, powered, sustained and manned flight of an aeroplane – 17 December 1903

Wilbur Wright
(1867–1912)

Orville Wright
(1871–1948)

governments would eventually have to come to them, they decided to sit it out in Dayton. In the next two years they built seven more aircraft but they stopped flying completely.

In those years there was a flurry of activity in France. Unaware of the pace of progress in Ohio, the Aero Club had announced prizes for powered flying at its dinner in October 1904. They were hardly generous when compared with the 100,000 francs which Santos-Dumont won in his airship: the Coupe Ernest Archdeacon was a silver trophy for a flight of 25 metres and 1500 francs for a flight of more than 100 metres; the Grand Prix d'Aviation Deutsch–Archdeacon was 50,000 francs for a circular flight of one kilometre. Would-be glider pilots were stirred into action both by the prizes and by the thought that Americans might triumph, for as long as the Wrights kept their machines under wraps there seemed to be a chance that the breakthrough might be made in France.

Many aspects of the Wrights' designs had been public for some time, but French pilots were reluctant to adopt wing-warping. Ferber used Wright-type wings with a front elevator and a tail; he flew briefly in October 1904 but without any means of lateral control. Robert Esnault-Pelterie, a gifted engineer, regarded wing-warping as structurally unsound and he took a stab at lateral control by adding separate ailerons to Wright-type wings; it failed to fly. Building on his experiences of April 1904 Gabriel Voisin, with his brother Charles, set up a business building gliders for wealthier experimenters. Archdeacon commissioned one with a tail like Ferber's; to test it they towed it behind a car without a pilot and it crashed. In 1905 he commissioned another, this time with box-kite wings based on the experiments of an Australian, Hargreave. It was built on floats and Voisin tested it behind a motor-boat on the River Seine; it flew, but little was learnt from it.

Perhaps the prizes and the exhortations had worked too well. European experimenters, unlike the Wrights, were impatient for results. Orville and Wilbur had refined their gliders over four years; they had built a wind-tunnel to test the shape of their wings; they had learnt how to be pilots step by step, starting with tethered flights, then short hops, before moving on with confidence to tip the aircraft out of the horizontal using the wing-warping, turning, then righting it again. European pioneers were impatient to get airborne; they were less inclined to follow ideas through methodically. Instead, they watched each other and copied the latest ideas.

Nobody personified French impatience better than Louis Blériot. He was an engineer who made a fortune manufacturing and selling automobile accessories. As fast as he made his money he spent it on flying. In 1905, following Archdeacon, he commissioned a float-glider from the Voisins; the results were more or less the same. The following year, on little more than a whim, he decided to try

The first sustained powered flight in Europe: Albert Santos-Dumont in the 14-bis.
He committed suicide in his native Brazil in 1932

ellipsoidal wings and commissioned a new float-glider; it failed to leave the water. His next machine, the Blériot IV, was a joint project with Gabriel Voisin who designed the main wings along Wright lines while Blériot, still clinging to his ellipsoidal theory, designed a tailplane. They agreed to add ailerons, copied from Esnault-Pelterie. It started life as a float plane but they later added wheels. On 12 November 1906 they took it to the Bagatelle, a large open space in the Bois de Boulogne. Fortunately for both of them it came apart on the ground while taxying.

But they were not alone at the Bagatelle that day. That afternoon Albert Santos-Dumont arrived with his latest aeroplane and Blériot and Voisin stayed to watch; they witnessed a landmark in European aviation.

Santos-Dumont was the son of a wealthy Brazilian coffee-plantation owner. He was tiny, barely five feet tall, but rarely went unnoticed in his floppy Panama hats and pin-striped suits. An eccentric even in aviation circles, he lived in an apartment on the Champs-Elysées where his dining-table was ten feet off the floor to acclimatise him to eating at altitude. He was a showman and his well-publicised flights in airships had won him not only prize money but widespread admiration. In 1904 he met Octave Chanute at the St Louis Exposition. Later that year he turned to gliding, and by 1906 had built his first powered aircraft – the 14-bis. It was an extraordinary machine: a pair of box-kite wings, from which a long neck extended supporting a forward elevator. Santos-Dumont stood in a balloon gondola at the back, next to the engine which drove a rear-mounted propeller.

After a series of test flights suspended underneath an airship, he took it to the Bagatelle in September 1906. It hurtled over the ground, raising great anticipation in the crowd; after a series of abortive attempts he finally found the right conditions and managed a hop of around twenty feet. The crowd roared its approval; nobody had never seen anything like it before.

Aviation circles in Paris began to stir again; another great moment in aeronautical history seemed to be at hand. On 23 October the Bagatelle was packed for Santos-Dumont's next appearance. Officials of the Aero Club's Aviation Committee were on hand to witness the attempt. The strange machine, nicknamed the 'canard' for its resemblance to a duck in flight, bumped into the air and covered 60 metres in seven seconds, well over the 25 metres needed to win the Archdeacon Prize. Few people cared that it had no means of lateral control; it was the first time that a heavier-than-air machine had made a real flight in Europe – and much more importantly it had been done in public and before official observers. More than satisfied, the Committee of the Aero Club fixed the date of the celebration there and then – a grand dinner on 10 November.

Henri Farman completing the first 1-kilometre circuit in January 1908.
The aircraft was built by Gabriel Voisin

The mood at the banquet was euphoric. Praise was heaped on Santos-Dumont; in a thinly veiled slur on the Wrights, Ernest Archdeacon emphasised his courage in flying in public. He claimed the 'official' conquest of the air for France. Carried away with patriotism and with the mood of the occasion, he came very close to saying that the Wrights were deceitful.

Two days later Santos-Dumont was back at the Bagatelle, having fitted ailerons to the 14-bis to give some control over lateral equilibrium. This was the day that Blériot and Voisin were in the crowd after their disaster in the morning. On his fourth attempt, Santos-Dumont made a flight of 220 metres in a straight line, winning the 1500-franc prize. Now, if he could just induce the 14-bis to fly in a circle over one kilometre, the last of the great prizes, the Grand Prix d'Aviation and 50,000 francs, would be his.

In 1907 all the French pioneers redoubled their efforts. At Issy-le-Moulineaux Leon Delagrange, another client of the Voisins, flew 500 metres, and at Buc Esnault-Pelterie, having quietly readopted wing-warping, covered 600 metres. Louis Blériot came up with three new designs: the Blériot V, which followed Santos-Dumont's 'canard' configuration but managed little more than hops; the VI, Libellule (Dragonfly), with tandem wings and an engine in the front, in which he at last took off, flying 150 metres; and lastly the Blériot VII,

Robert Esnault-Pelterie in a 1908 machine

in which he managed 500 metres. It was less than some contemporaries but he was now one of the leading French pilots, and the design, though itself not very successful, was prophetic. The engine drove a propeller at the front, pulling rather than pushing; the wings were amidships and the elevators and rudder were at the back of an enclosed fuselage.

But 1907 belonged to yet another pilot, Henri Farman, an Englishman living in France who had commissioned his biplane from Gabriel Voisin. He made three record-breaking flights: on 26 October he flew 771 metres, breaking the European record; on 9 November he flew just over one kilometre; then on 13 January 1908, before a huge crowd and official witnesses, he flew the first circular course in Europe, snatching the Grand Prix and the 50,000 francs from Santos-Dumont. The flight was more of a testimony to Farman's flying skills than to the design of the aircraft; it had no ailerons or wing-warping, no means of maintaining lateral equilibrium, and he skidded round the course using rudder only. Never mind how he did it, he had done it, and once again in public. For France and for Europe his flight represented the final conquest of the air by aeroplanes. The Aero Club claimed for Paris the distinction of hosting the second great triumph in the story of aviation, and at the inevitable banquet plaudits showered on Farman from all sides. The Wright Brothers were forgotten. They had disregarded challenges by Archdeacon to come to France and show what they could do; they had not flown for two and a half years; and they had failed to provide any proof that they could do what they said they could.

In February 1908 all that changed. After protracted negotiations by letter, the Wrights had signed satisfactory contracts with the US government and with a French company who would manufacture their machines under licence in France. They were ready to go public. But first they took Flyer III back to Kitty Hawk to brush up their flying skills. Wilbur then went to France, while Orville went to Washington to convince the doubters in the US Army.

Wilbur set up camp on the racetrack at Le Mans. Interest was intense – a lot was at stake for the French aeronautical establishment. Wilbur was unmoved. He shunned hospitality and lived on the job, preparing at his own pace with great care and saying little, which only added to the mystery. On Saturday 8 August he was finally ready. Archdeacon and Blériot were there but he was still not playing to the gallery. Taking off, he climbed away, banked into a turn using the wing-warping system, and then landed smoothly. It was a test flight round the field lasting $1\frac{1}{4}$ minutes. Not much, but enough to convince anybody who knew about flying that the Wrights had not been exaggerating or bluffing.

Any remaining doubters were quickly silenced. That autumn Wilbur made over 100 flights. Each time he flew the crowds grew bigger and the cheers grew louder. With little comment he flew further, higher, and for longer, answering

Alliot Verdon Roe built the first successful powered British aeroplane under railway arches in Hackney, East London, and made his first flight on 13 July 1909. In 1908 he cycled from London to Paris to meet Wilbur Wright

the critics by his actions. On 21 September he broke all records with a flight of 41 miles, staying aloft for an hour and a half. He then went on to set an altitude record of 360 feet (over a third of the height of the Eiffel Tower).

While Wilbur was stealing the limelight in France, Orville had a comparable triumph in Washington. Before a critical audience of officers from the Signal Corps he made a total of fourteen flights, four of them lasting over an hour. But it was a triumph marred by the first tragedy in powered aviation. On his last flight, on 17 September, he was carrying a passenger, Lt Thomas Selfridge. A propeller cracked and the loss of power on one side set up a vibration; the other propeller was torn loose and slashed through the bracing wires. Orville cut the engine and struggled to control the Flyer but it crashed, seriously injuring him and killing his passenger.

It was the Wrights' complete mastery of control which impressed officials in aviation circles and in government. Wilbur was awarded gold medals by the Aero Clubs of France and Britain, and when he returned to America President Taft

Orville Wright's crash at Fort Myer, Virginia

received both brothers at the White House. Congress awarded them another gold medal, and when they got home to Dayton the streets were decked with flags and lined by a delirious crowd.

Orville's crash did nothing to deter the US Army, and eventually they bought Wright Flyers. In Europe, however, the first firm to start building them was not French but British. At a national level Britain was very backward in aviation but a young entrepreneur, Eustace Short, heard about Wilbur's flights and went over to France to do business with him on the spot. Wilbur granted him a licence to produce six Flyers, and armed with the drawings he set up Short Brothers at Shellbeach on the Isle of Sheppey, establishing the first assembly line for aircraft in the world. All the aircraft were sold before he built them.

In Britain the pioneers of heavier-than-air machines were a tiny band. *The Times* had been quick to report Farman's British nationality when he flew his circle, but he did it in France in a French machine. At that time there had been no powered flying in England. Since the flight of the Nulli Secundus over London in 1907 (see page 24) the Army had been officially contemplating the use of airships, and in 1908 there were two projects under way at Farnborough: the construction of a second Nulli Secundus, and, in much more secrecy, the building of 'British Army Aeroplane No. 1'.

Colonel Capper, the superintendent of the balloon factory at Farnborough, had been the commander of Nulli Secundus in 1907. He had been to Dayton in 1905 to meet the Wrights but had no more success in learning their secrets than any other visitor. But he did come back convinced that powered flight was possible and set about gathering the funds from the War Office to carry out experiments. His right-hand man was an American, Samuel Franklin Cody, who had been in control of the Nulli Secundus engine and was officially the Army's chief kiting instructor.

Cody was the most unlikely figure ever to be involved in aeronautical experiments. Originally a Texas cowboy, he was illiterate and 50. He had reached the balloon factory by way of international horse trading, Wild West shows, music-hall entertainment, and finally by experimenting with man-carrying kites for the British Army, which saw them as a possible alternative to balloons for observation. He dressed in western clothes, with a stetson hat over shoulder-length hair, and rode around Aldershot on a grey charger called Bergamo. How the deeply conservative British Army, at the height of its Imperial grandeur, managed to acquire such an exotic figure as a test pilot and designer of its aircraft remains one of the curiosities of history. At the heart of the story lies Cody's extraordinarily warm and engaging personality: ordinary soldiers loved him for his informality and enthusiasm, and he charmed the colonels and the generals the same way he could hold a music-hall audience in his hands. Each time his contract came up for renewal, somehow the Army found him indispensable.

Cody had built British Army Aeroplane No. 1 – and it reflected his character. Robust and big in every dimension, the soldiers would eventually christen it the 'Flying Cathedral'. It was ready in the summer of 1908 but there was a problem: the Army only had one engine, a French Antoinette, which had powered Nulli Secundus and was now needed for Nulli Secundus II. But Capper quietly abandoned the second airship and Cody was able to hijack the engine for his aeroplane.

To test the engine he tethered the aircraft to a tree by its tail, set full power, and then measured the output using a spring balance. There was plenty of power and he moved on to little hops over Farnborough common. On 16 October 1908 he was ready for a test flight. Like most European aircraft of the period, 'No. 1' had no wing-warping system or ailerons, relying on the rudder to make turns. With the Antoinette at full power, it leapt into the air and Cody soon found himself flying towards a clump of trees. He managed to lift the machine over

SAMUEL F. CODY
Cody over Farnborough in one of his Flying Cathedrals. He was known as Colonel Cody though he never served in the Army; he gave as the reason that the King of England had once addressed him as Colonel and that was good enough.

them, only to be confronted with more trees. This time he tried a turn with the rudder, but the skidding slowed him down, a wing-tip touched the ground and he crashed. He was unhurt and jubilant – he had covered 1380 feet, over a quarter of a mile.

The Army had its aeroplane, and with time it could be made more controllable. But the Army, having achieved the first powered flight in Britain at government expense, in the very same month cancelled the whole programme. The Aerial Navigation Sub-Committee of the Committee on Imperial Defence had decided that aeroplanes had no military value. No aeroplane meant no need for a pilot, so the Army finally dismissed its chief kiting instructor. At least the Committee was consistent in its folly: when Cody asked if he could keep the machine they agreed; they even lent him the engine. Cody left Farnborough for the last time in March 1909, to set up in business as a freelance aircraft constructor with his sons.

If the Army had doubts about aeroplanes, they were not shared by the newspapers. Lord Northcliffe, the owner of the *Daily Mail*, announced a prize of £1000 for a one-way flight across the Channel. Wilbur Wright's demonstrations had raised the tantalising prospect of the dawning of an air age. What the European public needed was a demonstration of what aircraft could do, and flying the Channel was just such a demonstration. The obvious man to do it was Wilbur, but he was unmoved by such symbolic gestures; he knew what his aircraft could do and saw no need to take unnecessary risks flying over water when he could make money by selling aircraft.

That was not the mood among European aviators. Having grasped the value of wing-warping, and with ever more powerful engines being developed, Europe was catching up. By July 1909 there were three teams waiting near Calais for the right weather and Calais and Dover were bustling with excitement: hotels were booked out, trains brought sightseers from Paris and London, and the newspapers kept the atmosphere at boiling point.

The favourite was Hubert Latham, a French citizen of English extraction. He had already made one attempt, which ended in the water when his engine failed. His elegant new aircraft, the Antoinette, had been specially built by Leon Levasseur, the creator of the ubiquitous Antoinette engine. Next there was Count Charles de Lambert, an expatriate Russian aristocrat, who had bought two Wright Flyers. Lastly there was Louis Blériot. He was the underdog: broke (his whole fortune, over 750,000 francs, having been spent on pursuing his aviation career), he was attempting the Channel crossing on borrowed money. He was a terrible pilot, uncoordinated and impetuous; his aircraft was the smallest and the least tested; and his engine was the least powerful. And he hobbled around on crutches having severely burnt his foot on a hot exhaust pipe.

LOUIS BLÉRIOT

Behind the scenes there was consternation: some people thought that his flight had demonstrated that England could be invaded by air; but to the British people he was a hero.

A Blériot XI similar to that used to fly the Channel, preserved at the Shuttleworth Collection

An earlier model with Blériot's ellipsoidal tailplane

Louis Blériot about to set out, 25 July 1909

Crossing the French coast at dawn

Blériot's welcome to London

Count de Lambert crashed and dropped out, leaving Blériot and Latham cordially watching each other's every move as they waited for dead calm weather. Each of them was determined to be first, and not only for the prize – who would remember the second man to cross the Channel?

On the night of Saturday 24 July the blustery weather began to lift and both pilots left word that if conditions did improve they were to be woken. By 2.30 am it was dead calm and clear and Blériot went to the barn where he stored his aircraft. Despite the early hour a crowd soon gathered. Sunrise was at 4.40 and while he waited Blériot barked orders to his mechanics. The pressures were immense. Success could mean a new start to his career, failure could mean the end of it; the wind might get up; the engine might not be powerful enough to get him over the cliffs at the other end. But what Blériot lacked in resources he made up for in perseverance and sheer courage. As soon as it was light he started up, stowed his crutches in the fuselage and took off.

He had no compass, no instruments to help him, and when the wind did get up he had no real way of assessing its effect. After twenty minutes over the Channel he could see neither coast but he kept going until he sighted ships heading for Dover. Taking his course from them, he soon saw Dover Castle and headed for a meadow next to it. Overcome with relief and emotion he went straight in and landed. It was windy and he misjudged it, breaking the undercarriage and hitting the ground with the propeller. It was not an elegant arrival, but Louis Blériot was down and alive and he had conquered the Channel, the most convincing demonstration yet of what aircraft could do.

He became an instant celebrity and aviation's greatest hero. He was mobbed through the streets of London, where the damaged aircraft was put on display in Selfridges store and newspapers devoted lengthy columns to him and his machine. For France it was a national triumph; his reception in Paris was even more ecstatic. More than 100,000 people lined the streets, cheering him and his aircraft all the way to the Aero Club, not only for the usual sumptuous dinner but to present him with the Club's Gold Medal. Orders for Blériot aircraft poured in and he was on his way to another fortune. (Latham missed the opportunity which the calm weather presented; he tried the crossing two days later but his engine failed and he landed in the sea.)

Within a month France staged a second great aeronautical extravaganza. The City of Rheims, backed by the great champagne houses, organised The Great Aviation Week, the first truly competitive forum for aircraft and pilots. There were prizes for speed, passenger-carrying, endurance and distance totalling 200,000 francs, and the American publisher James Gordon-Bennett donated a trophy for the speed contest which became the premier prize of the meeting. The trophy was surmounted by a Wright Flyer but the Wrights were not there, once

RACING AT RHEIMS
Glenn Curtiss winning the
Gordon-Bennett Trophy; his
victory boosted his aircraft
business in the United States
in the same way that Blériot
had benefited from his cross-
Channel flight in Europe.

Left: Eugène Lefebvre in his
Wright Flyer.

again eschewing such lavish spectacles. Of the 22 competing aircraft three were Wright Flyers, the rest were French. All the French pioneers were there – Blériot, Farman, the Voisins, Esnault–Pelterie – but there was also a new breed of professional pilot, experienced men attracted by the prize money and the prospect of great fame. Latham was one; another was a doughty Frenchman, Eugène Lefebvre.

The races were staged in gladiatorial style. The course was marked out with pylons and surrounded by great pavilions where the spectators dined and sipped champagne. It was a fashionable occasion, a place for non-aviators not only to see aircraft but to be seen; pilots were presented to the President of France and Madame Fallières. Latham, bitterly disappointed at losing the race across the Channel, was a highly popular figure; he put up a stunning performance in the distance race, flying round the course for over two hours and covering 150 kilometres. Farman flew next, in a more streamlined aircraft of his own design, powered by a revolutionary Gnome rotary engine. Most aircraft engines were adaptations of water-cooled automobile engines and they frequently overheated, but the rotary engine was developed specially for aircraft: it was air-cooled and the cylinders spun round with the propeller. After $2\frac{1}{2}$ hours droning round the course Farman had easily beaten Latham, but he was not satisfied and went on into the night, finally landing after dark by the light of car headlamps. He had covered 180 kilometres in a little over three hours to win the Grand Prix and over 60,000 francs.

The Gordon-Bennett Trophy race was the high point of the week. After a promising start Lefebvre dropped back; his Wright machine was underpowered for racing. The event was dominated by two men: Blériot, who was favourite, and Glenn Curtiss, an outsider and the only American pilot there. In the fly-off Curtiss went first and managed a speed of 44 mph. Blériot was slower by six seconds, much to the disappointment of the crowd. Curtiss shot to stardom in Europe and in America.

Almost entirely thanks to the Wright Brothers the technical problems of mechanical flight had been overcome. As a result of Wilbur's demonstrations European aviation had surged ahead. But to what end? To the Wrights Rheims was merely a circus; they had no comprehension of the value of such meetings. They took a serious view of aviation, they wanted to sell aircraft to governments for military reconaissance and, longer-term, develop them for mail and passenger services. Rheims showed that, in its infancy at least, more than anything else aviation was a popular spectacle. The first practical use of aeroplanes was to thrill and to entertain.

Within months, meetings modelled on Rheims were being organised all over Europe and America, capitalising on the unerring ability of aircraft to attract a

crowd. The crowd attracted promoters, who put up money to attract pilots who wanted to win, and the thrill of competition increased the size of the crowd. It was not the way the Wrights had seen aviation progressing, but the evident truth was that big prizes and ruthless competition between pilots provided the sharpest spur to technical advance.

Aeroplanes sold newspapers too. In 1910 Lord Northcliffe put up £10,000 for a flight from London to Manchester – ten times the money he had offered for the Channel flight. By April *Daily Mail* readers, and then the whole world, were being thrilled by every edition as they followed the titanic struggle between a Frenchman, Louis Paulhan, and a debonair Englishman, Claude Graham-White, to win the money. Both flew French-built Farmans. Paulhan got away first and reached Lichfield at nightfall; Graham-White landed 57 miles behind, but decided to fly at night, something never before attempted. Paulhan heard about it and took off himself in the dark, just keeping ahead. As dawn came Graham-White was forced down by winds but Paulhan managed to fly above the turbulent air and made it to Manchester, physically exhausted by the journey.

In America Glenn Curtiss won $10,000 offered by the *New York World* for a flight from Albany down the Hudson River to New York City. Graham-White was offered $50,000 simply to appear at a Boston air meet. He took it, won another $10,000 on the day, and went on to Brockton, Mass., for another fee of $50,000.

To survive in the business the Wrights had to overcome their distaste for such events. So they formed a professional team of pilots to demonstrate their aircraft for them. Glenn Curtiss, who had become their chief rival as a manufacturer in the US, did the same. Both teams were at the Boston show, but their rivalry was not confined to the flying circuit.

The Wright Brothers were bitter. All around them pilots were profiting hugely from an invention which they had perfected for the world: without their wing-warping system none of it would have happened, certainly not as quickly. They held patents for wing-warping in all the leading aviation countries and they demanded royalties from any pilot using the system and flying for profit. If the pilot did not pay up, and many did not, they went to the courts. They made no exceptions – Paulhan, Graham-White and others had writs served on them at air meets by Wright lawyers, and promoters of meets received demands for twenty per cent of the posted prize money and ten per cent of the gate receipts. But they reserved their harshest treatment for Glenn Curtiss who was selling aircraft in direct competition to them. Litigation began to dominate their lives, and Wilbur especially spent long periods in the courts giving expert evidence against Curtiss. But it was a hopeless task. There were too many people flying, and even when they were awarded judgement the battles continued; there was always another

Claude Graham-White was a great socialite; he is flying his
Bristol Boxkite here for the members of the Ranelagh Club in 1910

pilot or promoter to sue or an appeal to attend. They would not settle out of court. It's hard to fathom what it was that made them go on; it had to be something more than the money. They were rich, they had sold aircraft to the Army as well as to professional pilots, and they received royalties from licensed manufacturers. In November 1910 the Wright company was incorporated with capital of $1 million, and the board was filled with Wall Street luminaries. The new company bought the patents from the Wrights for $100,000 and Wilbur became president and went on battling in the courts.

Their long-standing and fruitful friendship with Octave Chanute was severely tested by their pursuit of other aviators in the courts. Before he died in November 1910, the old man of American aviation exchanged a heated correspondence with Wilbur. As a friend, he questioned Wilbur's judgement and in his response Wilbur gave no quarter. To him it came down to a simple matter of right and

Konkurrenz-Fliegen
der erſten Aviatiker der Welt
26. September - 3. Oktober 1909
Flugplatz Berlin-Johannisthal
150,000 M. Geldpreiſe
Deutſche Flugplatz-Geſellſchaft ✳ Berlin

HOLLERBAUM & SCHMIDT · BERLIN·N·65·

wrong, a matter of Truth. They, not anybody else, had unlocked the science of aviation, and anything which smacked of a denial of that simple fact had to be challenged. But Chanute could see what the Wrights could not. They had taught the world to fly, but in so doing they had not simply invented a device, they had realised an ancient dream. Having unleashed it on the world, they could not then control it. Man would fly without paying the Wrights ten per cent.

Wilbur battled on in the courts and development of their aircraft suffered as a consequence. Meanwhile Europe forged ahead. Racing for cash prizes created a demand for faster and more reliable aircraft, and by 1911 pilots were competing over long distances between the major European cities. Once again they were dominated by French pilots and French aircraft, but the aircraft were unrecognisable from those of 1909. Among the favourites were Blériots and Deperdussins, sleek monoplanes with radial engines housed in streamlined fuselages; in the cockpit there were engine instruments and a compass.

The idea of a spinning engine came from the Seguin Brothers in France.
Its great advantage was that it was light and powerful, producing 1 hp
for every 3.3 lbs of weight, compared with the Wright water-cooled engine
which weighed 6.9 lbs for every horse power

Over 300,000 spectators turned out to see the start of the first race, from Paris to Madrid. The French Prime Minister, Ernest Monis, was at the front, but as the engines revved up for take-off the crowd surged forward, pushing the distinguished guests into the path of the aircraft. Monis was badly injured and his War Minister, Maurice Bertaux, was killed. After a delay of a day the race restarted, but all the pilots save one dropped out. When Jules Vedrines arrived alone in Madrid he was greeted by King Alfonso XIII. In June the first 'Circuit of Europe' was held – nine legs from Paris, through France and Belgium, across the Channel to England, then back to France. Fifty-two aircraft started; three pilots were killed on the first day and nine finished. The winner was Jean Conneau, a French naval lieutenant, whose £10,000 prize took his winnings that year to six times that figure.

America's great air race was a coast-to-coast marathon for which William Randolph Hearst had put up a prize of $50,000. To win, the pilot had to complete the journey in thirty days. All dropped out except one, Calbraith Perry Rodgers, flying a specially prepared Wright machine. Called the Vin Fiz Flyer after the soft-drink company who sponsored him with $5 for every mile he flew, it was still recognisably a derivative of the original Flyer, a pusher biplane with a pilot's seat on the lower wing and bicycle chains driving the propellers. He made it, but only after numerous minor mishaps and five major crashes, the last just twelve miles from the Pacific coast. The aircraft had to be more or less rebuilt and Rodgers suffered a broken leg and concussion; he flew the last leg after a four-week stay in hospital. He took 84 days and consequently failed to qualify for the prize, but it was a personal triumph and he became a popular figure. Sadly, however, Rodgers became yet another casualty of the use of aircraft for spectacle. On 3 April 1912 he returned to the place near Pasadena where he finished the journey to give a demonstration flight. Flying along the crowded beach he hit a seabird; it jammed the controls and he crashed into the sea and was killed.

By 1913, ten years after the Wright Brothers' first powered flights, the aeroplane had come of age. Wright aeroplanes were becoming obsolescent, and the achievements of French constructors and pilots were overshadowing American aviation. Within days of the Gordon-Bennett Trophy race in 1909 Blériot had broken Curtiss's speed record. By 1913 it had been raised to 127 mph, and every intervening record-breaking flight had been made by a Frenchman flying a French machine. Wilbur Wright's unofficial height record of 360 feet, set in 1908, had been raised to 20,079 feet by 1913 but the record books show no American entries after 1910. By 1913 too, French pilots and a lone Belgian had raised Farman's 1909 distance record to 634 miles. (Charles Lindbergh was the next American to hold this record, for his flight from New York to Paris in 1927.)

Two of the pilots who featured frequently in those record books were Jules

Vedrines and Roland Garros, both veterans of the Circuit of Europe races. In 1913 Vedrines flew 2500 miles in hops from Paris to Cairo, and Garros flew from the south of France directly over the Mediterranean to Tunisia in eight hours. Lord Northcliffe now put up £10,000 for a crossing of the Atlantic. Britain's American pioneer, Samuel Cody, and a German, Gustav Hamel, began serious work on aircraft to attempt it, but both were killed in crashes the same year.

The Wright Brothers had always believed that aircraft would one day span the oceans and the continents and that they would be used for military observation. As the first decade of the air age came to an end it was beginning to happen. The first experimental mail flights had taken place and the armies and navies of many countries were forming air corps. But by that time the Wrights' direct influence was marginal and Wilbur was spending an increasing amount of time in the courts. He did not live to see the aircraft fulfil his vision; he died of typhoid fever on 30 May 1912. He had been dealing with the court case against Curtiss from his sick bed and though his intellect still sparkled the strain of preparing testimony and touring the courts had weakened him. The Wright family saw the indirect hand of competitors in his untimely death.

Orville carried on the patent fight. In January 1914 the Circuit Court of Appeals in New York found in favour of the Wrights in their original 1909 suit against Curtiss, but Curtiss went back on to the offensive and the fight dragged on until 1917, when the US government ordered a pooling of aircraft patents as part of the war effort.

Wilbur and Orville had been fighting for money, but also for recognition of the truth of what they had done. The awards, medals, plaques, memorials, degrees and honorary memberships which were showered on them stand as testimony to the widespread recognition that they had given the world powered flight, but the Smithsonian Institution wavered. In 1903 Samuel Langley, with enormous financial support from the Smithsonian, had experimented with a tandem-winged aircraft in the Potomac River. In 1914 the Smithsonian gave it to Curtiss to prove that it could have flown before the Wrights. Curtiss made it fly, which Langley had never managed, but Orville's reaction was disgust – he could list dozens of alterations which had been made to make it fly. So in 1928, the Smithsonian still not having recanted, Orville shipped the 1903 Flyer to the Science Museum in London, a permanent reminder that America's premier scientific body did not accept what the rest of the world did. In 1942 the Smithsonian finally recanted, and in 1948 the Flyer came home to America to be displayed at the Smithsonian in Washington. Orville was not there to see it; he died of a heart attack earlier in the year.

THE GOLDEN YEARS OF RACING
Air racing found its way into every corner of Europe.

MAIN PICTURE: The Belfast to Dublin race of 1912
ABOVE TOP: One of the Deperdussin monoplane racers
ABOVE: The Wright response: two Wright Flyers flown by pilots called Bradley and Beatty at the Chicago Aviation Meeting 1911
RIGHT: Lt Jean Conneau used the name 'André Beaumont' for his professional racing appearances. Jules Vedrines was a chauffeur before he turned racing pilot. Roland Garros became a famous fighter pilot in the war (see p. 93)

Jean Conneau

Jules Vedrines

Roland Garros

CHAPTER THREE

THE AEROPLANE GOES TO WAR

When HMS *Dreadnought*, the world's first modern battleship, was launched in Portsmouth in 1906, she was the sensation of the age, capable of outshooting and outrunning any warship afloat: 17,900 tons, a top speed of 21 knots from revolutionary steam-turbine engines, and with ten 12-inch guns. She was the pride and joy of Britain's visionary First Sea Lord, Admiral Sir John Fisher.

By 1912 Britain was laying the keel of the ultimate warship of the day, HMS *Queen Elizabeth*, whose 15-inch guns could fling a one-ton shell over twenty miles. But even as technical advances increased the firepower and speed of the fleets, so one of the fundamentals of sea warfare remained constant. Finding the enemy fleet – a tiny thing in the vastness of the ocean – was still the highest priority in the prelude to battle. Navies had frigates, fast ships whose job was 'scouting' for the enemy, but naval commanders had always longed for a means of seeing over the horizon.

At the beginning of the twentieth century the Royal Navy experimented with kites. The irrepressible Samuel Cody demonstrated an ingenious system of ropes and lifter kites, towed behind a warship which supported a wicker basket for an observer. Airships offered another possibility, and by 1910 the German Navy had airships patrolling their coast. But an aeroplane, suitably adapted to fly from the water, or better still from a ship, could provide a perfect answer.

It was the US Navy which carried out the first flight by an aircraft from the deck of a ship. It was made in defiance of conservative admirals who regarded it as too dangerous – indeed, the pilot was not a naval officer but a civilian stuntman, Eugene Ely. On 14 November 1911 he dropped off an improvised ramp on the USS *Birmingham* and only just managed to reach flying speed. The following January he tried landing as well. He rigged up a system of ropes attached to sandbags on the deck of the USS *Pennsylvania* and was brought to a halt as he landed by a hook attached to his aircraft. The reception was mixed; some admirals grumbled that the ramps interfered with the guns.

Eugene Ely's Curtiss pusher biplane just after leaving the deck of the USS Birmingham; *he just touched the water and damaged a propeller, but managed to control it*

Britain was not far behind. In December 1911 the battleship HMS *Africa*, fitted with an improvised ramp, made a secret trip to the Short Brothers factory on the Isle of Sheppey. Lt Charles Samson, flying a Short S.38, made a successful take-off. His aircraft was specially designed for use at sea: it had wheels for take-off, and floats so that it could land on the water, then be hoisted back on board ship where folding wings made it stowable. The following January Samson made another flight in public and the Admiralty backed further experiments.

The technical advances of the nineteenth century which had so improved naval guns had much the same effect on the firepower of armies. But soldiers used artillery over much shorter distances: heavy guns were designed for battering down fortifications and could be directed by observers on the ground; light guns, field artillery, moved with the infantry and cavalry to give close support. Looking for the enemy was the task of cavalry, and once both armies were in position the commanders could see almost all of what was going on. But in the early twentieth century they faced an entirely new problem: armies had grown so large that they stretched out of sight. Generals now needed to know what the enemy was doing, where his reserves were, and how their own forces should be deployed to respond.

Balloons had been used in the American Civil War and in the Boer War, and although they made a contribution they were cumbersome, and unpredictable in rough weather. In 1908 Cody had flown an aeroplane for the first time in Britain, offering yet another means of putting a soldier in the air. Blériot's flight across the Channel in 1909 started a debate, but for a year aeroplanes barely featured in British military thinking. Even in France General Foch was still of the view that, while aeroplanes were good for sport, they had no military value.

Sir George White, a wealthy British financier and owner of a string of transport businesses, decided otherwise and in 1909 he began building aircraft. It was strictly a business venture: he fancied that the Army would eventually have to come to terms with the aeroplane and that, when it did, it would want to buy British. He set up the British & Colonial Aircraft Company with a factory at Filton in Bristol and either purchased or copied the technology from France. He was a man who got things done and by July the Bristol 'Boxkite' made its first flight. Sir George ordered Filton to produce another twenty; he would give the War Office a demonstration its more conservative figures could not ignore.

In September 1910 the Army held its annual manoeuvres on Salisbury Plain. Sir George sent two Boxkites to Salisbury, then approached Captain Bertram Dickson, an Army officer on indefinite sick leave, who was filling in time winning aviation prizes. When Dickson arrived in Salisbury he was treated with suspicion by some officers but he managed to attach himself informally to the headquarters of 'Red' Forces. At dawn on 21 September he took off and found 'Blue' Forces between Salisbury and Amesbury. He reported back, giving a detailed disposition of the 'enemy', then took off again; finding them once more, this time he landed in a field and just managed to report to headquarters by phone before being 'captured' by an enterprising 'Blue' corporal. The following day Robert Lorraine, an actor who had learnt to fly, hurriedly drove down to Salisbury to offer his services to 'Blue' Forces. The general agreed, though he did not brief him or make much use of his observations. The episode did bring about a small change in official policy thanks in part to ridicule in the press, though it brought little comfort to Sir George White: the War office bought two French aircraft.

The centre of all military aviation in Britain was the Balloon Factory at Farnborough. In April 1911 the Air Battalion of the Royal Engineers was formed and at long last purchased the first British aircraft – four Bristol Boxkites. Sir George White was delighted, although he had already sold eight to the Imperial Russian Army. The budget for the infant Air Battalion did not extend to training its pilots: officers had to pay for that themselves. Once again Sir George had anticipated events: he started a flying school on Salisbury Plain where officers could learn to fly for 75 guineas. If they passed the rudimentary test for an Aero Club licence and were acceptable to the new battalion the Army reimbursed the cost of instruction. By the end of the year eleven officers had been trained.

In December Farnborough unveiled the BE 1, an aircraft designed especially for military observation: stable, reliable, with two cockpits one behind the other. It came just as aircraft were being used in a real war for the first time. Italy,

RUNWAYS AT SEA

Launching and recovering aircraft on board ships has always been a challenge to the ingenuity of shipbuilders and the skill of pilots. Battleships had their own 'scouts', and after taking off on the guns the pilots either had to find their way to land or ditch in the sea. Towing a flat-topped barge (*below*) behind a fast destroyer was another way of launching; a scout launched in this way shot down a Zeppelin in 1918.

A Sopwith takes off on the guns of HMS Barham

HMS Furious, *the world's first aircraft-carrier, with two runways – one over the bow and one at the stern*

On 2 August 1917 Sqn Cmdr E. Dunning RNAS made the first-ever landing on a ship under way. He had to approach in a turn; the combined speed of the ship and the wind gave him a headwind of 47 knots. On 7 August he tried again in even stronger winds, overshot, stalled, crashed into the sea and was killed.

Geoffrey de Havilland designed the BE 1 at the Royal Aircraft Factory at Farnborough before setting up his own company; this one is on Army manoeuvres on Salisbury Plain in 1912

looking to expand its influence, occupied Tripolitania, a province of the sickly Turkish Empire in what is now Libya. The Italian Army had nine aircraft, mostly Blériots but including two Etrich Taubes from Austria; the Turks had none and the sight of Italian machines crossing their lines to snoop with impunity greatly irked them. With nothing to stop them save a barrage of rifle fire and with good weather, the Italians were able to make considerable use of aircraft to see what the Turks were up to. They also dropped bombs on the Turkish lines. The Turks swiftly opened negotiations to buy aircraft and borrow pilots.

The following year was one of progress in military aviation both on and off the battlefield. German volunteer pilots flew reconnaissance missions for the Turkish Army in their war against insurrection in their Balkan provinces. In America two enterprising officers of the US Army Signal Corps, Lts Chandler and de Witt, strapped a Lewis machine-gun to the rudder bar of their Wright aircraft and blazed away at a target on the ground, scoring several hits. It was the first time a weapon had been fired from an aircraft at the ground and a stunning demonstration of the potential in arming aircraft, but little notice was taken. In Britain an Army pilot flying a BE 1 on manoeuvres became the first to spot for artillery from the air; a Morse transmitter was installed in an aircraft; and pilots experimented with cameras.

It was also a year in which there was recognition that flying units needed an identity of their own. On 13 May 1912 the Royal Flying Corps was formed, covering military and naval aviation; it had a budget of £322,000 to include the purchase of land for a flying school. Farnborough, which was renamed the Royal Aircraft Factory, unveiled the first really fast single-seat 'scouting' aircraft, the BS 1; it could fly at over 91 mph. In all, 36 new aircraft were ordered, bringing the total to 50. (The French Army had around 200 aircraft and a budget approaching £900,000.) In October Germany formed its Military Air Service, and even countries not accorded 'power' status, Argentina for example, formed military aviation units.

With its new acquisitions the RFC had a very varied collection of aircraft: French and British machines built by private companies and Farnborough's own designs. In August 1912, to find out more about what were available from private companies and to evaluate them, the Superintendent of the Aircraft Factory, Mervyn' O'Gorman, conducted trials at Larkhill on Salisbury Plain. The rules were very tightly drawn, with tests for climbing, passenger-carrying and altitude, and there were substantial prizes. But the infant aircraft industry was playing for higher stakes – military contracts for aircraft. There were 31 entries: five all-British, thirteen British with foreign engines – mostly French, and the rest mainly all-French. One of the British entries was Samuel Cody, with a derivative of the original Army Aeroplane No. 1 of 1908. It was clearly obsolete and highly unsuitable, but his intimate knowledge of the Army and its curious ways, his understanding of an aircraft he had built himself and his awareness of the local flying conditions in poor weather all stood him in good stead. He won all the major prizes and the RFC was forced by its own rules to buy one of his aircraft.

The new British companies, formed around the pioneering efforts of men like Alliot Verdon-Roe, Thomas Sopwith, Frederick Handley Page, Geoffrey de Havilland, and businessmen like Sir George White, continued to lobby hard for the Army to buy their aircraft rather than develop its own designs at public expense at Farnborough. But the War Office continued to dither. It conceded a trickle of orders but never enough to provide funds for further development. It looked to Farnborough for development and pursued a policy of buying BE 1s produced in batches to War Office specifications, and other machines in ones and twos. Many of these were French and the first standard training aircraft for the RFC was a Farman.

The British companies turned to the racing market for developing their machines. Sopwith's racer was the Tabloid, a lightweight biplane built round

Father of the famous family of Sopwith fighters, the Tabloid, at the Schneider Cup Race in 1914

the famous French Gnome engine. In 1913 it outperformed the BS 1, proving that the British aircraft industry could produce fine aircraft. Still the War Office dithered. Sir George White brought out a similar design, the Bristol Scout.

In 1914 the Tabloid caused a sensation by triumphing in the premier race for seaplanes, the Schneider Cup. The first race was held in Monaco in 1913 and the trophy was presented by a Frenchman, Jacques Schneider, to a Frenchman, Marcel Prévost, flying a French aircraft, a Deperdussin, powered by a French engine, the ubiquitous Gnome. Second was Roland Garros in another French machine, a Morane-Saulnier. The next year, looking for a forum to show off the Tabloid, Sopwith entered a seaplane version powered by the Gnome rotary and flown by Howard Pixton, an Australian. He won a two-hour race at an average speed of 86 mph against French, German, American and Swiss competition.

So, as Europe moved towards war, the British aircraft industry was among the world leaders in design and performance, having caught up with the French. The RFC on the other hand had a motley collection of just over 100 aircraft divided between the Army and the Navy, many of them designed four years previously when European aviation was in its infancy. With war imminent, Vickers, the armaments conglomerate, sent its latest pusher design, the FB5, to Farnborough for tests. Approval was given within days but no orders placed. Vickers decided to gamble: they bought enough materials to build 50 and started production on their own initiative. At the British factory of the Gnome Engine Company production of rotary engines was increased from one to ten a week.

Some idea of the relative importance which military planners of the great

Many of the aircraft which started the war were 'pushers'; this is a Farman of the French Army

powers placed on aircraft is reflected by the size of their air services as Europe went to war. Between them they had under 1000 aircraft: Russia approximately 300, Germany some 240, France 150 and the military wing of the RFC 63. They were seen as an adjunct to cavalry. There was no perception of the aircraft as a fighting machine and virtually none of them was armed save with a rifle or a pistol. The RFC had only one aircraft fitted with a machine-gun and that was unofficial, the personal initiative of its pilot, Lt Louis Strange.

The RFC was deployed with the 100,000-strong British army at Maubeuge on the French border; to the south-east was France's Fifth Army. The Germans were advancing across Belgium and the Allied plan was to move up towards Mons to meet them. The Battle of Mons on 23 August 1914 was the first against superior German forces and the French, on the British right, started to retreat. The British fought on, not realising that the French retreat left them exposed to the south. During the day the RFC carried out reconnaissance flights and Lt Philip Joubert de la Ferté, flying to the north, reported German soldiers pouring along the roads. The Germans opened up on him with rifle fire, puncturing his fuel tank, and he had to hold his finger over the hole all the way back to base. Initially Sir John French, the British commander, was unmoved and decided to fight on. But when the report was confirmed by other pilots and, later, by cavalry, and when he heard that the French had retreated, he was forced to decide between retreat or being surrounded. He retreated.

The German plan was to force the French and their British allies back towards

FIRST WORLD WAR AIRCRAFT
Seventy years on a few original
aircraft are still flying; others are
faithful replicas, built for film-makers.

LVG CiV

Fokker EiII

Avro 504K

Sopwith Pup

Bristol F2b

LVG C1V: original German two-seater of 1915, now part of the Shuttleworth Collection. It was armed with forward- and backward-firing machine-guns.

Fokker E111 'Eindecker': a replica of Germany's first fighter with an interrupter-gear.

Avro 504K: original, built in 1918. One of the classic aircraft of all time, some 9000 were built. The RFC taught a generation of pilots to fly in 504s and this one was pressed back into service in 1940 to tow gliders.

Sopwith Pup: used by the Navy in deck-landing trials; on the Western Front it was soon superseded by its more powerful stablemate, the Sopwith Camel.

Bristol F2b: original of one of the most advanced aircraft of the war, with forward- and backward-firing guns. Some were still in service in 1932.

SE5a: classic British single-seat fighter.

SE5a

Paris, then send one army round the west of the city and attack in the rear. For the next ten days the French and British retreated just as the Germans had planned. It was a desperate time for France: half a million casualties in a space of weeks and their army in headlong retreat. On 30 August the Germans were within flying range of Paris and they sent aircraft over the capital to drop bombs; one person was killed and several wounded. Meanwhile General Joffre, the French commander-in-chief, had to wait until the German plan for Paris was clear. Information came from prisoners, from spies, from cavalry and from aircraft, but much of it was uncoordinated and for a time there was confusion. Then on 3 September a French pilot, Lt Watteau, brought back the first definite reports of the German armies moving from west to east in front of Paris, indicating that they did not have the strength to envelop the city. Joffre still hesitated until more French and British pilots confirmed the German move, but then, prompted by General Gallieri, moved against the Germans on the River Marne. The British moved into a gap between two German armies; the Germans felt exposed and started to retreat, and any chance of a swift victory was gone. For the first time aircraft had played a part in preparing for a decisive battle.

In a series of outflanking manoeuvres the opposing forces finished up in a more or less continuous line of trenches stretching from Switzerland to the Channel coast. A war of seemingly endless movement had suddenly turned into a static confrontation. It was a war for which the armies were not prepared; the trenches were protected by barbed wire and the ground between them was swept with machine-gun fire and shelled by artillery. Massed cavalry was held behind the lines ready to exploit any breakthrough and to reconnoitre the enemy positions, but faced with trenches horses could no longer reconnoitre. The new air arm replaced them.

On a static front, artillery became the principal means of waging war; aircraft became the handmaiden of the guns. Pilots took daily photographs which were turned into maps to enable the ground spotters to adjust their fire with pinpoint accuracy. Aircraft also spotted for the guns directly, giving the corrections by Morse code. From their vantage point aircraft could also give advance warning of the movement of enemy reserves; they quickly became the principal source of military intelligence in a trench war. By the war's end over two-thirds of all military information was either obtained or verified from the air.

Once the 'Front' had been established, both sides started building airfields some twenty miles to the rear. As demands for photographs and visual obser-vations mounted, replacement aircraft were hurried out from Britain: two-seater BE 2cs, the first single-seater Sopwith Tabloids and, in October, the first of the Vickers FB 5s which had been built without an order. In a short time the reconnaissance effort settled down to a gruelling, systematic, daily survey of the

THE EYE IN THE SKY
In the last two years of the war, the RFC took over half a million photographs of the Western Front from many different altitudes, daily updating information and making maps.

The Front from high level and the map made from the photograph

The Front from low level, with German soldiers sheltering in a shellhole. INSET: *A camera on an Avro 540*

Front, spotting targets for the artillery, correcting their fire, photographing the trenches whenever the weather was good enough, looking for changes in the pattern of trenches or a build-up of enemy forces.

Clearly neither side allowed the other unrestricted access. In the early days pilots met a barrage of small-arms fire if they flew within rifle range of the trenches, and before long both sides installed anti-aircraft guns firing explosive shells. But fire from the ground could only ever be partially effective and many pilots felt that war in the air, like war on land or at sea, needed its own tactics, and that the best way to shoot down an aircraft was from another aircraft. To do that they would have to learn how to fight in the air, and they would have to learn on the job, finding the appropriate weapons and developing tactics. In the headlong plunge into war they armed themselves with whatever they could find, rifles, pistols and even grenades, which they hoped to drop on their adversaries. It took extraordinary skill to be effective with such small weapons fired from one moving aircraft at another and, though some pilots possessed those skills, clearly aircraft could be much more effective against each other if they were more heavily armed.

On 5 October 1914 a German Aviatik scout was flying near Rheims looking for signs of the French Army. It was spotted by Cpl Quénault, the observer in a Voisin pusher flown by Sgt Joseph Frantz. Quénault had acquired a Hotchkiss machine-gun which he had installed in the front cockpit, giving him an unrestricted forward field of fire. The German aircraft was unarmed but the unsuspecting pilot took no evasive action as Frantz manoeuvred towards him. At close range Quénault opened up with his machine-gun, riddling the Aviatik and setting it on fire. It crashed immediately, the first aircraft shot down in air-to-air combat. The lessons for pilots were simple: if you want to survive treat any enemy aircraft as lethal and arm yourself as heavily as possible.

The British were slower to arm than the French but faster than the Germans. Observers in the BE 2cs began to carry machine-guns to fire against attacks from the rear, and pushers like the Vickers FB 5 were supplied already armed with a machine-gun in the front, earning the nickname 'Gunbus'. But the new and much faster single-seat scouts, the Bristol Bullet and Sopwith Tabloid, which offered the best chance of catching enemy aircraft, were much more compact with a whirling engine and propeller right in front of the pilot. Forward-firing guns would have to clear the propeller, but rear-facing guns meant the pilot would have to face in two directions at once. Experiments were made with guns firing sideways from the cockpit, missing the propeller and the wing-struts, but it was highly unsatisfactory.

What single-seater pilots wanted was a gun firing directly forward, over the propeller or through it. A French manufacturer, Raymond Saulnier, came up

Aerial Combat 1915

with the most elegant solution, an interrupter-gear in the engine which only fired the gun when the propeller was out of the line of fire. He experimented with the Hotchkiss, but its fire was so erratic and so many rounds went off late that he shot off propeller after propeller. With the help of Roland Garros, the pre-war racing pilot now in uniform, he worked on a much cruder idea, fixing deflector plates to protect the propellers by spinning away those rounds which would otherwise hit it. The first experiments were disastrous and cost a few more propellers, but gradually they got the plates just the right shape and strength, and by 1 April 1915 Garros was ready to test the system in his Morane scout. Officially he was on a mission to drop bombs on a railway station near Ostend; in fact he was looking for a likely quarry. When he found one he dived straight at it. The German pilot remained steady while his observer blazed away with a rifle, not expecting fire from the front of a single-seat monoplane. Garros fired in the dive and raked the German aircraft, but it went on flying. He made two more firing passes before it eventually caught fire and crashed.

It was a crude device but it worked. Garros' whole aircraft felt like a weapon; it could be aimed directly at the opponent, flying and firing all in one flowing movement. On 15 April he was back again and shot down another German aircraft. Air activity was still very sparse in 1915, and the loss of two aircraft in quick succession to a single-seater caused concern on the German side. On 18 April Garros despatched another, then the same afternoon he was hit by ground fire and forced to land behind enemy lines where he was captured. The Germans now knew the secret of his success and hurriedly set about producing their own system for firing through the propeller.

But such incidents, though dramatic, were still comparatively rare; although they were now armed, the daily task of pilots remained intelligence-gathering. The generals were facing a new problem which arose from the sheer scale of the armies they were commanding: they could no longer see, with their own eyes, what was going on. An advance would take place along several miles of the Front while they were remote from the battle in their headquarters, and they would quickly lose touch with developments; what is more, their ability to influence events once the battle had started was virtually nil. So, in addition to their general surveys of the Front, the RFC was tasked with gleaning information while the battle was in progress, and in some detail.

Pilots developed what they called contact patrols – flying over the battle area low enough to distinguish the colour of uniforms; sometimes flying between the opposing forces, noting their positions. Such flying took a particular kind of soldier/pilot, one who could be brave alone and still stay calm enough to make useful and accurate observations; inaccurate or incomplete information could only add to confusion.

One such pilot was Capt. Lanoe Hawker. He made something of a speciality of contact patrols and his reports were so good that his services were constantly in demand. In April 1915 he was based at Poperinghe near Ypres, where the British Army held a precarious salient jutting into German territory. At 5 pm on 22 April the Germans launched a huge artillery bombardment, accompanied for the first time on the Western Front by poison gas. In the immediate confusion, in some cases panic, the Germans advanced under cover of darkness. The British commander, General Sir Horace Smith-Dorrien, rushed up reinforcements, but in the morning he had no idea where they would be best placed, not knowing how far the Germans had advanced or where his own troops had finished up. Hawker was sent to find out. Flying against the wind in his slow and cumbersome BE 2c he was an easy target, and his first contact with the enemy was a salvo of

FIRING THROUGH THE PROPELLER
Roland Garros in the cockpit of his Morane-Saulnier soon after the gun and deflectors had been fitted. After his capture he escaped from the Germans to fly again, but was killed in action.

The deflector plate

Roland Garros

TACTICS

These diagrams were used by the RFC as
visual aids for pilots in training for combat.
The top two scenes show how important it
was to be suspicious of what appeared to be an
easy target; 'Jackals' (*bottom*) was designed to
instil the need for disciplined formation-flying.

rifle and machine-gun fire; it was a start and told him where some Germans were. By roaming over the whole area of the battle, noting a bridge down here, hostile fire there, French troops moving in this or that direction, empty trenches and, crucially, a line of new German trenches dug during the night, he was able to give a complete picture of the situation. Over the following days he had a grandstand view of the Second Battle of Ypres.

On 24 April, flying low over a farm to see who occupied it, he was hit in the foot by a sudden burst of fire. Clearly it was occupied by Germans but he was determined to place it accurately on the map, and also he did not want to give them the satisfaction of having beaten him off, so he flew over again just to make sure. It was just the aggressive spirit needed and fostered in the RFC, where the policy was always to carry the fight to the enemy. Despite the wound, which made walking difficult, he stayed with the squadron until the worst of the battle was over. For his work that month he was awarded the DSO.

In June he was given a much faster, single-seater Bristol Scout, fitted with a sideways-firing machine-gun. On 25 July he was patrolling alone near Ypres when he saw two German reconnaissance aircraft flying just to their side of the lines. He dived into the attack and opened fire from about 400 yards, only to be met by a hail of ground fire. Realising he could not get close enough he broke off the attack. Thirty minutes later, he saw another; this time it was on the wrong side of the lines. He climbed to a position above the enemy, between him and the sun, then dived, waiting until he was very close before firing a stream of bullets into it and sending it crashing down behind the British lines. A great cheer went up from the thousands of troops below, who later confirmed that one of the first aircraft he had shot at had been forced to land on the German side. Valuable maps showing the location of German guns were found on the body of the observer in the German machine. It was a classic air battle and the high point of a period of ascendancy for the Allies. Lanoe Hawker was awarded the Victoria Cross, the first for aerial combat. The fight showed some of the basic tactics of aerial combat emerging: get above your opponent and use surprise where possible, coming out of the sun.

Within the RFC Hawker was acknowledged as an expert fighter as well as observer and he became something of a hero inside the Army as well. But to the public at large he was virtually unknown; the British policy was not to single out individuals for special praise. The French did things differently: with little to show for the huge loss of life on the ground, the French Army used the success of their airmen as symbols of victory. Adolphe Pegoud, the pre-war aerobatic pilot, who had shot down his first German in February and had five aerial victories by that time, was a national figure in France. The psychological effect of such lionising on German pilots, who were already suffering from a technical disadvantage, was the reverse: they felt inferior and stayed close to their lines, avoiding combat.

However, one day in July 1915 a tiny monoplane landed at the German airfield at Douai. It was flown personally by Anthony Fokker, a famous Dutch pilot and aircraft manufacturer. Holland was neutral and he had sold his services to Germany. He had come to demonstrate the Fokker EI, a pure fighting machine. In the time since the capture of Garros' deflector-equipped Morane he had succeeded where Saulnier had failed, perfecting an interrupter-gear which could fire a machine-gun reliably through the propeller. One by one the pilots squeezed into the cockpit with him for a demonstration flight. Two, Max Immelman and Oswald Boelke, were particularly thrilled, and when the new machines started coming into squadron service they were among the first to try them out.

On 1 August Allied aircraft came to bomb Douai airfield. Immelman and Boelke took off in their EIs in pursuit. Boelke's guns jammed, but Immelman managed to shoot down his first enemy aircraft. It was a turning-point: by the end of the month Boelke had shot down his first, and within days the Douai pilots managed to shoot down a whole flight of French aircraft on a bombing mission. The technical pendulum was swinging in favour of the Germans and with it went a psychological advantage; in September it was the Allied pilots who were avoiding combat, a period they referred to dolefully as the 'Fokker Scourge'.

The German Air Service now introduced new reconnaissance aircraft and an intensive programme of training pilots. At the same time it built and improved the Fokkers. In the autumn of 1915 they virtually had command of the air but they failed to exploit their advantage fully. The pilots, Boelke in particular, wanted to form squadrons of Fokkers and carry the fight over the lines, using much the same policy as the French and the British, but senior German officers were more cautious and deployed the Fokkers piecemeal up and down the Front, with strict orders to the pilots not to fly across the lines lest their secret be found out. It was a mistake. The Allied air commanders appreciated that air warfare was offensive in nature and they carried out a policy of crossing the lines even when they were at a technical disadvantage and suffering the consequences.

One of the architects of the aggressive policy was General Hugh Trenchard. Since the beginning of the war he had been a senior staff officer, but in August he had been appointed commander of the RFC in France. In the face of the Fokker Scourge he ordered the squadrons to practise formation-flying, and further, that reconnaissance flights would continue to be aggressive though the aircraft would be protected by three or more armed machines.

By January 1916 Immelman and Boelke had each shot down eight aircraft and news of their exploits had reached the German public. The German High Command took the same view as the French of their value as symbols of heroism

'Mick' Mannock

James McCudden

Lanoe Hawker

BRITISH PILOTS

Major Edward 'Mick' Mannock, VC. The RAF's outstanding fighter-leader, he shot down 73 enemy aircraft; before the war he was a telephone linesman; he was killed in action in 1918.

Major James McCudden, VC. The RAF's tactician, he shot down 57 enemy aircraft; started as a bugler and worked his way through the ranks.

Major Lanoe Hawker, VC. The professional soldier, observation pilot and fighter pilot.

Capt. Albert Ball, VC. The first British ace to receive publicity, he shot down 47 enemy aircraft.

Albert Ball

and success, and the Kaiser awarded them both Germany's highest military decoration, the Pour le Mérite. A new word entered the German language, coined to describe their new heroes – Oberkanone, literally 'top gun'.

On 21 February the Germans launched a huge offensive against the French fortified lines at Verdun. It was a bloody battle of attrition fought with horrendous artillery bombardments which lasted until December the same year. It was Germany's attempt to 'bleed France white'. The contribution of the German pilots at the outset was dwarfed by the effort on the ground but it was considerable: 140 reconnaissance machines and 21 of the new Fokker fighters. German air policy was still defensive – to protect their reconnaissance machines and to deny the French access to their airspace. As the battle opened French aircraft were pushed back but Commandant de Peuty, the commander of the French Air Services, went on to the offensive. He reinforced Verdun with four squadrons of the latest French single-seater scout, the Nieuport, which was fitted with a machine-gun on the top wing, firing over the propeller. It was faster than the Fokker – up to 120 mph against 80 mph, was stronger and highly manoeuvreable. The French pilots took on the Germans in a fight for control of the sky over the battlefield, enabling their photographic aircraft to work away underneath.

By 1916 the French had a highly developed system of photographic reconnaissance which was providing up to 5000 photographs a day of any particular section of the Front. In some cases prints were flown from the developing unit and dropped to hard-pressed commanders on the ground within an hour of being taken. In the mud and smoke of battle below over a million men died at Verdun alone in indescribable anonymity; thousands of men reduced to nothing save a few unidentifiable bone fragments. By contrast the tiny numbers who fought in the air thrived on the cult of the individual. In the skies over Verdun new French 'aces' were born and the names of Georges Guynemer, Charles Nungesser and Jean Navarre became official national heroes, with whole columns of newsprint devoted to their exploits.

The Germans did the same. By June Max Immelman's personal score had reached fifteen and amongst Allied and German pilots alike he was known as the 'Eagle of Lille', ascribed mystical, even superhuman powers. Then on 18 June he came up against two FE 2bs, new two-seater pushers which were coming into service with the RFC. Whether through structural failure or as a result of bullet-fire, his aircraft broke up in the fight and he crashed to his death. Having projected him as a national saviour, his death was a national tragedy for Germany and his funeral was fittingly elaborate. Lying in state at a military hospital, among the many who came to pay their respects were the Crown Princes of Bavaria and Saxony and twenty German generals.

FRENCH PILOTS

Capt. René Fonck, Croix de Guerre with 28 palms. Arguably the most successful pilot of all; his official score was 75, but his own estimate was 127.

Capt. Georges Guynemer became the darling of France for his 54 kills; he disappeared on a flight in 1917.

Lt Charles Nungesser raced cars before the war; frequently wounded and shot down, he survived the war with 45 kills.

Adolphe Pegoud became the first 'ace' but was killed in 1915. The Germans dropped a wreath to his funeral.

Georges Guynemer

Charles Nungesser

Adolphe Pegoud

Edward Rickenbacker

Raoul Lufbery

'Billy' Mitchell

AMERICAN AND
GERMAN PILOTS
Capt. Edward Rickenbacker
scored 26 and was active in
aviation for the rest of his life.
Major Raoul Lufbery fought
for France before America
joined the war; killed in 1917.
General 'Billy' Mitchell,
flamboyant leader of US
airmen in France.
Hauptmann Oswald Boelke,
the architect of air-fighting
tactics, and his partner
Leutnant Max Immelmann.

Max Immelmann (left) *and Oswald Boelke*

If the German General Staff valued the image of its pilots more than their skills, Boelke, now the leading fighter pilot with eighteen kills and a master tactician of air fighting, did not share them. When the generals decided to take him off flying duties because he was too valuable he was furious, but even a direct appeal to the Kaiser himself was useless; he was sent on a tour of inspection of other Fronts.

On 1 July, after an extensive artillery bombardment, the British Army started its offensive on the Somme to relieve the hard-pressed French at Verdun. General Trenchard was in a much better position than Commandant de Peuty: he had two new pusher aircraft, the two-seater FE 2 and the single-seater DH 2, both armed with guns facing forward. But it was clear that for fighting, the single-seater biplane with its engine at the front and guns firing through the propeller was the best configuration and he also had the first allied examples of these: the Bristol Scout and the Sopwith $1\frac{1}{2}$ Strutter, both fitted with synchronised guns firing through the propeller, and the French Nieuport. However, his main advantage was numerical – 386 aircraft, of which 138 were fighters, as against 130 with 19 fighters on the Somme Front alone. When the land battle opened the RFC controlled the sky. British reconnaissance aircraft were free to observe and give constant help to the British artillery.

In the dogfights above them a new name began to find its way into the newspapers, despite Army disapproval. In the space of three months Capt. Albert Ball, a moody but thoroughly aggressive twenty-year-old, became the highest-scoring fighter pilot on all sides, accounting for 30 German aircraft. In the air the Allies were once again in the ascendant.

In the autumn of 1916, after their setbacks on the Somme, the German Air Service underwent great changes. Boelke, who had been tirelessly promoting the idea of forming fighting squadrons, got his way and 33 Jagdstaffeln (literally 'hunting squadrons') were formed. They were equipped with a new fighter, the Albatross single-seater with two synchronised machine-guns firing through the propeller and a powerful Mercedes engine which gave it a good rate of climb and top speeds of well over 100 mph. Boelke was to lead one of the new 'Jastas'. He knew from experience that he would need a particular kind of aggressive, yet cool-headed pilot. On his tour of the Eastern Front he had found a young and aristocratic cavalry officer flying observation patrols, but whose name would soon become greater than any other fighter pilot – Baron Manfred von Richthofen.

That autumn the new German fighting squadrons were superior in aircraft, tactics and fighting spirit, and they brutally wrested the initiative back from the Allies. It was in large part due to Boelke's leadership and example. They never had as many aircraft as the Allies, yet between September and November his Jasta 2 shot down 76 Allied aircraft for the loss of seven. It was the flowering of a personal talent and understanding of the principles of air fighting which was unrivalled. He was leader, instructor, mentor and fighter and his team was a tight and cohesive unit. (Jasta 11, formed at more or less the same time, accounted for only one enemy aircraft over the same period and that was unconfirmed.) Sadly, one of those seven losses was Boelke himself. On 28 October the squadron attacked two British aircraft. As they dived, Boelke's wing just touched that of a colleague; the wings buckled and he spiralled down. His personal score was 40, eclipsing Ball. Germany went into mourning again and Jasta 2 was renamed Jasta Boelke in his memory, a tradition which the Federal German Air Force retains to this day.

Within a month it was England's turn to mourn. On 23 November Manfred von Richthofen saw a lone DH 2 and went into the attack in his Albatross. He quickly realised that he was up against a skilled opponent; the DH 2 was inferior in all respects but Richthofen, who had already shot down ten enemy aircraft, was no longer a novice. They were fighting over German airspace and as they tangled they flew lower and lower. At 100 feet the RFC pilot broke off the fight and headed for home, zig-zagging over the trenches. He nearly made it, but one of Richthofen's bullets went straight through his head. He was Lanoe Hawker VC, Britain's first real fighter pilot and tactician. Richthofen retrieved the machine-gun from the wreckage and had it mounted in pride of place among the trophies of his battles.

On 16 January 1917 Richthofen shot down his sixteenth victim and became the leading living German fighter pilot. Two days later he was awarded the 'Pour le Mérite' and command of his own Jasta, No. 11, which had yet to improve on its record. On his first flight with the squadron he doubled its score to two and his own to seventeen, and within a short time he had brought it the same inspiration which Boelke had instilled in Jasta 2.

Late in 1916 the German Army started preparing new defensive positions, known to the Allies as the Hindenberg Line. The Allies wanted to know all they could about them and pilots had to fly deeper into German territory. Jasta 11 was at Douai and throughout the winter part of their job was to stop the photographing of the new positions. Many of the British reconnaissance machines were still the old and vulnerable BE2cs, but Trenchard never let up on the offensive policy: he had superiority in numbers and a new generation of fighters. The single-seater Sopwith Pup, Sopwith Triplane and SE5a, and the Bristol Fighter, a formidable weapon with synchronised guns firing forward and a gun for the observer in the rear cockpit for defence, gave him a technical advantage. But the new fighters came in only slowly and, though they were more than a match for the Albatross, their pilots had yet to discover their full potential and the Germans were highly effective. The fight for information was a costly one.

The Last Flight of Captain Albert Ball

The air battle on the Arras Front reached a crescendo in April 1917, 'Bloody April' to the RFC. In a single month they lost 151 aircraft, 21 of them to Richthofen alone, bringing his total to 52. German losses for the same period were 70, in part because there were simply more British aircraft to shoot at – 385 fighters compared with 114 – and in part because the RFC policy of always being on the offensive made them more vulnerable. But the German tactics, still inspired by Boelke and directed mainly by Richthofen, were precisely what was needed. They concentrated their best pilots into individual, élite squadrons and wherever possible went for the more vulnerable observation aircraft which were doing the real damage. In the mêlée the ever-aggressive Captain Ball died: Richthofen's brother, Lothar, was officially credited with shooting him down but some reports suggest that he became disorientated in cloud and crashed.

The aeroplane came of age as a fighting machine over the battlefields of Arras. The scale of air operations in France would continue to grow massively through 1918, and as new types of aircraft sent the pendulum swinging back and forth the fortunes of pilots soared and crashed, but in their essentials the roles which aircraft could perform in support of armies on the ground, and the tactics which went with them, were defined by the summer of 1917. For the soldier the most profound change was the use of aircraft for observation – their original function.

Substantial troop movements had to be carried out at night or run the risk of the enemy finding out exactly what was happening.

Aircraft could also drop bombs on soldiers, their supplies and communications and they were used extensively for that purpose, although causing only minor casualties. Soldiers could also be strafed from the air. On 11 May 1917 the RFC made the first co-ordinated attack in support of infantry. After the customary artillery barrage had stopped, the German infantry came out of their dugouts to defend themselves and found they were not only facing advancing British soldiers but low-flying FE 2bs and Nieuports with machine-guns blazing. In July the Germans made use of the same tactics and formed squadrons specially trained to support soldiers in attack. Tactical ground-attack aircraft made their début.

But the most profound development was in the air itself. The sky, like the sea and the land before it, was now a place to do battle. Airmen had to fight for the airspace over the battlefield and a new type of aircraft – the fighter – had been born. Fighting in aircraft was a highly individual form of combat which took a particular kind of personality: aggressive, ruthless, cool in combat, competitive, even élitist; the spirit of the fighter pilot was central to the ethos of a new fighting arm which was only truly effective when on the offensive.

By 1917 soldiers had come to accept that without an air corps an army was incomplete. In 1914 when the US Army formed its aviation section with six aircraft, 60 officers and 260 soldiers it was far behind even Britain; as America went to war on 6 April 1917 Congress voted $640 million for military aviation.

The Air Services saw quite another role for aircraft in war – striking directly at the population and economic centres of the enemy. The potential for aircraft, and airships, to drop bombs on strategic targets away from the battlefield was obvious even before 1914, but the first efforts were puny. Airships could carry more weight and had a much longer range. The day following the declaration of war ZVI approached a fortress at Liège carrying eight artillery shells, but as it descended through the clouds it was riddled by ground fire from rifles and machine-guns and turned back leaking, only to crash-land before reaching its base. On 30 August a single German aeroplane flew over Paris and dropped several small bombs; the damage was negligible, and on subsequent raids Parisians, far from being terrorised, came out into the streets to watch.

The RNAS had been given the task of defending mainland Britain from attack by airships and they decided that attacking them in their home bases was the best policy. On 21 September they sent three Avro 504s from Belfort, close to the Swiss border, to Friedrichshafen. They bombed the sheds and destroyed the gasworks but failed to hit any airships. On 8 October two Sopwith Tabloids took off from Antwerp to bomb the Zeppelin sheds at Düsseldorf and Cologne. One destroyed an airship shed with a Zeppelin inside but the other bombed Cologne railway station. These were the first strategic bombing raids and they were made against specifically military targets. In range and carrying capacity they showed clearly how limited the aeroplane of 1914 was. Nevertheless both Germany and France formed air units specially for bombing, and on 4 December the French bombed Freiberg-im-Breisgau and on the 24th the Germans bombed Dover. In the same month the Royal Navy launched the first-ever air attack from on board ship, sending seaplanes to the Zeppelin sheds at Cuxhaven. They missed the sheds and went for the German fleet instead without causing much damage; all the aircraft were lost.

What the air services on all sides wanted were bigger aircraft with longer ranges. Commander Murray-Sueter of the RNAS, who had planned the Cuxhaven raid, went to see Handley Page and asked them to build what he graphically described as a 'bloody paralyser of an aeroplane'. What he had in mind was on the lines of Russia's four-engined giants, the Ilya Muromets, which had been built for reconnaissance but were soon turned into bombers. The Germans and French came to the same conclusions and by late 1914 the aircraft industries of all combatant powers were looking at the problems of producing long-range bombers. Meanwhile the airship was the only strategic bomber available and Germany was far ahead of the others in airship technology (see p. 28)

Germany started planning to attack London with aircraft in late 1916. On the direct orders of General Ludendorff a special squadron, Bombengeschwader 3, was formed with the sole purpose of bombing England and, he imagined, terrorising the population. Equipped with 30 of the latest Gotha IV long-range bombers, its first attempt to bomb London came on 25 May 1917. Bad weather stopped the raiders at Gravesend and they bombed Folkestone instead, killing 95 people. But on 13 June a force of fourteen Gothas attacked London in broad daylight. The aircraft sent up to intercept them were mainly ageing BE 2cs, one of which was the only aircraft to be shot down. Unhampered by fighters, the Gothas unloaded their bombs and turned back for their base in Belgium: 162 people were killed and 432 injured. Eighteen of the dead and 30 of the injured were children from Upper North Street School in Limehouse. The British public was outraged: the Zeppelins had been beaten but this new threat seemed both more deadly and more humiliating since all the raiders had escaped. Inevitably there were calls for retaliation.

The first action taken by the War Cabinet was to put General J. C. Smuts, the South African soldier and statesman, in charge of an enquiry into Britain's air defences. The first part of his task was relatively simple, to reorganise and improve the existing defences which had been installed against the Zeppelins.

THE GERMANS RAID LONDON
The first of the heavy bombers
was the Gotha IV. On 7 July
1917 (*opposite top*) bombs fell
close to St Paul's Cathedral in
the City of London and in
Cox's Court, Little Britain,
EC1. By January 1918
(*opposite below*) anti-aircraft
defences had made bombing
London expensive.

The Gotha IV

Cox's Court and St Paul's Cathedral

This Gotha was shot down at night in January 1918

Two fighter squadrons were brought back from France, to the annoyance of some generals. Home Defence started to absorb defences badly needed in France. The latest fighter, the powerful, fast and manoeuvreable Sopwith Camel, was also ideal for intercepting bombers, and the RNAS squadrons tasked with defending Britain were re-equipped with it in June.

Intercepting bombers was clearly a more difficult task than catching the slow and highly visible Zeppelins, but the first interception was made on 4 July when Camels attacked sixteen bombers returning from a raid on Harwich and one Gotha was shot down in flames. The improved defences caused the German planners to think again and the last daylight raid on London took place on 7 July. In late August three Gothas were shot down, and by the end of the month daylight raids stopped altogether. Then on 3 September the Gothas came back at night. They flew in a stream rather than in formation, making interception even more difficult. On 25 September the first night-raider was shot down by anti-aircraft guns but it was January 1918 before the first night interception was made. On the night of 19/20 March 38 bombers set out; only thirteen reached their targets and six were shot down. The night bombing of Britain was stopped.

Fewer than 1000 people had been killed in a total of 28 day and night raids and the damage to property and disruption to industry was not of any great economic or strategic importance, but the long-term effects of the campaigns were far-reaching. Civilians had been killed and Britain humiliated; air warfare now had a political as well as a military dimension. General Smuts's report to the War Cabinet in October 1917 unsurprisingly recommended retaliatory raids against Germany but it went much further: 'The day may not be far off when aerial operations with their devastation of enemy lands and destruction of industrial and population centres on a vast scale may become the principal operations of war, to which the older forms of military and naval operations may become secondary and subordinate.'

The whole report, but particularly that theme, was anathema to fighting soldiers: there was moral opposition to the very concept of waging war on civilians, but the main objection was that it reduced the air effort in France where the Army saw the primary task of aircraft as supporting their operations on land. But Smuts did not stop there. He proposed that the air arms of the Army and Navy be hived off from their parent services and formed into a completely new body to be called the Royal Air Force. To free it from interference by generals and admirals it would even have its own Ministry and its own ranks. Within the RAF would be a bomber force to strike against Germany and quite independent of all requirements of the Army.

There were powerful objections inside the military establishment, but politically it was just what the Prime Minister, David Lloyd George, needed. The

'BLOODY PARALYSERS'
Russia built the first four-engined bomber to go into service in 1914, Igor Sikorsky's Ilya Muromets: 73 were built, it had a crew of 16, and its first raids were in Poland in 1915.

The 'bloody paralyser' Cmdr Murray-Sueter asked for in 1914 was the Handley Page 0/400.

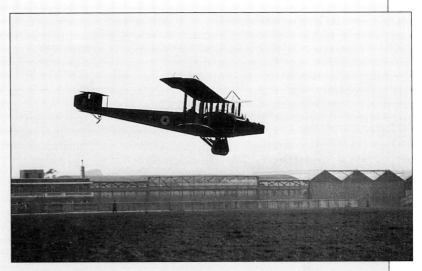

The Handley Page 0/400

The Ilya Muromets

French Army was riven with indiscipline and even mutiny, and the burden of fighting was falling more and more on Britain; Russia, preoccupied with revolution, was all but out of the war; and America had yet to provide a decisive advantage. Smuts was offering the tantalising prospect of a radical new route to victory. Given enough bombers Germany could be brought to her knees without mass casualties on the Western Front.

A Bill was passed by Parliament in November 1917 setting the date for the formation of the Royal Air Force, the world's first independent air force, for 1 April 1918. General Trenchard was appointed as its first Chief of Staff. But in October 1917, before Parliament had even passed the Bill, the Independent Bomber Force was being formed at Nancy in France, the closest point from which to reach the German industrial areas. The first aircraft were DH 9 single-engined light bombers which had been used for bombing targets at the Front; they could carry just 460 lbs of bombs. They were soon backed up by Handley Page O/400s, the 'bloody paralyser' which Murray-Sueter had asked for in 1914, which had already been used by the RNAS to bomb the Gotha bases in Belgium; they could carry nearly a ton of bombs.

Before the end of October both types were used in raids against industry in the Saar. By June 1918 they had made 57 raids into Germany. Berlin was out of reach though Handley Page was working on its V1500 bomber which would bring it within range. The Germans responded by bringing fighters back from the Front; they were highly effective – on one occasion a force of twelve DH 9s set off to bomb Mainz; two got back. The raids had similar results to those carried out by Germany against Britain: casualties were never measured in more than hundreds and frequently in tens; the total killed in the rest of the war, 746, was less than Germany had inflicted on Britain and they were no more than an irritation to industrial production. The principal effects were indirect: they drew fighters away from the German Army sorely pressed at the Front, and they hurt the pride of the German people. Germany could no longer bomb Britain and Germans at home were already suffering privations due to the war effort and the naval blockade. The raids were tangible evidence of the creeping realisation that Germany could not sustain the war.

The last great German offensives at the Front began with the 'Kaiserschlacht' in March 1918. With Russia out of the war, they were Germany's last chance to win before the American effort and the British blockade made it impossible. They came perilously close to success. The RFC threw everything it could into strafing and bombing the advancing troops, taking very heavy losses from ground fire and from the best German fighter pilots. Of these the most feared was still Manfred von Richthofen, but on 21 April in a dogfight near Amiens, after he had just shot down his 80th opponent, making him the highest-scoring fighter

A replica Fokker Triplane in the colours of the Red Baron

THE RED BARON
Manfred von Richthofen was
a charismatic and instinctive
leader whose pilots adored
him. He had an enthusiasm
for souvenirs of his victims,
which he kept in his trophy
room (*left*); Lanoe Hawker's
machine-gun is over the door.

pilot of the war, in an unguarded moment he let a Canadian Camel pilot, Roy
Brown, get into a firing position which he put to good effect. Richthofen's loss
was a grievous blow to the German Air Service and to Germany.

By June the German offensive had been stemmed. The losses on the ground
were, as usual, measured in tens of thousands but the losses in the air too reflected
the higher level of air activity by both sides: in May alone Germany lost 180
aircraft, the Allies over 400. Where Allied aircraft had once operated in flights
of four or six they now flew in squadron formations of twelve and these were
stacked up over the Front, each operating at its best operational height. The
Bristol fighters gave top cover at 18,000 feet; SE 5s roamed around 12–14,000
feet; the Camels took on the low flyers and strafed the enemy on the ground.
Sopwith had also developed the Dolphin specifically for the role of ground attack.

So strong was the legend that in 1925 the German government brought
Richthofen's body back to Germany where it was reburied in Berlin

When the Allies launched the inevitable counter-offensive on 8 August aircraft were involved along the whole 35-mile front. Pursuing the same aggressive policy, the RAF offered the Germans plenty of targets and lost 83 aircraft in the day, more than the entire strength of the RFC four years earlier; the Germans lost 49. But the RAF came back in strength and attacked German airfields in force. On 16 August it could muster 65 aircraft for a *single* raid on La Bassée airfield.

By 1918 the RAF was not only the world's only independent air force but by far the biggest: 22,500 aircraft and nearly 300,000 men, more than three times the size of the whole army which had crossed to France in 1914. Aircraft made decisive individual contributions in many battles on many Fronts, but their overall contribution to the Great War was never more than a spur to victory. The notion in the Smuts report never came close to even a full test; that would have to wait for another war. But the lessons were all there and twenty years later, when war came again, many of them had to be relearnt.

The Ford Trimotor: one of the first all-metal airliners

CHAPTER·FOUR

SHRINKING THE WORLD

Readers of *The Aeroplane* in 1919 became familiar with variations on the following theme: 'Avro 504K in perfect order: £40.' On the Western Front alone the combatant nations had produced over 200,000 aircraft between them; Britain had built 56,000. Many were destroyed in combat but even before the Peace Conference at Versailles was over the RAF had been cut by over half and there were thousands of surplus aeroplanes up for sale at a fraction of their original cost.

In another column *The Aeroplane* reader might find another familiar plea: 'RAF Captain requires post as pilot. Practical knowledge of rigging. Any type of machine.' Britain had trained 26,000 pilots: most were young men who went straight from school to war with little experience of life in between. Plucked from a gruelling yet stimulating experience, they were restless, press-on types looking for exciting outlets for newly redundant skills. Their options were few. There was talk of a long-term future flying mail and passengers but in 1919 it was a hazy prospect. There was barnstorming, stunting at air displays, which attracted some flamboyant souls. It offered a familiar thrill of closeness to death and Jean Navarre, who had captured the heart of France over Verdun in 1916, survived two more years of war only to die flying through the Arc de Triomphe. In America Hollywood hired experienced pilots to re-create their epic battles for the cameras but the number needed was tiny.

For an even small number there was a tantalising, more glamorous and potentially even more rewarding prospect – Lord Northcliffe's prize, offered in 1913, of £10,000 for a direct flight across the Atlantic. Aircraft had improved greatly in the interval and the prize was now £13,000, but even in 1919 the flight remained a daunting prospect. At its narrowest point between Newfoundland and Ireland the Atlantic is nearly 2000 miles across, a moody ocean prone to violent and unpredictable storms. But the challenge of the unknown was the whole point and there was no shortage of pilots willing to have a go.

By April 1919 four British teams were preparing to try. They were backed by aircraft companies for whom the prize offered a different prospect – publicity for what their aircraft could do. Sopwith's entry was designed for the flight; christened 'Atlantic', its pilot was Harry Hawker, the company test pilot, with Lt-Cmdr Kenneth McKenzie-Grieve as navigator. The Martinsyde Company entered another single-engined two-seater and took on Freddie Raynham as pilot. Handley Page and Vickers both entered their long-range bombers which had been denied the opportunity to bomb Berlin. Handley Page's four-engined V1500 was under the command of Admiral Mark Kerr, while Vickers' two-engined Vimy had an ex-RAF pilot and navigator, Capt. John Alcock and Lt Arthur Whitten Brown.

The prevailing winds blow from west to east, so the company teams set off by sea for Canada; but the first attempt was made in the opposite direction. On 8 April Major J. C. Wood set out from England in a Shorts seaplane; it was an ill-prepared attempt, and fortunately for him the engine failed over the Irish Sea, close enough for him to be rescued.

Meanwhile the teams were settling into the Cochrane Hotel in St John's, Newfoundland, and when the press booked in too, it became the unofficial race headquarters. There were no airfields and as they arrived each 'bagged' the largest flat space they could find. At Trepassey Bay the US Navy was preparing three Curtiss flying boats. They were not competing for the *Daily Mail* prize, since they planned a refuelling stop in the Azores. It was a naval exercise with 41 destroyers positioned along the route to help them navigate. They set off on 16 May but ran into bad weather; two had to land in the sea short of fuel; the third made it to the Azores.

On 18 May the weather lifted and the stage was set for the race to begin. Neither Admiral Kerr nor Alcock and Brown were ready. At 3.40 pm, in high spirits, Hawker and McKenzie-Grieve took off in the Sopwith without incident. Two hours later Raynham and his navigator boarded the Martinsyde. It was more powerful and they confidently expected to overtake the Sopwith team, but as the heavy machine trundled over the rough ground it hit a bump and briefly shot into the air, then belly-landed and nosed over into the soft ground. Both occupants were injured, but mercifully it did not catch fire.

News of the crash added more drama for the millions waiting for news of the Sopwith. Long after its fuel would have been exhausted there were still no sightings. Reluctantly, the flags in St John's were lowered to half-mast; it looked as if the cruel ocean had claimed its first victims. A week later the mood changed to jubilation: Hawker and McKenzie-Grieve arrived off the Hebrides aboard a Danish ship. Their engine had overheated in bad weather and having found the ship they had ditched alongside it. London gave them a heroes' welcome and Northcliffe gave them £5000. Two days later, after a long wait in the Azores, the remaining US Navy Curtiss arrived in Portugal to complete the first-ever aerial crossing of the Atlantic.

The American success and Hawker's rescue raised interest on both sides of the Atlantic. Vickers sent cables to Alcock and Brown demanding to know what was causing the delay, but on 14 June they were ready and a team of local men was recruited to push the overloaded Vimy to the take-off point of a hastily prepared runway of finite length. The Vimy's engines roared as it built up speed right to the end, where Alcock hauled her clear of a stone wall. Then, just skimming some trees, he began to climb slowly over St John's.

From the start the Atlantic did its best to defeat them. Within an hour they flew into a fog bank and Brown had nothing by which to navigate. They managed to climb above it and caught sight of the moon in a dark sky, but thick clouds barred the way ahead; they had no alternative but to fly into them. Alcock had no horizon with which to orientate himself – the instruments were only rudimentary and of little help in thick cloud. The airspeed indicator had jammed at 90 mph and, without knowing it, they were slowing down; eventually the Vimy shuddered into a stall and plummeted down through the murk. Waiting for the inevitable crash into the sea, they suddenly emerged from the cloud just 100 feet above the waves and Alcock managed to right the aircraft. Just after 8 am they crossed the Irish coast near Clifden, Co. Galway, but as they approached to land on an open space they saw people were waving. Alcock and Brown thought it was a welcome, but it was a warning: their chosen site was a bog and the Vimy finished up on its nose; they climbed out unhurt. They had been in the air for 16 hours 28 minutes.

Now it was their turn to be heroes. Aircraft escorted their train and crowds greeted them at every station. By the time they reached London the streets were packed, on a par with Blériot's reception just a decade earlier. Northcliffe was too ill to present the prize and his place was taken by the Secretary of State for Air, Winston Churchill. The following morning King George V knighted them both. (Admiral Kerr abandoned his attempt when he heard of their success.)

Sixteen years after the Wright Brothers had flown just a few yards, an aeroplane had crossed the Atlantic. Alcock and Brown's flight gave a glimpse of the possibilities of the future, a world in which journeys between continents were shrunk from weeks to hours. The Australian Prime Minister, William Hughes, in Europe for the Peace Conference, was moved to put his country on the aviation map. He offered £10,000 for a flight from London to Australia. Vickers prepared another Vimy and on 19 November Keith and Ross Smith, Australian brothers and RAF flyers, flew home from the war to the warmest of welcomes. Knighthoods were conferred on them by the King too. Four months later there were two more knighthoods. Two South Africans, Lt-Col. Havan van Rynveld and

On take-off, Alcock and Brown's
Vimy carried 870 gallons of fuel,
40 gallons of oil, a black toy cat
called Twinkletoes as a mascot
and 300 specially stamped letters
which were changing hands for
£175 in London. After the flight
Alcock stayed with Vickers and
died in a crash in France in
December 1919; Brown retired
from flying and died in 1948.

The US Navy Curtiss NC-4 flying boat which flew from
Newfoundland to Lisbon with a stopover in the Azores

Lts Keith and Ross Smith with Sgts James Bennett and Wally Shiers
at the start of their 28-day flight from London to Darwin, Australia

Quintin Brand, set out from London for Cape Town. They had three serious mishaps on the way and eventually Vickers had to supply a total of three Vimys and the South African government had to buy an ex-RAF DH 9 for them to finish the journey. They arrived in Cape Town on 20 March 1920.

Such flights made headlines and brought honours for the airmen and they gave a tempting vision of the future, but they also demonstrated the physical dangers and practical difficulties which would have to be overcome before the world could be girdled by long-distance passenger-carrying aircraft. But over shorter distances, between European capitals, there were more immediate possibilities. Commercial flying had been banned by all nations during the war but Germany got off to a good start by lifting its ban in January 1919. On 5 February Deutsche Luft Rederie started the first daily passenger service by air, using five-seater AEG biplanes for the 120 miles from Berlin to Weimar, the new site of the National Assembly.

This 'first' – by the defeated nation before the Peace Treaty was signed – dented French pride. Ever mindful of France's heritage in aviation, Farman Brothers arranged a symbolic passenger flight to England in a converted bomber, but since Britain had not lifted its ban all the passengers had to be military personnel. For their first truly civil flight the Farman company looked instead to Belgium and started flights over the battle-scarred countryside from Paris to Brussels on 22 March.

Britain lifted its ban in May but it was August before the first daily international service was established between Europe's two most important capitals. On the 25th a DH 4a of Air Transport and Travel (AT&T) took off from Hounslow, the only airfield with customs facilities, with one passenger, some Devonshire cream, leather, grouse and newspapers. It arrived at Le Bourget $2\frac{1}{2}$ hours later. The fare was £21 and in the afternoon four more passengers were carried in a DH 16.

Victorious Britain had five tiny airlines in 1919; by 1921 they had shrunk to three. Defeated Germany looked in on itself for an outlet for its energy and its nationalism and became intensely air-minded: local communities, towns, cities and the states wanted to be on the air map and offered financial incentives to the fledgling airline industry, and the central government gave the airlines a direct subsidy. Despite the impoverishment of paying war reparations and the restrictions on aviation imposed by the Treaty of Versailles, seven civil airlines started operations in 1919 and another six in 1920.

Germany was debarred from building military aircraft but ironically these restrictions helped to spur their designers into fresh ideas. Aircraft manufacturers teamed up with shipping companies to form airlines. They used the subsidies to stimulate the designers and builders still further, and in record time Junkers

Start of the first international air service from London to Paris

produced the first all-metal cabin airliner, the F.13. But large aircraft were a particular worry to the Allies and they forbade them from flying over Germany. Undaunted, Junkers looked east and offered technical assistance to the new airlines of Eastern Europe if they purchased Junkers aircraft; in aviation Eastern Europe became a German province.

In 1920 there were eight French airlines. Each one was awarded its own sphere of influence where it could develop without competition. Lacotière looked south from Marseilles to French North Africa; CFRNA eastward from Paris, in time extending their routes to Constantinople. The policy of helping airlines went even further than in Germany: in addition to direct subsidy, departments of government were formed to encourage technical innovation, to study the needs of the industry, and to provide navigation and weather information. By 1924 twelve foreign countries were linked to France by air. National pride was then, and has been ever since, a formidable force in the development of national airlines and the policy of subsidy was firmly rooted in French nationalism.

The British did things differently. They handed out knighthoods to the trail-blazers who generated spontaneous popular enthusiasm, but failed to grasp the real need of civil air transport: to survive beyond infancy it would need to be nurtured by subsidy. The first step was a good one: in March 1920 Waddon airfield, near Croydon, was turned into an air terminal. The most prestigious

FLIGHT ROUND THE WORLD
On 6 April 1924, four Douglas
World Cruisers with US
Army crews took off from
Seattle to fly round the world.
Two of them, 'Chicago' and
'New Orleans', landed back
there on 28 September after
flying for 363 hours in 175
days, covering 26,400 miles.

During the flight the crews
posed at Croydon. *From left:*
Lt Lowell Smith (leading
pilot), Lt L. P. Arnold (pilot
of 'Boston', which came
down), Sgt H. H. Ogden
(mechanic, 'New Orleans'),
US military attaché, Lt J.
Harding (mechanic,
'Chicago'), Lt Leigh Wade
(pilot, 'New Orleans') and Lt
Erik Nelson (pilot, 'Chicago').

route was London to Paris but passengers were few and competition was intense, and by July 1920 rivalry and the French subsidy to its airlines had reduced the £21 fare to £10. The British airlines, AT&T, Handley Page and the Instone Airline, lobbied for a comparable subsidy but their pleas fell on deaf ears. In December 1920 AT&T stopped flying; the following February the other two British operators stopped, leaving the new Croydon airport to the foreign airlines.

British prestige was hurt. Stung into action by a flurry of political and press comment, Winston Churchill set up the 'Cross Channel Committee', which managed to find £25,000 each for Instone and Handley Page, who resumed the service in March, flying on alternate days. By 1923 10,000 passengers a year were flying between London and Paris, the majority of them on British carriers. Several lessons had been learnt. Unfettered competition between airlines in a limited market meant that none would survive; some sort of subsidy was essential, especially on international routes where the competition was subsidised. In peacetime, without healthy airlines there could be no healthy aircraft-manufacturing industry. Lastly, whether governments liked it or not, airlines were inextricably bound up with national policies and national prestige.

One lesson that British ministers learnt quickly was that payment of subsidy gave them plenty of room to influence airline development and they saw that subsidising many small airlines was inefficient. A single big airline would be far easier to deal with: it was also a more potent national symbol. In 1924 the subsidy system was formalised: £1 million over ten years payable on the number of miles flown. But there was a political quid pro quo: in return the independent airlines must combine into a single national airline. The purpose of Britain's 'flag carrier' was evident in the name – Imperial Airways.

The idea of linking the British Empire by air was a powerful one; the new airline was to be as much an instrument of policy as a commercial enterprise and imperial thinking was to dominate civil air policy in Britain for over thirty years. One of the first priorities of the newly appointed Director of Civil Aviation, Sir Sefton Brancker, was to establish an air route to India. The RAF had established military airfields in many parts of the Empire, but for civil flights the route would have to be surveyed in detail and refined for the needs of passengers. Sir Sefton decided that he would carry out the survey himself; what he needed was a pilot.

He found the ideal candidate in Alan Cobham who managed the de Havilland Air Taxi Service at Stag Lane, near Hatfield. He was a jolly, outgoing man and a great enthusiast for civil flying; he had made a number of charter flights round Europe and North Africa. They set off on 20 November 1924 in Cobham's DH 50, G–EBFO, and after a gruelling four months collecting information on the routes, details of the facilities, friendly and hostile areas and potential hazards, they arrived in Rangoon on 17 March 1925.

But Cobham had developed a taste for survey-flying and the following year he planned an even more ambitious flight for Imperial Airways, backed by the aircraft industry. He would fly to Cape Town and make a film on the way to publicise air travel. It was a masterful flight: across Europe, down the Nile through British Africa, to the Cape in 93 days. Coming back, without the problems of film-making and with a greater knowledge of the route, he took sixteen days. Cobham was a doer: he organised everything from fuel to labour to smooth out the runways in the bush; he dined en route with local colonial settlers and administrators, making himself an ambassador for civil aviation. He had scant regard for politicians but he knew who was paying the piper, and when he tried to wake them up to aviation he played the right tune with style and humour.

He announced his next trip as a flight from Rochester on the River Medway to the Thames outside Parliament – via Australia. He took the wheels off EBFO and replaced them with floats and set off on 30 June 1926. After an epic round trip in 90 days, wearing himself to exhaustion in the process, he flew up the Thames to Hammersmith with ships hooting their welcome and people waving from the streets, before turning and slipping low over Westminster bridge to land before barges filled with the Great and the Good.

For his three odysseys Cobham joined aviation's other knights. As a national figure his mission was to make Britain air-minded. He organised air shows, personally taking members of the public on joy rides in an Avro 504, and National Air Days, and chartered aircraft in which he took young people for 'air experience' flights. But turning enthusiasm into a viable business for Imperial Airways took time. Few people in Britain could afford to fly, except occasionally for fun, and passengers were drawn almost exclusively from the home and colonial ruling élite.

There were also political problems. British aircraft were denied flying rights over Italy because the British government would not allow Mussolini, who wanted to dominate the Mediterranean, reciprocal rights at Gibraltar and Malta. It was a short-sighted policy by Britain which stunted the development of the route to India, and in the early days passengers going east first had to make their way by train and ship to Port Said before boarding an aircraft for Basra. When the route was opened to Karachi in 1929, the journey was still more of an adventure than a convenience. Passengers paid £130 and boarded an Armstrong-Whitworth Argosy at Croydon to fly to Basle. There, to avoid flying over Italy, they boarded a train for Genoa where they embarked on a Shorts Calcutta flying boat for Alexandria. Here they changed to a DH 66 Hercules which took them through Gaza, along oil pipelines across Arabia, with night stops at desert camps fortified against local tribesmen (a forced landing might mean being held for

BRITISH AVIATION'S GREAT POPULIST

After the triumphs of his route-proving flights, Sir Alan Cobham went on with his airshows and joy rides and he started a business developing in-flight refuelling systems; he died in 1973.

Crowds greeted Cobham at Westminster on 1 October 1926 after his return from Australia; his engineer had been killed while they were flying over the desert by a bullet from a Bedouin tribesman.

ransom). Leaving the Gulf for Karachi, Imperial pilots had to fly a lonely southerly route away from the Persian coast, where tribesmen shot at aircraft. At Karachi the service stopped, save for those bold enough to continue to Delhi in a tiny Puss Moth of the local flying club.

While Cobham and Imperial Airways were looking east and south, another race was regularly hitting the headlines – first to fly over the North Pole. Apart from Eskimos, a handful of ancient mariners and the American explorer Robert Peary, who had reached the North Pole on foot in 1909, nobody had seen much of the huge expanse to the north of Canada. There was still talk of an undiscovered land-mass. The aeroplane was the perfect answer for the polar explorer, and in the longer term the polar regions represented a shorter route for passenger aircraft between Europe and parts of America and the Pacific.

The Norwegian explorer, Roald Amundsen, was the first to try. He had sailed the North-West Passage between 1903 and 1906 and in 1911 he was the first to reach the South Pole. In 1925 he mounted an aerial expedition to the North Pole from Spitsbergen using two Dornier–Wal flying boats adapted to land on ice. Amundsen, his pilot and a Dornier mechanic were in one; Lincoln Ellsworth, an American colleague, was in the other with a similar crew. After take-off, their first problem was a huge fog bank which made navigation difficult, but when it broke up they found themselves staring down on vast ice-fields. After eight hours flying half their fuel was gone and they decided to land. One of Ellsworth's engines failed in the descent and he was forced to come down in a gap between two ice-floes. Amundsen landed three miles away on shifting ice. They were 150 miles from the Pole.

Ellsworth struggled in vain to repair the engine, then set out on foot to join Amundsen. His aircraft was airworthy but there was no room to take off. The six men worked for days, dragging the Dornier to a large ice-floe where they shifted tons of ice and snow by hand to form a runway. The first attempt to take off failed, then on 15 June, after unloading every non-essential item, they managed to bounce the Dornier off the ice and find their way back to Spitsbergen. A faulty rudder forced them to land on the north shore and they were picked up by a sealing ship.

Amundsen was back the following year with an airship, the 'Norge', piloted by the Italian Umberto Nobile. This time he had competition: a U S Navy officer, Commander Richard E. Byrd, was at Spitsbergen with a ski-equipped Fokker Trimotor named the 'Josephine Ford', after the daughter of his principal backer, the motor manufacturer Henry Ford. Both teams stressed that they were there in the interests of science, but both were eager to be first, and when the Norge arrived from Leningrad on 7 May 1926, Byrd made his first attempt the next day. The Trimotor never left the ice; it was too heavy. After stripping every

Amundsen's team clearing a runway for the Dornier–Wal to take off from the polar ice-cap

spare item they just managed to get off, and after eight hours flying north their compass and dead reckoning indicated they were above the Pole, though it looked no different from the miles of ice they had already flown over. The flight back to Spitsbergen was uneventful.

On 11 May Amundsen made it to the Pole in the Norge, then flew on across the Arctic to land in Alaska, the first-ever trans-polar flight. Both teams were given heroes' welcomes but behind the ceremonies the atmosphere was marred by controversy. Byrd's claims to have flown over the Pole were widely disputed, while Amundsen and Nobile fell out over the matter of which one of them should receive credit for the flight. However much the trail-blazers protested the contrary, personal and national prestige went hand in hand with their scientific endeavours.

Watching the Norge arrive in Alaska was an Australian adventurer, Hubert Wilkins. He was in Fairbanks with an American pilot, Carl Eilson, and another of Fokker's Trimotors intending to fly across the Arctic to Spitsbergen. His ambition was to establish weather stations in the Arctic to improve forecasting but he was also going to look for any undiscovered land-mass. But before they

The Norge at Spitsbergen

ACROSS THE ARCTIC BY AIRSHIP

National prestige was a great part of all trail-blazing flights. Two years after piloting Amundsen over the Arctic in the Norge, Nobile was back with an airship called the Italia; he crashed on the ice and Amundsen was amongst the first to fly out to find him. Nobile was rescued but Amundsen was never seen again.

Roald Amundsen – explorer

Umberto Nobile – pilot

could set out that year the Trimotor was badly damaged on a test flight and put away in store. The following year they were back with a American Stinson powered by a single Wright Whirlwind radial engine, and on 29 March 1927 they set out on a 600-mile exploratory flight. In case they were able to find a landing site, Wilkins carried explosives which he would detonate in the ice to determine the depth of water underneath. Hundreds of miles from land the engine started misfiring and they were forced to land. While Eilson fiddled with the engine, restarting it from time to time to keep it warm, Wilkins set off his charges and listened for the echo off the ocean floor. It was thousands of feet deep. They took off again but the engine was still misfiring and they had to land again. Once more Eilson fixed it and they set off for the nearest land, but sixty miles from Point Barrow in Alaska they ran out of fuel and were forced to land on the ice again. This time a storm blew up and they had to sit in the cockpit for four days before setting off across the moving ice, arriving on land ten days later.

They were back in Alaska in 1928, once more intending to fly to Spitsbergen. Wilkins had sold the remains of his Trimotor to a pair of restless Australian ex-RAF pilots, Charles Kingsford-Smith and Charles Ulm, and he used the money to buy a brand-new Lockheed Vega. The Vega had a single Wright Whirlwind engine, and with extra tanks it had a formidable range of well over 2500 miles. It was equipped with skis and painted bright orange so that it would be highly visible from the air if they were forced to land on the ice again. They finally set out from Point Barrow on 15 April. Visibility was unlimited but they saw no trace of land in fifteen hours flying. They made pre-planned landfall off Ellesmere Island, then turned north of Greenland for the last leg. North of Spitsbergen they ran into storms and were forced lower and lower until they were flying in a snowstorm whipped by fierce winds. They were only a short distance from their goal, but the only prudent thing was to land and Eilson put the Vega down on Dead Man's Island, just north of Spitsbergen, in a snowstorm. This time they had to spend five days in the cockpit before the storm abated and they managed to fly the last few miles to Green Harbour. Pilots had blazed trails over oceans, deserts and mountains, but their flight was a truly epic journey; if the engine had failed there was little hope of rescue. Wilkins, the Australian, was knighted.

The year was good for Australians: Charles Kingsford-Smith and Charles Ulm repaired Wilkins' old Fokker Trimotor, installed three of the latest Wright Whirlwinds and, renaming it 'The Southern Cross', on 31 May took off from Oakland, California, for Australia. The leg to Honolulu took $27\frac{1}{2}$ hours, to Fiji 35 hours, and finally on to Brisbane: nine days after setting out they completed the first crossing of the Pacific. Kingsford-Smith joined the British Empire's aviation knights.

Later the same year Sir Hubert Wilkins flew to Antarctica. His long-term

*Charles Kingsford-Smith over Sydney, Australia, in the Southern
Cross, approaching Mascot airfield after his epic flight*

aim was to fly across the subcontinent looking for sites for weather stations, as
he had done in the Arctic. That summer he and Eilson made a ten-hour exploratory flight, then left their two Lockheed Vegas tied down on Deception Island
aiming to return the following spring.

This time there was competition. Richard Byrd, having been the first to fly
over the North Pole, was also determined to be the first to fly to the South Pole.
He was on a different financial footing. With over 80 men, he set up a base on
the Ross Ice Shelf called 'Little America': it had tall radio masts for continuous
communication with home and he planned to spend the winter there and attempt
to fly to the Pole the following spring. Which is exactly what he did, becoming
in November 1929 the first man to fly over both Poles. Having made quite sure
of his position he told Little America by radio and the base passed on the news
to the US where it was announced over loudspeakers in Times Square in New
York even as he was still airborne.

Richard Byrd's triumph over the South Pole was evidence of another development in aviation which was to have profound long-term implications – the gradual

*One of the many aerial photographs taken by Ashley McKinley on Cmdr Byrd's
Antarctic expedition: their supply ship,* New York City, *moored at the Ross Ice Shelf*

stirring of the giant American economy to the potential in civil aviation. In 1926 when he went to the North Pole he had flown a European aircraft, the ubiquitous Fokker Trimotor, albeit with American engines. In 1929 he flew a Ford Trimotor with Wright Whirlwinds. Both aircraft and engines were symbols of the rapid growth of civil aviation in America in that three-year interval. In 1926 Germany was the leading passenger-carrying nation, far ahead of Britain, France and Italy, while America had only scarce and erratic passenger services. By 1929 Ford Trimotors (see page 114) were regularly crossing the United States coast to coast and the USA had overtaken not only Germany in total passenger miles flown but all the European nations put together. It was an astonishing achievement, which led to American domination in civil aviation.

Passenger flying got off to a slow start in America after the war. It was partly because the US aircraft industry had not been subject to the same impetus of producing large numbers of military aircraft. But America had a highly developed

On 3 April 1933 the Marquess of Clydesdale and Flt-Lt D. McIntyre were the first pilots
to fly over the summit of Mount Everest; the aircraft were a Westland PV-3 and a Wallace

rail network undisrupted by the war, and the speeds of aircraft of the day gave
passengers little if any advantage for the inconvenience and danger of air travel.
The only use for aircraft for the first half of the 1920s was in carrying mail.

In 1920 there was no question of private companies doing this. The US Post
Office launched the whole enterprise with public funds, using its own aircraft
flown by its own pilots. The backbone of its fleet was the British DH4 light
bomber, with American Liberty engines built in America. The goal was a coast-
to-coast airmail service and the first leg, between Chicago and Cleveland, was
opened on 15 May. By September the route had been established. Over short
distances air mail was not of much value since the railways were faster, but
a transcontinental service did make sense. As aircraft became faster the Post
Office invested $500,000 in beacons to enable their pilots to fly at night and the
time was cut to between 30 and 35 hours using a relay of pilots. By 1925 there
were close to 100 mail-planes, with an overnight service from New York to
Chicago, and a full day had been cut off the rail time from New York to San
Francisco.

All-metal Junkers G-24

In-flight movies were introduced in 1925

GERMANY – EUROPE'S MARKET LEADER

Germany's airlines were highly innovative and by 1930 they were carrying 120,000 passengers, as many as France, Britain and Italy put together.

But there was a strong political feeling that the mail should be carried by private companies under contract to the Post Office. President Calvin Coolidge and his Secretary of Commerce, Herbert Hoover, were supporters of privatisation, and in 1925 Congress passed the Air Mail Act which handed the operation of the services to private companies. These had to bid for sections of the route and they were paid by the pound for the mail they carried.

In January 1927 William Boeing bid for the Chicago–San Francisco sector, putting in a very low tender – half what the Post Office was prepared to pay – because of his expectations for a new aircraft, the Boeing Type 40, which in addition to mail could carry two, and later four, passengers. It was designed around a new Pratt & Whitney Wasp radial engine which proved very reliable, and in the two years which followed Boeing Air Transport carried 1300 tons of mail for the government and 6000 fare-paying passengers.

It is just one example of the pace of growth in air traffic in America. There are many such stories of entrepreneurial skill and technical know-how in the best dynamic tradition of American business, but behind them all was a combination of forces and factors which found the perfect environment in which to flourish. The companies took over an established mail route which had been developed at public expense. Men like Ford, Boeing and Donald Douglas saw the opportunities and gave America a superb first generation of reliable, fast airliners; Daniel Guggenheim endowed a fund with $2.5 million to promote aeronautics; Congress provided forthright and enlightened financial support for private endeavour. But there was one even more important factor: the extraordinary level of air-mindedness in America, the sort of enthusiasm which Cobham strove to create in Britain. From 1927 onwards a great wave of popular interest in air travel developed on the back of one man making one flight and capturing the hearts of the whole world.

Charles Lindbergh was too young to fly in the war, but in the years which followed his aviation career encompassed the whole range of flying jobs. Starting as a barnstormer, he then joined the Army Reserve for a fuller training before working for the new private mail-carriers. It was while flying the mail between St Louis and Chicago in 1926 that he first heard of the Orteig Prize: $25,000 for a flight from New York to Paris or Paris to New York. It was tempting, not only for the money but for the prestige, but New York to Paris was a far greater distance than Alcock and Brown's flight. Only now were aircraft which could do it becoming available.

The first pilot to try it was René Fonck, the French war ace who with 75 victories had been the highest-scoring Allied fighter pilot. His aircraft was the S–35, a three-engined monster built by the Russian émigré Igor Sikorsky, who had designed bombers in Russia before the Revolution. Sikorsky was a methodical

*Many of the aerial explorers of the 1920s and 30s chose the tough
Lockheed Vega for their flights: Hubert Wilkins, Amelia
Earhart; and in July 1933 Wiley Post, an American, became the
first pilot to fly round the world solo, in 7 days and 18 hours*

man and he was anxious to test the aircraft thoroughly by gradually increasing
its load with each test flight. Fonck was interested in just one thing – making the
trip before winter closed in over the Atlantic. He prevailed, and early in the
morning of 20 September 1926, with a crew of four and 2500 gallons of fuel, the
overloaded S–35 rolled down the runway at Roosevelt Field, New York. Sikorsky
was watching with thousands of sightseers as it hit a bump and shot into the air.
It fell back on to the field and burst into flames. Fonck and his copilot escaped
injured, but the engineer and the radio operator were both killed.

The tragedy only boosted the prestige of the Orteig Prize; there was no
shortage of new takers. Richard Byrd, fresh from his triumph over the North
Pole and not yet started on the South, began preparing a Fokker Trimotor with
backing of $100,000 from a New York department store. Another US Navy pilot,
Lt Noel Davis, began converting a bomber with the backing of the American
Legion. In France Charles Nungesser, another French war ace, was preparing a
naval aircraft, which he named 'L'Oiseau Blanc', to attempt the flight in the
opposite direction.

The Boeing 40B could carry 3 passengers as well as mail, increasing its profitability

The US Mail used converted British bombers, DH 4s, powered by the Liberty water-cooled engine

FLYING THE MAIL

Mail flying in America was a hazardous business; the pilots were adventurous spirits, following in the traditions of the Pony Express, and they took great pride in always getting the mail through.

LEFT: Charles Lindbergh in his days as a mail pilot, standing in the midst of the wreck of an aircraft from which he had baled out when it ran out of fuel over fog banks en route for Chicago

RIGHT: William 'Wild Bill' Hopson, one of the characters of the mail-flying fraternity; he died in a crash in 1928

Charles Lindbergh had savings of $2000 and no backing, but he was a very experienced pilot, used to long and lonely journeys by air. He believed the aircraft the other entrants were using were too heavy; with the right machine he could do it alone. He was well known in St Louis and when he approached local businessmen for finance in exchange for a promise to call his aircraft 'The Spirit of St Louis' he met a positive response. He contacted Ryan, an obscure aircraft builder in San Diego, and they agreed to build an aircraft to his specification around the Wright Whirlwind engine. He finally placed the order in February 1927 and work started immediately.

During the spring of 1927 the pace of the preparations quickened. Another Wright-powered aircraft, the Wright/Bellanca, flown by Clarence Chamberlin, joined the race. (Lindbergh had tried to buy the aircraft but it was not for sale.) On 13 April Chamberlin showed what it could do, staying aloft for 51 hours to break the world endurance record. Three days later Richard Byrd went for a test flight in his Wright-engined Fokker with Anthony Fokker at the controls. They crashed on landing but fortunately nobody was killed. On 26 April Lt Davis and his copilot were killed when they crashed on their final test flight. Two days later Lindbergh took his new Ryan monoplane for its first test flight in California; it had been built from scratch in just two months.

The crashes and the deaths heightened interest in the flight and by early May it was at fever pitch as the world waited to see who would get off first. There were three possible contenders: Chamberlin and the Bellanca in New York, Nungesser in Paris, and Lindbergh, largely unknown and still in California. On 8 May Nungesser and his navigator Coli took off from Le Bourget. For a whole day millions tuned in to their radio sets for the latest news; crowds lined the waterfront in New York, waiting for a first glimpse. There were reports that they had been seen off Newfoundland but, long after their fuel would have been exhausted, it was clear that they had gone down. There was still hope of rescue by ship but that slowly dwindled; unlike Hawker and McKenzie-Grieve there was no reprieve. They were never seen again.

On 12 May Lindbergh arrived in New York after a record-breaking flight across America all alone. He was a new face, a new lamb for the slaughter, and crowds thronged Curtiss Field to catch a glimpse of him. Then, even as he was shyly giving his first interview to reporters, Byrd landed in the repaired Fokker.

At this point the weather closed in for a week; while nothing happened in the air the newspapers on both sides of the Atlantic sustained the interest with the latest twists and turns in the story. Byrd, the gentleman, was not quite ready and offered the use of his runway and weather reports to Lindbergh. Chamberlin was ready but his team fell out with their backers over contracts; both sides reached for their lawyers and the aircraft was grounded by a judge.

Replica of Charles Lindbergh's Spirit of St Louis

On the night of 19 May the forecasts indicated that the storms would clear the following day. In the morning the only contender at the starting line was the lone outsider, Lindbergh. He took off early in drizzly rain, which did nothing to keep away sightseers attracted by the frisson of another crash. Conditions were not ideal, but Lindbergh decided to go and once in the air he was glad to leave behind a world which seemed to have gone mad with interest. But the pressures of the last few days soon began to take their toll and he started to feel sleepy. His main enemy for most of the rest of the flight was fatigue.

Over St Johns, Newfoundland, he moved slightly off course to fly over the town in a farewell salute. The gesture was picked up by the press and flashed round the world. Out over the ocean he found the same storms which had nearly done for Alcock and Brown and on occasions, as he flew into them, 'The Spirit of St Louis' became encrusted in ice. To fight the sleepiness he stuck his head out into the icy slipstream. He daydreamed and nodded off to sleep; the aircraft dived and he was woken up by the changing note of the engine. Night came, then dawn, then the first signs of life – sea birds, fishing boats – and finally the coast of Ireland.

Now he was exhilarated: there was plenty of fuel left and he was ahead of time. Ireland and Cornwall slipped by, then the Channel and, as his second night aloft approached, the coast of France. He had no difficulty finding Paris: its lights shone out and the airfield at Le Bourget was alive with car headlamps as Parisians flocked to see him arrive. He landed and in an instant the aircraft was surrounded by onlookers swarming over the airfield; he had to shut off the engine. After 33 hours of loneliness and serenity he was back in the mad world.

In the space of a few weeks Lindbergh had gone from obscure mail pilot to world superstar. Paris went wild; he waved to the crowd from the balcony of the US embassy. It was an emotional welcome but the emotions were mixed, the ghosts of Nungesser and Coli still fresh. But he did everything just right, acknowledging the courage of the French pair and visiting Nungesser's distraught mother. Here was a star who was no product of publicity hype: a quiet, courteous, unassuming young man, a hero whom millions could easily warm to. The King of England, the President of France, ambassadors – all sought his company and he gave it willingly, shyly, without being overwhelmed by it. His strong and silent personality shone through and the crowds loved him. He flew to London in 'The Spirit of St Louis' where the welcome was even more spirited than in Paris. Croydon airport had never seen anything like it: as he came in to land both sides of the runway were packed; when he stopped, the aircraft was immediately submerged in people.

Within a week of Lindbergh's flight Chamberlin and Byrd both crossed the ocean. Chamberlin nearly made it to Berlin, but by then the world had its solo

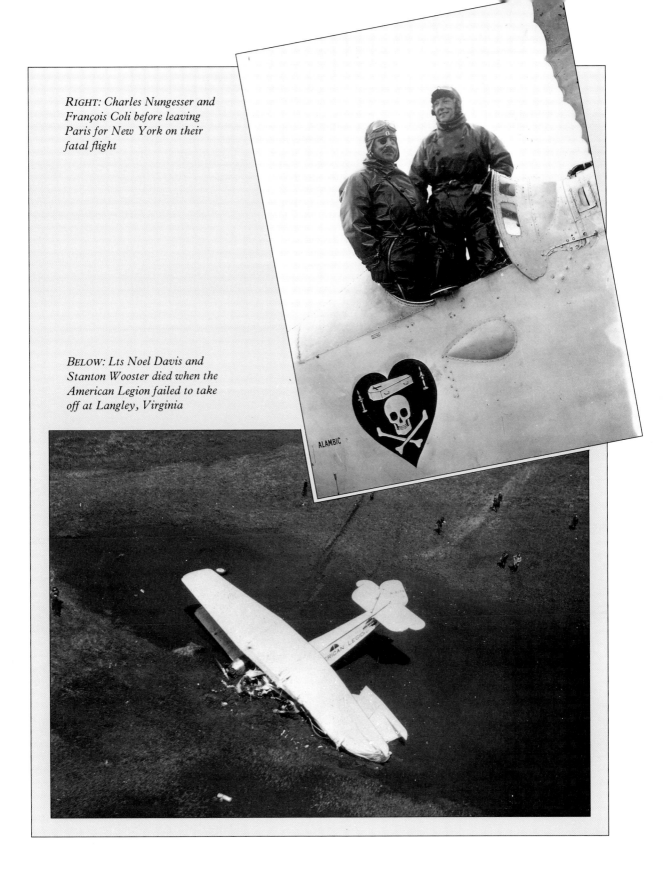

RIGHT: *Charles Nungesser and François Coli before leaving Paris for New York on their fatal flight*

BELOW: *Lts Noel Davis and Stanton Wooster died when the American Legion failed to take off at Langley, Virginia*

AVIATION'S GREATEST HERO
Charles Lindbergh's extraordinary popularity brought fame, wealth and personal tragedy; but he was disgusted by the crazed hero-worship in America and when it led to the murder of his son, he left for Europe. He spoke out against US involvement in World War 2 and resigned his reserve commission after a row with President Roosevelt. He spent some years in semi-disgrace, turned to conservation after the war and died in 1973.

LEFT: Before the Atlantic flight
RIGHT: Lindbergh worked with
Juan Trippe for many years
OPPOSITE: New York welcomes
Lindbergh in its usual fashion
BELOW: His reception in Paris

hero and all attention was focussed on Lindbergh. President Coolidge sent a US warship to bring him home. By the time he arrived in Washington, America was determined to outdo any welcome in Europe. When the USS *Memphis* hove to the banks of the Potomac were crowded for miles, aircraft flew overhead and pigeons were released. His mother was there to see the President pin the Distinguished Flying Cross on his lapel. Congress struck a special medal for him, as they had done for the Wright Brothers; he went to Dayton to meet Orville Wright. In New York he was presented with the $25,000 Orteig Prize. The souvenir industry went into top gear, turning out millions of items from buttons to slippers to sheet music.

Lindbergh was hot property for America and not for the last time he became a diplomatic instrument: Coolidge asked him to fly to America's sometimes tricky southern neighbour, Mexico; the Mexicans responded with thunderous acclaim. It seemed that wherever he went he was assured of an emotional welcome.

He was even hotter property for commercial aviation. His first task was a tour of the country in 'Spirit of St Louis', sponsored by the Guggenheim Fund for the Promotion of Aeronautics, to promote civil air transport. At every stop the whole town would turn out to greet him. Business offers poured in but the only ones he took were consultancies with the fledgling airlines, and when he made speeches they were confined to promoting civil aviation. He was the perfect instrument and image for commercial aviation.

In 1928 the whole vision of air transport as a business in America changed. Financiers and industrialists took more interest and progress accelerated. One turning-point was the formation on 16 May of a new company: Transcontinental Air Transport (the forerunner of TWA). It was well financed with the backing of prominent industrialists from the aircraft industry and the Pennsylvania Railroad. The chairman of its technical committee was Charles Lindbergh, charged with surveying their routes. At a technical level, drawing on his experience as a mail pilot, they could not have done better; but much more important was his publicity value: when the company made 'Coast to Coast in 48 Hours', a film to publicise its service, there was Lindbergh flying alongside the Ford Trimotor as it raced the trains across America.

In 1926 there were twelve companies operating mail services and carrying a few passengers; by the end of 1928 there were 25. Traffic continued to grow but the number of airlines then fell as amalgamations were forced by competition. By the end of 1929 America was the world's leading carrier by volume with just eleven airlines. A year later America was carrying twice the traffic of the whole of Europe with just four airlines; they were amalgamations of the smaller lines and became known as The Big Four: TWA, United, Eastern and American.

The Big Four had strong political friends. When Herbert Hoover became

TRAIL-BLAZING WOMEN PILOTS

In 1932 Amelia Earhart (*right*) became the first woman to fly the Atlantic solo, starting from Newfoundland and landing in Londonderry, NI; in 1935 she flew from Honolulu to Oakland, Calif.; two years later on another flight over the Pacific she disappeared without trace.

Amy Johnson (*below*) qualified as an aircraft engineer before learning to fly; in May 1931 she flew alone to Australia in a de Havilland Moth, the first of many record-breaking flights. She served in the war as a ferry pilot in the Air Transport Auxiliary and was killed when she crashed into the Thames on a delivery flight.

MISS AMY JOHNSON, O.B.E.

President in 1929 he appointed as Postmaster General a man whose dedication to the US airline industry had far-reaching effects. Walter F. Brown wanted to see airlines flourishing and in turn channelling the money into the aircraft-manufacturing industry, stimulating new ideas and new aircraft. In short, he saw the beginnings of a new transport industry, but he recognised that without subsidy it would falter. He wanted the smaller and less efficient operators out of business, leaving the way clear for a smaller number of bigger, efficient operators. As a result of the lowest-bidder method of awarding mail contracts, operators had bought cheap, old aircraft which did nothing to advance the industry. To feed them money he amended the Air Mail Act so that instead of tendering for mail contracts on a rate-for-weight basis, they received a straight payment of $1.25 per mile for the space available, effectively a straight subsidy to the operator. It was subsidy on a far grander scale than anything in Europe.

Brown also engineered amendments which gave him real powers over the industry. He used these to pursue his far-sighted policy, but by manipulating the contracts in favour of certain airlines and holding secret meetings with them, he enabled the Big Four effectively to carve up the domestic routes between them. In the end it became a national scandal, and when Franklin Roosevelt became President in 1933 Brown's methods were put under close scrutiny. The new Postmaster General, James Farley, alleged that a total of $78 million had been paid out to the favoured airlines and that the secret arrangements were outrageous. A special committee found the allegations substantially true, and Brown was disgraced, though later cleared of fraud.

Roosevelt cancelled all mail contracts and brought in the Army to do the job. Lindbergh used all his prestige to back the airlines, warning that the Army was not up to it. He was proved tragically correct: five Army pilots died in the first week of operations and six more were injured. At a conference to put the mail business on a new footing the Big Four got back much of what they had lost, except that the level of payment was reduced from $1.25 to 40 cents a mile. The subsidies had had their effect: by then the Big Four were healthy businesses.

On the day before the contracts were cancelled the airlines gave a demonstration of what the Brown years had achieved. Wartime US air ace Eddie Rickenbacker of Eastern and Jack Frye of TWA flew across America, from Los Angeles to Newark, NJ, in thirteen hours. The aircraft was the DC–1, an all-metal, purpose-built airliner with two Wright Cyclone engines, the first of a line of aircraft from the Douglas company which culminated in 1935 with the DC–3. The DC–3 revolutionised air transport in America and, eventually, worldwide. By 1939 world passenger traffic had quadrupled; two out of every three passengers were on US domestic routes and 75 per cent of all US domestic flights were made on DC–3s. Over 50 years after its début there are still examples in com-

The DC-3 – the most widely used airliner of the 1930s

mercial service. It was a major factor in the subsequent US domination in the building of airliners.

If US performance on domestic routes was spectacular, its performance on international routes was no less so. Throughout the 1920s and 1930s Germany was the leading European carrier, with routes to the East and to South America. Britain, France, Holland and Belgium used their flag-carriers in Europe and to link their far-flung Empires. The view in Washington in the late 1920s was that the US needed a foreign airline to compete with the Europeans and to protect its investments and influence in Latin America and the Pacific. German interests had founded an airline in Colombia as early as 1919 and followed it by establishing others in Bolivia and Brazil. The first multi-engined aircraft to fly in Brazil was a Dornier-Wal which was operated between Rio de Janeiro and Buenos Aires in 1926 by a German trading company. The US needed its 'flag carrier', but to provide it and catch up with the Europeans would need heavy subsidy.

Once again mail contracts were the ideal vehicle for the subsidy. In July 1927 the first overseas air-mail contract, from Key West in Florida to Havana, Cuba, was awarded to Pan American Airways, a company which had been formed at least in part by people in Washington who were nervous of the security implications of Germany's moves into South America. Pan American had very little cash and no aircraft and they had to start the service by 19 October. There was one other major problem: President Machado of Cuba had already granted exclusive landing rights to the Aviation Corporation of America (AVCO), in the person of its 28-year-old and infinitely energetic president, Juan Trippe.

Clearly there would have to be some kind of compromise but Trippe had no such intention: he wanted control. In the negotiations which followed he wore the opposition down with ruthless obduracy backed up by enormous stamina. When the first mail flight took place on the appointed day, in a hastily chartered aircraft, it was still in the name of Pan American, but in reality the company had simply become the operating subsidiary of AVCO, with Trippe in complete control. By January 1928 Pan American had bought Fokker Trimotors and started carrying passengers to Cuba.

Trippe understood that the overseas airline business was inextricably bound up with politics, and that for his airline to succeed it would have to be well connected in Washington. When the Foreign Air Mail Act was passed in March 1928, the rate for carrying mail was $2 per pound per mile, and Postmaster General Brown had virtually absolute power in allocating the contracts. The next two foreign routes were from Cuba onwards to Trinidad and Panama. When both were awarded to Pan American there was criticism, but there was little anybody could do since, apart from preparing the ground well in Washington, Trippe had negotiated exclusive rights along the route well in advance.

Pan American was just what the US government needed: a highly efficient business, innovative in its use of aircraft and the latest aviation technology, with a vigorous man at the top. It became a 'chosen instrument', and in exchange for the generous subsidies it became almost an extension of US foreign policy in Latin America. South American governments liked doing business with Trippe because once they were on his route map American business and investment inevitably followed. Each time a new foreign-mail contract came up, Trippe used his contacts in South America to put Pan American in an unassailable position to get it. If there was competition he found a way to buy it or neutralise it. By 1930 Pan American's routes stretched down both coastlines of South America, finally meeting at Buenos Aires after a trans-continental leg.

There were few runways anywhere, and especially in South America. The only type of aircraft which could fly the routes were flying boats. Trippe had thought of that well in advance. As early as 1928 he commissioned Igor Sikorsky to build him just what he wanted. In the early days Pan American bought a succession of Sikorsky S40 and S41s which put the company on its feet and became the backbone of the Pan American fleet.

Backbone of Pan American's Clipper fleet: the Sikorsky S42 flying boat

*Charles Lindbergh and his wife Anne with the Lockheed Sirius in which
they flew along the great circle route from Washington DC to Tokyo in 1931*

Trippe took on Charles Lindbergh as technical consultant to survey new routes and act as ambassador for Pan American and the United States at the same time. They were a powerful team, a mailed fist in a velvet glove: the ruthless businessman hand in hand with the world's international hero. Even romance was harnessed to the cause: Lindbergh's marriage to Anne Morrow stirred millions of hearts worldwide, and when Pan American's Trinidad route was extended to the mainland of South America Lindbergh flew the inaugural flight taking his new wife with him.

Latin America was not the limit of Trippe's vision. In 1931 Lindbergh made a proving flight from New York through Alaska and over the Arctic to Japan and China, the polar route. In the back seat of his Lockheed Sirius was his wife. But the flight was just a prelude to Trippe's next challenge – the Pacific. In 1935 he opened an office in San Francisco; later the same year, to little surprise, Pan American was awarded the trans-Pacific mail contract. All his energy went into the new venture. He had planned and ordered new flying boats from Sikorsky and Martin. The S42, built to Pan American's specifications, was the first American aircraft capable of long-distance sea crossings and carried 32 passengers in some luxury.

In 1935 there were no aircraft which could cross the Pacific without stopping several times on the way. Honolulu was 2400 miles from mainland USA and there were huge stretches of ocean beyond with no facilities. But no obstacle was too great for Trippe. He surveyed the uninhabited islands of Wake and Midway, then sent construction teams to build ports and hotels on them. His island bases were then supplied with everything they needed by air. By October 1936 weather forecasting, radio aids and survey flights were complete and the first passengers were flying to Manila. By April 1937 the route was extended to Hong Kong.

By now Trippe had set his sights on a global service. He asked the manufacturing companies, this time including Boeing, to come up with the aircraft while he set about negotiating the routes. His first target was the Atlantic. Germany with her giant airships was the only country making regular crossings but 1937 was the year of the Hindenberg disaster. Trippe opened negotiations with France and Britain, but they demanded reciprocal rights and the US government at first resisted such an arrangement. The State Department eventually made a fifteen-year deal, but Britain would not let Pan American start until it had aircraft capable of flying the route too.

The end of the first flight from America to China: a Boeing 314 Clipper about to land in the harbour at Hong Kong

IMPERIAL AIRWAYS 1924–1939
Top: Britain's trimotor, the DH 66 Hercules, the first new type ordered by the new airline in 1927, for use on the Cairo to Basra section of the route to India.
Above: The 20-passenger Armstrong-Whitworth Argosy.
Right: The backbone of the Imperial fleet in the 1930s were eight 4-engined Handley Page 42s which could carry 38 passengers in great style; no passenger was ever lost.

Canopus, greatest of Imperial's 'C' Class flying boats;
the Caledonia made the first return flight across the Atlantic

Imperial Airways used flying boats on its Empire routes, but none had the range to cross the Atlantic without in-flight refuelling or by reducing the load to an uneconomic level. In June 1937 Pan American and Imperial started a parallel service from New York to Bermuda, Pan American using Sikorsky S42s and Imperial a lone Shorts S23 'C' class flying boat. Shortly afterwards both airlines started experimental flights from New York to Southampton via Newfoundland and Ireland.

Then in early 1939 Boeing unveiled the giant Type 314 flying boat it had developed for Pan American. It was the wonder of its day, bigger than anything else in the world. It was powered by four double Wright Cyclone engines which gave it a cruising speed of over 170 mph and a range of 3500 miles. It had passenger accommodation for over 70, with sleeping berths, lounge and dining-room all equipped for luxury living. With these Trippe could outflank the British, whose next class of flying boats would not be ready until the summer of 1939. Pan American started a $375 29-hour service to Lisbon via the Azores. In July Britain agreed to flights via the northerly route but by the time their own flying boats were ready Europe was on the brink of war. Pan American continued its service throughout the war, flying high-priority passengers and mail, and the Boeing 314 'Clippers' became their standard-bearers across the Pacific.

Generously subsidised by the US government, Pan American like its domestic counterparts ploughed money into the home manufacturing industry. Abroad it fulfilled the 'imperial role' of airlines far better than any of its European counterparts and far outstripped them in its network of routes. Technically it was far ahead too, pioneering radio navigation for flights over the sea. Its aircrews in their smart, military-style uniforms became ambassadors, exuding the confidence that America was the world's leading country in commercial air transport. By 1939 it unquestionably was. As a flag-carrier Pan American had no equal.

CHAPTER FIVE

THE QUEST FOR SPEED

Juan Trippe was not the first to envisage a global transport system based on giant passenger-carrying flying boats. Thirty years earlier, in 1911, the same idea had captured the imagination of the French Under-Secretary for Air, Jacques Schneider, holder of both balloon and aircraft pilot's licences. With 70 per cent of the world's surface covered by oceans, rivers and lakes, he argued that it was logical to build more aircraft which could operate from the water rather than from land. To encourage the development of seaplanes, Schneider offered a prize to compete with the Gordon-Bennett Trophy which had given such a boost to technical progress in land-planes. The 1912 Gordon-Bennett race was held in Chicago, and at the inevitable banquet which followed Schneider announced 'La Coupe d'Aviation Jacques Schneider': £1000 and an even more magnificent trophy for a contest exclusively for seaplanes. The rules had been tightly drawn to encourage technical progress; there were tests for seaworthiness and the ability of the hydroplanes to taxi on water. But in the end it was a race and the choice of pilots and aircraft was dominated by the quest for speed and the urge to win.

Far from starting a line of passenger-carrying seaplanes, the early Schneider Cup races (see p. 84) spawned the most famous family of land-based fighters of the First World War – the Sopwith Pups, Camels and Triplanes and their French counterparts. All these fighters used variants of the French Gnome and Le Rhône rotary engines. Rotaries were ideal to power fighters since they cooled themselves while running, even at high power settings. But there were disadvantages: they had a large frontal area which added to drag; the spinning cylinders thrashed the air, adding yet more drag; and there was mechanical loss from all the moving parts. As their size and power grew, so another problem limited their development: torque. The centrifugal force of the spinning mass at the front of the aircraft pulled the nose in the direction in which it spun, making it difficult for the pilot to control, especially on take-off.

In the wartime quest for speed rotaries were superseded by a new range of water-cooled, in-line engines, like the Rolls-Royce Eagles which powered Alcock and Brown's Vickers Vimy and the American V-12 400-hp Liberty which powered the DH 4s of the US Mail Service. Water-cooled engines still had a tendency to overheat if run at high power continuously, but they were powerful, and power was the legacy which war left the air-racing fraternity in 1919.

For five years the Schneider Cup had stood in The Royal Aero Club in London. Having won in 1914, Britain hosted the 1919 contest at Bournemouth against a strong challenge from France and a lone Italian. It was something of a farce: the course was shrouded in fog and the judges issued contradictory orders for start times. Some confused pilots withdrew before the race, others retired, leaving only Sgt Guido Janello of the Italian Air Force to cross the finishing line, but the judges decided that he had missed one of the markers. The official result was a compromise: the race was declared void, the Italians were to host the contest the following year, while the trophy stayed in Britain.

One of the French pilots who had withdrawn was Sadi Lecointe, a war veteran with a lust for speed. In February 1920 he set a new record of 171 mph in his Nieuport–Delage 29; by the end of the year he had raised it to 194 mph. In the same year he romped home in the Gordon-Bennett Trophy race at Étampes outside Paris, giving France that trophy for ever and marking the end of an era in air-racing.

To rekindle the competitive spirit and to provide a new forum for the pilots, Madame Deutsch de la Muerthe established a prize of 20,000 francs in her late husband's memory. Lecointe always did well in practice but on race-day he invariably crashed, leaving slower contestants to win. The new prize failed to earn the prestige of the Gordon-Bennett and in 1922, when only one entrant crossed the finishing line, it was abandoned.

Meanwhile in America a new era in the quest for speed was dawning around a new prize and a new engine. The prize was the Pulitzer, sponsored by the Pulitzer family of journalism fame. The new engine was the D-12 'wetsleeve monobloc', built by the Curtiss company, winners of the first Gordon-Bennett Trophy race in 1909. The blocks were cast in aluminium, into which holes were bored for steel sleeves which housed the pistons. Water circulated through the block to cool it, but the steel sleeves were encased in aluminium and the water never came into direct contact with them. In the Curtiss D–12 the designers managed to put the water jacket right against the steel, hence the name 'wetsleeve'. The D–12 ran cooler and could run longer at higher revolutions; it was also very compact, with a small frontal area, enabling the airframe around it to be more streamlined. With a lightweight metal propeller it was ideal for racing.

The D–12 needed a forum and the Pulitzer provided it. The first race was in 1921 and it was won convincingly by an adaptation of a Curtiss naval biplane fighter powered by a D–12 and flown by a Navy test pilot, Bert Acosta. In 1922

D–12-powered aircraft took the first four places in the race at Mitchell Field, Long Island; and on 13 October at Detroit General William 'Billy' Mitchell of the US Army Air Corps used a D–12 to wrench the world speed record from Sadi Lecointe with a run at 222 mph.

In 1920 and 1921 the Schneider was held in Venice. There was only weak opposition from France and the Italians won in both years; a third win would give them the prize for ever. For 1922 the venue was Naples: Italy and France had strong government-sponsored teams; Britain had a one-man, one-aircraft team sponsored by the industry. The pilot was Henry Biard and he was flying the Supermarine Sea Lion II, a flying boat powered by a 450-hp Napier Lion engine. He was a canny competitor: the Sea Lion was the most powerful machine there, but he kept the speed down in practice not to give the game away. In the Schneider races the competing aircraft made a staggered start, each one being timed round the circuit. On race-day Biard was first off and he completed the first lap in record time. The Italian team of three were desperate for a third win and as they joined him on the course they started flying tactically, ganging up in front of him as all four aircraft headed for the turning points. Climbing over them would lose him speed, but choosing his moment carefully Biard was able to pull up at full throttle, then dive flat out for the next turn, passing them on the way. He stayed flat out to win at an average speed of 145 mph.

Biard's victory, and the way he snatched permanent possession of the Trophy from the Italians by sheer nerve and skill, injected new vitality, new prestige and a fresh streak of nationalism into the contest. International competitiveness was even further enhanced in the 1923 race at Cowes on the Isle of Wight, when Britain and France came up against an American team for the first time. Having decided to compete, the Americans did not use half measures. The US Navy put together a team of three professional pilots, Lts Rutledge Irvine, David Rittenhouse and A. W. Gorton. Like the pre-war racers they had float-planes – a slender fuselage which looked like a fighter mounted on twin floats. There were two Curtiss CR–3s powered by a new 465-hp D–12 engine, and a Wright NW–2 with a brutish 600-hp engine. But apart from professional pilots and aircraft fresh from success in the Pulitzer races, what made the American team a really formidable opponent was its backing, its organisation and attention to detail. The pilots had no other duties and they were given months to prepare; they arrived at Cowes well before the race to acclimatise themselves; and a US warship was at hand to give practical and moral support.

All the European aircraft were flying boats. The British started out with two entrants: the Supermarine Sea Lion III flown by Biard, and a Blackburn Pellet which capsized on its first launching. The French entered a team of five, but one diverted to Littlehampton and was damaged on the beach and another collided in France before departure. The American float-planes had their problems too: Gorton crashed the Wright during full-throttle tests; he was thrown clear.

On race day Rittenhouse and Irvine took off first in the CR–3s; Biard was next in the Sea Lion, but the two Americans had completed their first lap before he was airborne. A single French aircraft started out, only to retire on the second lap, leaving the two Americans to fight it out with Biard. He was flying faster than ever before and finished with an average speed of 157 mph, but the superiority of the Americans was clear: Rittenhouse finished first at 177 mph, followed by Irvine at 174 mph. It was a triumph for the American pilots, their sleek float-planes, their engines and, above all, their organisation, but *The Times* sounded a rather sour note: 'British habits do not support the idea of entering a team organised by the State for a sporting event.' The British Air Ministry took a rather more practical view: they bought D–12 engines, and in time they were manufactured under licence in Britain and powered the fastest British fighter of its day, the Fairey Fox. Two found their way to Britain's leading engine manufacturer Rolls-Royce.

In the quest for the world speed record there was no lessening of international competitiveness. In February 1923 Sadi Lecointe had wrested it back from 'Billy' Mitchell, pushing his Nieuport–Delage to 233 mph. Only weeks later Lt R. L. Maughan in a Curtiss R–6 grabbed it back with an improvement of 3 mph. Lt Alford Williams won the 1923 Pulitzer in another Curtiss, then on 2 November Lt A. Brown became the fastest man alive in another at 255 mph. Two days later Lt Williams was back with 267 mph. America looked unstoppable; but early in 1924 the French test pilot, Florentin Bonnet, flew a Ferbois V–2 to 278 mph.

None of the European nations was ready for the Schneider Cup in 1924. All the Americans had to do to win was fly round the course. Sportingly, they declared the contest void. In 1925 the French pulled out again, Britain and Italy challenging the US at Chesapeake Bay. The American team flew their record-breaking float-planes and the Italians were brimming with hope for their new Macchi M33 flying boats, now powered by D–12 engines. Britain had switched to float-planes: the Gloster III, a biplane flown by Hubert Broad, and the first monoplane to enter the contest since before the war, the Supermarine S4, flown by Henry Biard. Both British aircraft had exceeded 200 mph in practice thanks to a new Napier engine. Biard crashed the S4 during a high-speed practice run, though miraculously he managed to swim clear. When the race day came the Americans revealed a new secret weapon, Army test pilot Lt James Doolittle. Rather as Biard had done in Venice in 1922, he blasted his way to victory by nerve, skill and stamina, rounding the markers more tightly than anybody else

OPPOSITE: The Schneider Trophy

Lt Alford Williams USN on becoming the fastest man
alive in his D-12-powered Curtiss R-2 in 1923

and suffering the higher G forces. He used the engine power wisely to win at
232 mph; Broad came second in the Gloster III at 199 mph.

The cost of challenge was mounting; a new generation of aircraft would have
to be developed to beat the Americans. The contest was no longer for the
pittance in prize money but for the prestige that went with winning and thereby
demonstrating national technological prowess. Prestige meant a lot to Mussolini,
who decided that Italy must have the Cup back at all costs – and those costs
would be met by the Italian Government. The Air Ministry in London began to
stir too, forming a High Speed Flight to train RAF pilots and funding further
aircraft research. The American government, with its pilots needing just one
more victory to retain the Cup for ever, took a different view: Congress chose
that moment to cut off further funds, leaving the Curtiss company to defend the
Schneider Cup in 1926. They entered a single aircraft flown by Lt George
Cuhiddy.

Britain was not ready for the 1926 contest but the Italians had worked wonders
in twelve months. The flying boats had gone, replaced by Macchi M39s, a new

*The Macchi M39: 60% of the upper surface of the wing was
a brass radiator to cool the water circulating from the engine*

monoplane with twin floats and a sleek fuselage housing a huge 12-cylinder Fiat engine. Mario di Bernardi, Italy's top pilot, had reached speeds of 260 mph in practice. The M39 was a temperamental aircraft, however: one caught fire in practice, another's engine blew up during the race, but di Bernardi led the contest in a third and, when Cuhiddy's oil pump failed, went on to win at an average speed of 246 mph.

Without government finance America backed out and the 1927 race, in Venice, was a straight duel between Italy and Britain. But it was also a battle of refinement between designers and engine builders. With government money, Mario Castoldi of Macchi and R. J. Mitchell of Supermarine minutely tailored their earlier M39 and S4 designs to accommodate the new 1000-hp engines under development at Fiat and Napier. The British had a professional military team and a fleet of new aircraft: three Supermarine S5 monoplanes and three Gloster IV biplanes, all powered by Napier Lion in-line engines, and a single Shorts Crusader which introduced a radial engine for the first time. The Italians all had the latest Macchi, the M52.

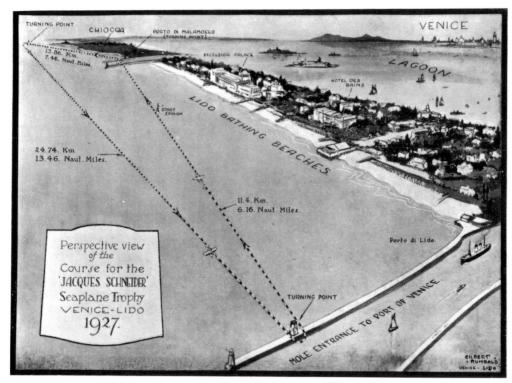

*The triangular 50-km course had to be completed seven
times; to count the laps, the RAF pilots poked a finger
through papered-over holes in a board in the cockpit;
even so, they occasionally lost count*

Only three pilots from each team could compete, and 200,000 people crammed
on to the Lido beaches for the gladiatorial spectacle. Flt-Lt S. M. Kinkead's
Gloster was away first, followed by Major di Bernardi in an M52, then Flt-Lt
S. N. Webster in an S5, Capt. F. Guazelli in another M52, Flt-Lt O. E. Worsley
in another S5, and lastly the M52 of Capt. A. Ferrarin. The crowd got its
spectacle: Ferrarin's engine caught fire on the start line; the Gloster pulled out
on the fourth lap with a cracked propeller-shaft; then, after lapping at 275 mph,
di Bernardi's engine failed on the sixth. Guazelli fought on alone for Italy, but
the two S5s were steadily improving their early lead. Their progress owed as
much to the pilots as to the aircraft: the Italians tended to climb at the turns
whereas the High Speed Flight pilots had been trained to make steep-banked
turns at low level. Suddenly it was no longer a race; there was a groan from the
Italian crowd as Guazelli veered away from the course and landed, a fuel line
having broken and sprayed him with petrol. Webster and Worsley finished first
and second at 281 and 275 mph.

*Echoes of the Schneider Cup: this faithful replica of the Supermarine S5,
the winning British aircraft in 1927, was built by Bill Hosie and flown in
1987; he crashed in it in May of that year and was killed*

Unofficially the two RAF pilots and di Bernardi had broken Bonnet's world
speed record. Five weeks later di Bernardi made an officially timed run in a
re-engined M52 at 297 mph. Schneider Cup aircraft, though freakish creations
to comply with the rules for the contest, were the fastest machines on earth.
But when Jacques Schneider died in January 1928, the M52s and S5s, designed
solely for speed, had contributed little to his dream of a world linked by seaplanes.

There was no contest in 1928; all the participating nations agreed that at least
a two-year gap was needed between races to give time for development work.
But that did not stop the pilots trying to break the official world speed record.
In March 1928 Kinkead attempted the record in an S5; he crashed into the sea
off the Isle of Wight and was killed. Before the month was out di Bernardi in an
M52 had broken his own record with 318 mph. This was beaten by 1 mph in
November by Flt-Lt D'Arcy Greig in an S5, but it was deemed to be too small
an increase to count officially.

164

THE SCHNEIDER CUP RACES

In the post-war years Britain won the trophy 4 times, Italy 3 times and the US 3 times.
Opposite top: Sadi Lecointe with his Spad at Bournemouth in 1919; after a trial flight, 15 inches were lopped off each upper wing to get more speed.
Opposite bottom: Lt David Rittenhouse winning for America at Cowes in 1923.
Left: All Italy celebrated when Mario di Bernardi snatched outright possession from the US in 1926.
Above: The British team about to celebrate outright possession with a dinner at Claridges in 1931.

By early 1929 Mitchell and Castoldi had both refined their basic designs yet again to accommodate new engines. Britain had the S6 with a new Rolls-Royce engine, the R. The Napier Lion was lighter but it had reached the peak of its development, and the R with a supercharger produced 1900 hp, nearly twice the power. Getting it ready for the contest, however, was itself a race against time – the first examples chewed themselves up on the test-bench; but by August the first engine was ready for trials in the S6. The Italians had an engine of comparable power but they had achieved it by increasing the number of cylinders to eighteen. Castoldi modified the airframe to take the new engine and the result was the M67. On 22 August, in trials for the race, Giuseppe Motta reached 362 mph over Lake Garda, then crashed and was killed.

The race itself took place at Calshot on the Solent in September. The S6 established its dominance from the outset. Flt-Lt H. R. D. Waghorn was first away and on his first three laps recorded 324, 329 and 331 mph respectively. The two M67 pilots were lucky to escape with their lives: on the first turn fumes started pouring into Lt R. Cadringher's cockpit; he could not see where he was going and veered off inland to clear it. Lt Giuseppe Monti suffered from fumes too, but then the cooling system exploded and sprayed him with boiling water and steam; he managed to land but was carried off to hospital. Waghorn won with ease, at an average speed of 328 mph. There was a celebratory dinner at which Prime Minister Ramsay MacDonald expressed the hope that Britain would gain its third victory to win the Trophy outright, but once the euphoria was over the Government announced that official finance would not be available.

Italy and France, who had re-entered the fray, were determined to stop the Trophy falling into British hands for ever and the 1931 contest promised to be a scorcher. France was developing the H.V. 120, a high-speed seaplane, specially for the contest. Italy established its own high-speed flight at Lake Garda to train its pilots, and the Italian design team delivered a new aircraft, the Macchi–Castoldi MC72. It was a menacingly beautiful aircraft: an elongated snout housed a new engine from Fiat, the AS6, two of the latest AS5s bolted front to back to give 24 cylinders. The sheer power of all the later Schneider Cup aircraft gave the pilots new problems: not only did the torque pull the nose in the direction of rotation, but the float on that side was forced lower in the water with potentially disastrous results on take-off. To overcome the problem, the MC72 was fitted with two propellers which spun in opposite directions, cancelling out each other's torque.

The MC72 was still a lethal machine and death now added a new twist to the prestige and mystery of the Schneider Cup. On a test flight over Lake Garda Monti's propellers touched and he was killed. In France an H.V. 120 crashed, killing its pilot. Then, as race day approached, the engine in another MC72 backfired in flight, setting a fuel tank alight; it exploded in mid-air. The Italians and French asked for a postponement but the British refused: without further government finance, the 1931 contest would be their last chance for an outright victory.

But for the intervention of the deeply patriotic Lady Houston, Britain might not even have made it to the start line. She underwrote £100,000 to get whatever more could be squeezed out of the S6 and the R engine. Instead of adding cylinders Rolls-Royce refined and supercharged the R to produce 2000 hp. At

The last Schneider Trophy winner, the 2600-hp Supermarine S6b: the floats contained the fuel tanks

full power the engine had a useful life of less than an hour, but it promised to pull the S6b which housed it past the 400 mph mark. On race day it was the only entry. A million people turned out to see the walkover. Flt-Lt John Boothman averaged 340 mph, just enough to ensure permanent possession of the Trophy. Then, to thrill the crowd and with the Cup no longer in dispute, Flt-Lt George Stainforth broke the world speed record with a run of 379 mph in another S6b. It was Britain's turn to dominate. Two weeks later, on 29 September, using a sprint version of the engine he broke it again at 407 mph.

Italy had one last card to play. In April 1933, after a lot of work on the fuel system, Warrant Officer Francesco Agello of the Italian Air Force took an MC72 over Lake Garda and raised the record to 423 mph. The following year he took it to 440 mph, a record which would stand until 1939, and a seaplane record which stands to this day.

The Schneider Cup as a forum in the quest for speed was gone. Germany had begun to plan an entry, but with Britain possessing the Cup outright the magical contest was finished and another era was over. No other trophy could command the resources of governments, and with its passing the public money went too. The huge cost of coaxing a few more miles per hour out of purely racing aircraft could no longer be justified, however prestigious. Schneider aircraft had no practical use, yet they had shown the way forward for anybody who wanted speed. Their secrets – the aerodynamics of speed which had been honed by racing, and the engines, particularly the Rolls-Royce R – were of interest to senior European air force commanders. As Europe rearmed in the face of a resurgent Germany, many of those secrets became the building-blocks of a new generation of fighters. It was competition of a different kind and no less fierce, but for a time it went on largely behind closed doors.

Just as air racing was dying in Europe, however, it began to flourish again in America as a spectator sport after a brief hiatus. The tightening of military budgets that had kept America out of the Schneider had also put an end to the Pulitzer, which had become little more than straight competition between Army and Navy pilots. Then Charles Lindbergh ignited an explosion of interest. In 1928 National Air Races were held in Los Angeles and were a great success. So the following year the promoter Clifford Henderson decided to use the popularity of air racing as the basis for an aviation extravaganza. From the start they were conceived as a commercial venture, heavily promoted and tailored to the needs of the crowd. Gladiatorial in concept, they took place before a grandstand, with the contestants taking off together and racing round in front of the crowd.

In 1929 the races were held in Cleveland, Ohio, where 80,000 people packed the stands. As part of the process of making America air-minded, Henderson's idea was to create a market-place for aviation where manufacturers could show

*The fastest seaplane ever built: Francesco Agello with
the MC72; in 1934 the engine was boosted to 3000 hp
to set his 440.6 mph record*

off their wares. But the key to popular interest lay in the spectacle which aviation
could provide: there was barnstorming, closed-circuit racing, women's racing,
and races to Cleveland from other parts of the US. The Army, Navy and Marines
had display teams, led on occasion by Lindbergh himself.

The climax of the festival was a 50-mile closed-circuit race featuring military
and civilian pilots. The military flew variants of current biplane fighters and
with a reputation built on the Pulitzer and Schneider races were favourites. They
were up against two civilian monoplanes powered by versions of the latest radial
engines: a Lockheed Vega, and a Beech Travel Air Model R, known as 'Mystery'
because the company kept it shrouded in secrecy until the last minute. It was
flown by an ex-barnstorming pilot, Doug Davis, who took an early lead but lost
valuable time when he missed a turning point, and was overtaken by an Army
pilot. He fought back and steadily closed the gap to win by a whisker. The Army
was second, the Vega third and the Navy fourth. The military were embarrassed:
they had been beaten not only by a civilian but by a bunch of under-financed
garage mechanics. The National Air Races were to become increasingly dominated
by this new breed: ex-barnstormers in pursuit of speed, prestige and the cash
prizes and sponsorship which competing could bring.

ABOVE: A record of a different kind: John and Kenneth Hunter stayed aloft for 23 days 2 hours, 554 hours, flying above Chicago in July 1930

RIGHT: In 1938 Jacqueline Cochran won the Bendix Trophy, the second woman to win the race against men. During the war she was the first woman to ferry bombers across the Atlantic and in 1953 she became the first woman to fly faster than sound, in a Sabre jet; she died in 1980

For the 1930 races in Chicago Clifford Henderson persuaded a Cleveland industrialist, Charles Thompson, to sponsor the major race and commission a suitable trophy, and so the Thompson Trophy joined the array of glittering prizes in the quest for speed. The race was another triumph for the new breed of buccaneers. The tiny Laird company sold aircraft in kits for people to build at home. They had built some small commercial aircraft but racing seemed to offer some instant rewards. Just four weeks before the race they started work on what they called their 'Solution', a biplane. Flown by Charles 'Speed' Holman, it took off on its first test flight just hours before the race, and made it to the start line with only minutes to spare. Another bizarre entrant was Benny Howard, who built his first machine from the parts of two completely different aircraft, then expanded his business by adapting his products to carry bootleg whisky. He entered a biplane he called the Howard DGA3. When the pilot he had hired failed to show up, Howard flew it himself. The Marines entered a much modified Curtiss Hawk biplane which led for much of the race but crashed and the pilot was killed. Holman won in 'Solution' at 202 mph, a Travel Air was second and Howard's DGA third. A little more money flowed into the coffers of the struggling entrepreneurs.

In 1931 there was another new trophy. The Bendix, sponsored again by an industrialist, was for distance racing. Laird built another biplane, the 'Super Solution', and Jimmy Doolittle, hero of the 1925 Schneider Cup, romped home

Benny Howard and the DGA4; DGA stood for Damned Good Aeroplane

at an average speed of 223 mph. Laird's biplanes had won both trophies but in fact they marked the end of an era – it was the last time a major race was won by a biplane. The 1931 Thompson Trophy went to a stubby little monoplane, one of the most lethal aircraft ever built – the Granville GeeBee.

The Granville Brothers had a garage business in Massachusetts. They were attracted by the cash prizes and started building aircraft in a disused dance hall. The GeeBees were little more than the minimum of fuselage and wings needed to get a pilot and the Pratt & Whitney radial engine airborne together and racing. Design was compromised in favour of speed; they were like highly-strung stallions and a pilot needed skill just to stay alive.

Jimmy Doolittle winning the 1932 Bendix. He said of the GeeBee:
'If you let go of it, it took over in an effort to destroy itself and you with it'

The GeeBees were dangerous but they were fast and Jimmy Doolittle chose one for the 1932 Thompson Trophy. Flying close to the ground in such an unpredictable machine took all the skill he had acquired in a decade of racing; he managed to get ahead at the start and stay there, lapping all but one of the other contestants to win at over 250 mph. In seven years he had won the Schneider, the Thompson, the Bendix and broken the world speed record for seaplanes; but after his flight in the GeeBee he saw how the stakes were rising and retired from racing. There were plenty of pilots looking to fill his shoes, however. Roscoe Turner, a flamboyant figure, went on to win the Thompson three times and the Bendix once. But, though the races pushed up speeds, even in 1939 pilots were still winning at under 300 mph and the races contributed little to the general progress of aviation.

There was one American caught by the speed bug who was certainly no buccaneer. Howard Hughes was meticulous, a perfectionist. His racer was not put together in a back-street garage; money and care were lavished on it from the start. The Hughes H–1 was a superb piece of engineering: the skin was of burnished aluminium, the rivets which held it together were smoothed flush to reduce drag, the undercarriage was retractable, and the radial engine drove a variable-pitch propeller enabling the pilot to change its 'bite' on the air according

Jimmy Doolittle with his GeeBee

The Pulitzer, 1920–1925

The Thompson, 1930–1949

THE AMERICAN TROPHIES

The Bendix, 1931–1949

to the speed. It was the ultimate racing aircraft, and even had a different pair of wings for long-distance or closed-circuit racing. But it never entered a race.

It did, however, break a world speed record. By 1934 Bonnet's 278 mph had stood as a record for a land-plane for a decade. That year Raymond Delmotte, a fellow Frenchman, flying a Caudron C–460 finally beat it with 314 mph. That was a challenge which excited Hughes. By 1935 the H–1 was completed to his satisfaction and he began test flights. In September he was ready and flew it to a measured course near Burbank, California. He made four passes and that was enough, but he made two more just to make sure, before running out of fuel and landing in a nearby field. He had averaged 352 mph. He went on to beat the US coast-to-coast record with a flight of seven hours, but the absolute world record was well out of reach: the H–1 was nearly 100 mph slower than Francesco Agello's 440 mph in the MC72 built for the Schneider. Hughes's engineering was superb; what the H–1 lacked was power. His radial engine was the best that money could buy, but radial engines, which dominated the American industry and were perfect for the airlines, lacked the brutish power of the in-line, water-cooled engines which were the legacy of the Schneider in Europe.

Howard Hughes with the elegant H-1 racer

A Victim of the Quest for Speed

In 1931 Lowell Bayles won the Thompson in a GeeBee at over 240 mph. In December he set out to break Bonnet's 278-mph record. He managed 281 mph which was not enough to take it officially and so tried again; on his first run he was timed at 314 mph then tragedy struck: a fuel cap came off and smashed into the windscreen; he was just 50 feet above the ground, crashed immediately and was killed.

*Roscoe Turner with his Weddell Williams racer, one of the most successful of the period;
the radial engine was a Pratt & Whitney Hornet, four of which could lift a Pan American
Clipper with 38 passengers*

In 1935, as Europe began rearming, aircraft designers were called upon to give fighter pilots more speed. That meant a monoplane and air forces round the world issued more or less the same specification for the new generation of fighters: an all-metal monoplane, machine-guns or cannon mounted in the wings, with a fully enclosed cockpit and a retractable undercarriage. Hughes had tried to interest the US Army in the H–1 as the basis for a fighter, but was turned down because it did not meet with their specification. The first of the new breed in America was the Seversky P–35 with a Pratt & Whitney radial engine. It was not as refined a machine as the H–1, and the undercarriage, although retractable, was exposed; with two machine-guns, it had a top speed of around 280 mph and entered service in 1937. In a modified form it won the 1937–9 Bendix races. The French equivalent was the Morane-Saulnier MS–405. With an Hispano-Suiza in-line engine giving a top speed of just over 300 mph, it did not go into squadron service until 1939. But the fastest entrants in this unofficial, and largely secret, quest for speed were Germany and Britain.

In May 1935 Flugkapitän 'Bubi' Knötsch took off in the prototype of the Messerchmitt Bf 109 at Willi Messerschmitt's factory at Augsburg. The in-line engine destined for it was not ready and the first prototype was powered by a Rolls-Royce Kestrel which gave it an unimpressive speed at the outset. Later production models still only had a top speed of 292 mph when they were delivered to Richthofen's old squadron in 1937.

On 6 November 1935 Britain's first monoplane fighter made its début. The Hawker Hurricane had a top speed of 322 mph and that came from its Rolls-Royce Merlin engine, a direct descendant of the R racing engines. The following March Supermarine had the prototype of its new Spitfire ready. Its lines were distinctly reminiscent of the S6b, which was unsurprising since it was designed by R. J. Mitchell. It too was powered by a Merlin engine, but it was faster than the Hurricane with a top speed of 350 mph. Mitchell's old Schneider Cup adversary, Mario Castoldi, also turned his skills to fighters, and in 1937 the first of Italy's new generation of fighters, the Macchi C200 Saetta (Lightning), flew for the first time. It had a Fiat radial engine and a top speed of 313 mph.

The quest for speed was no longer for glittering prizes. The goal was a fighter which could outperform the opposition. The essence of the fighter is speed and climbing ability, and to draw attention to the performance of their products companies in Germany and Britain set out to break the absolute speed record. Supermarine prepared a Spitfire specially for the task, but it was Germany which now made the running. Heinkel and Messerschmitt were locked in a contest to supply the Luftwaffe with their fighters. The Bf 109 made its public début at the Olympic Games in Berlin in 1936, and the following year Messerschmitt installed a specially prepared engine in a 109 and beat Hughes's record for land-planes with 379 mph. The Heinkel He 100 was ready early in 1939; fuelled by a mixture of ether and methanol, which strained the engine to its limits, Hans Dieterle managed to set a new absolute world speed record of 463 mph on 30 March. The record of Francesco Agello was beaten at last.

OPPOSITE: The Supermarine Spitfire, the result of racing developments for the Schneider, flew for the first time in 1937. Apart from the power of the Merlin engine, its frontal area made it much more suitable than the radial for high-speed fighters

Frank Fuller completing a record 9 hrs 35 min coast-to-coast flight from Los Angeles to New Jersey in 1937 in the Seversky; in the same year, Howard Hughes reduced the time to 7 hrs 28 min in the H-1

But Willi Messerschmitt was back inside a month with another machine, supposedly a variant of the Bf 109 but in fact a completely new design known internally as the Me 209. It was the smallest machine which could house Germany's record-breaking Daimler Benz DB601 inverted-V engine and was extremely difficult to handle. On 26 April Messerschmitt's test pilot, Fritz Wendel, just beat the Heinkel with a run of 469 mph. It was the last piston-engined aircraft to hold the official world speed record. (Wendel's piston-engined record stood for 30 years until, in 1969, Darryl Freenamyer raised it to 482 mph in a Grumman Bearcat. The present record of 499 mph was set in August 1978 by Steve Hinton flying a North American Mustang powered by a Griffon engine which was a derivative of the Rolls-Royce Merlin.)

Unofficially Wendel's record was broken both in combat and in trials during the six years of war, though never by a large margin. Both sides squeezed every last drop of power out of their engines and propellers, but just 40 years after the Wrights' first flight both had reached their maximum potential in the quest for speed. Rolls-Royce improved the Merlin to power faster fighters and bigger bombers, but the piston engine had reached a plateau of development. There was an even more fundamental problem with the propeller: as the tips of the spinning blades came close to the speed of sound, they suffered a great loss of efficiency. To go faster a completely new system of propulsion would be needed. On 20 June Erich Warsitz, Heinkel's test pilot, made a 50-second flight in the rocket-powered He 176; then in the last days of peace, on 27 August, he flew the He 178, the first aircraft powered by a jet engine.

GERMANY SURGES AHEAD
Above: Hans Dieterle with the Heinkel team after bringing the record to Germany in March 1939.
Right: Willi Messerschmitt congratulates Fritz Wendel on beating Dieterle a month later.

CHAPTER·SIX

AIR POWER

Guernica is the ancient capital of the Basques. In April 1937 it was held by government forces, the Republicans, in the Spanish Civil War. It occupies a naturally good defensive position and with Basques fighting for their home ground it would be a tough obstacle for General Franco's Nationalist army. Monday 26 April was market-day and even with fighting just ten miles away the town was busy. In the late afternoon He 111 and Ju 52 bombers of the German Kondor Legion, sent by Hitler to support Franco, appeared over the town. It was undefended against air attack and high explosive bombs and incendiaries rained down for three hours, reducing buildings to rubble and starting many fires; low-flying aircraft machine-gunned the streets. The raid had one purpose: to terrorise the defenders and destroy their will to resist. In this it succeeded; two days later the Nationalists took what remained of Guernica without a fight. There was outrage round the world. A quarter of the inhabitants, over 1500 people, had been killed and nearly a thousand injured. It was a test of the use of air power. As was Madrid. Bombed repeatedly from the beginning of the war, its inhabitants suffered even greater casualties, but it held out for two years. If anything the bombing stiffened the resolve of the defenders, but their fortitude tended to be forgotten in the outrage at the destruction of Guernica.

The Spanish Civil War was the first real test of air power and apparently confirmed the theories of the Italian, Col. Giulio Douhet, who had prophesied as early as 1911 that countries would wage war using aircraft independently of ground forces by bombing each other's population and industrial centres. In 1921, in *Command of the Air*, he argued the case even more forcefully and by 1927 his theory had been developed to the point that some believed that wars could be won using air power alone. In America his ideas were taken up by General 'Billy' Mitchell, and in 1932 Stanley Baldwin gave them a sense of inevitability with the chilling phrase: 'The bomber will always get through.'

OPPOSITE: The instrument of Air Power: Britain's heavy bomber the Avro Lancaster

The church of San Juan, Guernica, before (inset) *and after the raid*

Guernica and Madrid were symbols of the horror and effectiveness of air power and the instrument of their destruction, the Luftwaffe, became feared throughout Europe. That suited Hitler perfectly; even the implication that the Luftwaffe might be unleashed elsewhere became a powerful political tool, and when the Nazis marched into Austria and Czechoslovakia, as Europe appeased Hitler, there was always the feeling that Guernica might be repeated. Goering built on the awesome image of the Luftwaffe; he invited Charles Lindbergh to inspect it. Lindbergh was impressed with what he saw and broadcast his view far and wide, adding to its image of invincibility. Goering and most of his senior officers believed that they could win a war by making the Luftwaffe the handmaiden of the Army; despite a few dissenters, they largely ignored Douhet's ideas of an independent strategic force and did not build long-range heavy bombers to strike at an enemy's heartland.

In Britain, the RAF had been fashioned by a different hand and from a different experience; its architect was Marshal of the RAF Viscount Trenchard. It had been independent of the Army since 1918 and he had struggled to keep it independent. He was in step with Douhet and Mitchell, but he adapted the theory for the needs of the British Empire, using light bombers to police recalcitrant tribesmen. At home the emphasis was on bombers and in 1936 Fighter

The Junkers Ju 87 Stuka dive-bomber served on all fronts as a ground-attack bomber

Command was equipped entirely with biplanes. But thanks mainly to its first commander, Air Marshal Sir Hugh Dowding, 500 Hurricanes and 300 Spitfires were on order. Dowding was a far-sighted and professional airman who saw a possible defence against the bomber in an effective fighter force. He had initiated the design of the new monoplane fighters based on the Schneider Cup racers, and he vigorously supported the development of radar to detect aircraft approaching Britain.

To get enough new fighters Dowding had to change attitudes. His intellectual honesty, his mastery of detail and the quiet and persistent force with which he put his case gradually won him more resources but few friends in the RAF and Whitehall. But in the autumn of 1938 he persuaded his superiors that air defence had to take priority: when war finally came 536 of the RAF's total of 1566 aircraft were bombers and 608 were fighters. The Luftwaffe not only had twice as many fighters and bombers but 600 reconnaissance aircraft to the RAF's 96 and 366 dive-bombers to the RAF's none. In all, Goering had 3609 aircraft.

Early in the morning of 1 September 1939 the Luftwaffe bombed Warsaw as the German Army invaded Poland. Over one million men supported by 1600 aircraft, mainly bombers, attacked bridges, military positions, railways and air-fields. It was 'Blitzkrieg', the combined use of motorised troops, advancing behind a spearhead of armour, supported by the 'flying artillery' of the Luftwaffe. Poland waited for her allies, Britain and France, to bomb Germany in retaliation, but nothing happened. On 3 September Neville Chamberlain, the British Prime Minister, finally issued an ultimatum to Germany: withdraw or face war. The time limit passed at 11 am and Britain and Germany were at war. But still no bombs dropped on Germany or, though air raid sirens sounded soon after the declaration of war, on Britain either. The government acted in the expectation of air raids: streetlights were extinguished, houses blacked out, shelters built, gas-masks issued to civilians, and children living in obvious targets such as London were evacuated to the country, but neither side wanted to provoke the other into unleashing their bombs on each other's population.

On 17 September the Soviet Union invaded Poland from the east. Crushed between the two, and with their Air Force all but wiped out, on 25 September the Poles made a last stand in Warsaw. A force of 400 He 111 and Do 17 bombers, Ju 87 Stuka dive-bombers and ground-attack fighters pounded the city all day long. Warsaw surrendered on the following day.

Europe entered on the 'phoney war'. The British Expeditionary Force in France sat tight, supported by ten squadrons of single-engined Fairey Battle light bombers, three squadrons of twin-engined Blenheims for long-range reconnaissance and four squadrons of Hurricanes. Bomber crews risked their lives dropping nothing more deadly than propaganda leaflets; bombs were restricted to military targets, mainly the opposing navies. On 18 December 24 Wellington bombers set out for Wilhelmshaven in daylight unescorted; twelve were shot down by fighters and three more badly damaged.

The Allied strategy was to build up their strength, but in the spring of 1940 it was Hitler who was ready: in April Denmark and Norway succumbed to Blitzkrieg; on 10 May Germany invaded neutral Holland, and simultaneously forged through Belgium towards France. The Dutch only had 52 fighters and the Luftwaffe dropped paratroopers on the Hague and Rotterdam. The Dutch Army resisted for four days, then Luftwaffe bombers tore the heart out of Rotterdam and the Dutch surrendered the same evening. By 12 May the second German thrust had reached the River Meuse. Here, so the French thought, was a natural obstacle which would hold up the advance; the Germans would bring up artillery. Instead, the Luftwaffe concentrated 1500 aircraft over Sedan and bombarded the French positions all day. By nightfall they had crossed the river; France had suffered not only a severe defeat but a savage blow to its morale. It was the most effective demonstration yet of tactical air power supporting an army.

Winston Churchill replaced Chamberlain on 10 May. As the allied armies

BATTLE OF BRITAIN AIRCRAFT
The aircraft which fought the
Battle of Britain have retained
a fascination for nearly half a
century. There are a number
of Spitfires still flying but
fewer Hurricanes, yet Hurricanes outnumbered Spitfires
by nearly two to one during
the Battle and accounted for
more enemy aircraft than all
the other defences put
together. More Me 109s were
built than any other aircraft
except the Soviet Il-2
ground-attack fighter.

This Me 109 is privately owned in the United States

*A Hurricane IIc of the RAF Battle of Britain Memorial Flight. The Heinkel He 111 (inset) is
preserved by the Confederate States Air Force in Texas; it has been re-engined with Merlins*

fell back the French Premier, Paul Reynaud, requested ten squadrons of RAF fighters to help stem the German advance. Dowding thought this would be a grave error since sooner or later the Luftwaffe would be turned against Britain. He showed Churchill a simple graph of what would happen if losses in France were replaced from Britain: in two weeks there would be no Hurricanes left on either side of the Channel and Britain would be defenceless. It worked, and though some Hurricanes were sent over they were quickly brought back when it was clear that France was going to collapse. The BEF was evacuated from the beaches of Dunkirk under repeated attack from the Luftwaffe. Fighter Command gave what protection it could from the south of England.

Britain was alone, but thanks to Dowding most of her fighters were intact. Churchill appointed the newspaper tycoon, Lord Beaverbrook, as Minister of Aircraft Production; he and Dowding were given a six-week respite while Germany swallowed France, then in mid-July Hitler's plans for the invasion of Britain were ready. There was one important prerequisite: Hitler wanted the RAF cleared from the skies over the Channel, making it safe for paratroop-carrying aircraft and invasion barges.

The Luftwaffe started by trying to blockade Britain by closing the Channel to British shipping. Both sides had learnt how vulnerable bombers were in daylight, so Goering sent over Messerschmitt Bf 109s and the slower, twin-engined Me 110s to escort them, planning to draw the Hurricanes and Spitfires into fighter-to-fighter combat and shoot them down. As shipping came under attack, so Dowding was pressed by the Admiralty to throw everything against the Luftwaffe, but he resisted. He mounted convoy patrols, but he never committed all his squadrons at once. The climax of this phase came on 8 August when three successive waves of Ju 87 dive-bombers attacked a convoy off the south coast. The Stuka was good at pin-point bombing of ships, but it was hopelessly vulnerable in a dogfight. The RAF pilots were under instructions to leave the fighters alone and go for the bombers; Stuka crews suffered badly: of the 31 Luftwaffe aircraft lost that day most were Stukas; the RAF lost 20. Up to that point the Luftwaffe had lost 300 aircraft to the RAF's 150, but more importantly in the same period Beaverbrook had squeezed 300 replacements out of the factories and Fighter Command's strength had actually increased.

Goering changed his strategy. In Poland and France the Luftwaffe had destroyed many of its opponents on the ground and he believed that a four-day concerted attack on Fighter Command's radar stations and airfields would give him command of the air over southern England. But hitherto the Luftwaffe's opponents had been either tiny or ill-prepared. Now, for the first time, it was up against a sizeable, well-trained, well-disciplined, well-equipped, and above all well-led force, fighting in its own sky for its own airfields.

The start of the new campaign, code-named 'Adlertag' (Eagle Day), was set for 13 August. On the 12th Luftwaffe units attacked the chain of coastal radar stations, putting several out of action for a time – Ventnor, on the Isle of Wight, was out for eleven days. Adlertag itself was less of a success. A force of 74 Do 17s took off from northern France heading for the Thames estuary. Then a weather flight reported a deterioration over England and orders went out to abandon the raid; only the fighter escorts heard them, leaving the bombers unescorted. On the way in the tail end of the raid was attacked by Spitfires of 74 Squadron; the remainder managed to bomb Eastchurch airfield, but on the way back 111 and 151 Squadrons shot down five and damaged five more. Later in the day 30 twin-engined Me 110s took off though the bombers they were to escort stayed on the ground; a far smaller force of Hurricanes shot down six. Then 40 Stukas escorted by as many Me 110s were attacked by thirteen Hurricanes while Spitfires fought Bf 109s above; nine Stukas were lost. The final tally for the day was 45 German planes shot down, and many others damaged beyond repair, for the loss of thirteen to Fighter Command. Worse still for Goering, faulty intelligence had sent the bombers to Coastal Command airfields and the effort was wasted as far as the immediate battle was concerned.

Goering believed that the RAF's strength in the south of England had been achieved at the expense of stripping protection from further north. On 15 August he mounted a maximum effort, with even closer fighter protection for the bombers. The day started with Stukas diving on airfields on the south coast; then, around midday, Luftwaffe units from Norway set out across the North Sea for Scotland and Newcastle. The RAF squadrons in the north had plenty of warning and were manoeuvred by radar into ideal positions to butcher the raiders over the sea. The attacks switched back to the south, inflicting some damage, but the Luftwaffe had lost another 75 aircraft to the RAF's 34.

Beaverbrook kept the aircraft coming by setting the manufacturers near impossible targets, but Dowding's more immediate problem was pilots. His ranks were swelled with Czech, Polish, French, Fleet Air Arm, Empire and American volunteers, but between 8 and 18 August he lost 94 dead or missing and a further 60 wounded. As in the First World War there were aces, pilots whose individual scores mounted fast: 'Sailor' Malan, leader of 74 Squadron, a tactician whose dictum was 'always turn to face the enemy'; Sgt 'Ginger' Lacey, top-scoring non-commissioned pilot; 'Johnnie' Johnson, officially the RAF's top scorer. But the backbone of Fighter Command were the many pilots who accounted for just one or two enemy, young officers and sergeants who wore the Luftwaffe down, four or five missions a day and giving battle whatever the odds. (There was one occasion when six Hurricanes met 100 bombers and went straight into the attack.) Eleven Group, covering south-east England, bore the brunt of the fighting and

Dornier 215s over the River Thames

Of 2940 RAF aircrew who took part in the Battle, 507 were killed and 500 wounded

SUMMER 1940
The Battle of Britain, like
Drake's defeat of the Spanish
Armada in 1588 and Nelson's
victory at Trafalgar in 1805,
saved Britain from invasion
and turned the tide of history.

*RIGHT: Hermann Goering (here
with Hitler and Doenitz) led the
Luftwaffe until the end of the war;
he committed suicide in 1946*
*LEFT: Final moments of an Me
110: tracer shows the RAF fighter
pilot that his aim is high; by
correcting it he brings his fire on to
the enemy's port engine*

*Air Chief Marshal Sir Hugh Dowding with the King and Queen on 6 September 1940.
After the war Dowding turned to spiritualism; he died in 1970*

suffered the highest casualties; pilots often returned only to fall asleep until the next scramble. The whole country sensed the decisiveness of the battle; Churchill articulated the feeling in the House of Commons on 20 August: 'Never in the field of human conflict was so much owed by so many to so few.'

Without radar they could not have done it. Dowding and Air Vice Marshal Keith Park, commander of Eleven Group, watched the formations build up over France from their operations rooms; once there was a clear picture the response could be planned and the orders given, and the pilots could stay on the ground until they knew where they were wanted. Without radar, they would have had to fly standing patrols, adding to exhaustion, burning valuable fuel and spreading themselves too thinly. Dowding and Park saw eye to eye on deploying the fighters. Where possible they waited until the Bf 109s, the Luftwaffe's best fighters, were at the limit of their range, then engaged them with faster Spitfires while the Hurricanes went for the bombers. The Bf 109's lack of range was a great drawback; Adolph Galland, one of Germany's fighter aces, likened it to being like a dog on the end of a leash, always just out of reach of his quarry.

Between 15 and 18 August the Luftwaffe lost 194 aircraft, then the weather closed in and Goering took stock. He felt his fighter pilots lacked aggression, but he was too eager to blame them. Many of the problems lay in their aircraft: the Me 110 and the Stuka were very vulnerable in a dogfight. On 19 August the Stukas were withdrawn from the battle and held ready to support the invasion. But the problem was deeper than that: the Luftwaffe lacked a clear idea of what it was doing. Goering agreed to attack Bomber Command stations, to frustrate the attacks on German invasion forces gathering in the Channel ports; he ordered sporadic raids, often at night, against cities, especially those with aircraft factories; other bombers went on bombing shipping. The main thrust of the offensive remained against fighter stations but by late August it was gradually drifting from what started as a concerted battle for air superiority into a general, strategic attack on Britain, her population and industrial base, a task for which the Luftwaffe was neither equipped nor trained.

Late on 24 August the battle entered a new phase. A German crew missed its target and jettisoned its bombs over London. The following night 29 Wellingtons bombed Berlin. It was a turning-point: Hitler was humiliated; he decided on retaliation and wholesale air war against Britain now became policy. On 7 September London was attacked for the first time. For once Fighter Command was caught napping; nobody expected it and the raiders did a great deal of damage. Goering continued to attack London, letting Fighter Command off the hook. The climax to this phase of the battle came on 15 September: 1000 fighters and bombers went for London. They came in waves and Dowding had to commit everything he had. There were no reserves: every fighter pilot who could join the battle did so, and at the day's end they claimed 185 shot down. In fact it was only 60 but the RAF lost only 25 aircraft and thirteen pilots.

The Luftwaffe could not keep up that pace, and with Fighter Command clearly unbeaten Hitler gave up his plans for invasion. The idea that the bomber would always get through was shown to be false, and though the margin of victory was extremely narrow, the Battle of Britain was won.

Within a month of his triumph Dowding was replaced at Fighter Command. His single-mindedness and his manner had made him enemies and the RAF was now looking to go on the offensive. Yet he was the sole architect of victory in the first great all-air battle in history: in peacetime he fought to get the fighters, then fought to retain them in opposition to other demands; he husbanded them in battle and deployed them with consummate skill.

In four hectic months of air combat the Luftwaffe had lost 1733 aircraft but it was still a formidable force. Hitler now decided to try to bomb Britain into submission, to destroy her economic base and the will of her population to resist. To whose who suffered it, it became known as the 'Blitz'. Daylight was clearly

Bomb damage, London

too expensive in men and materials, so from mid-October the Luftwaffe bombed at night, which was far less accurate. German scientists developed an electronic means to guide bombers right over their targets. A device called Knickebein sent a narrow beam from Europe; the bombers flew along it until another beam intersected it right above the target, giving its precise position. A battle quickly developed between the scientists on both sides to counter each others' devices. At first the British simply jammed the beams, but later they developed a more subtle countermeasure, bending them so that the bombs fell harmlessly. The Luftwaffe also trained selected crews as pathfinders, to find the exact target and mark it for the main force. Then they developed a more advanced beam system called X-Gerät; British countermeasures took several months to develop.

In early November the Luftwaffe switched entirely to night operations, bombing provincial cities as well. Coventry was first: on 14 November 437 bombers were guided right over the city centre and bombed the heart out of it. In the same week Britain's first radar-equipped nightfighter, a twin-engined Bristol Beaufighter, had its first success. On the night of 19/20 November the radar operator guided Flying Officer John 'Cat's Eyes' Cunningham right underneath his target until he had visual contact and opened fire at close range. Defences of all kinds were improved: more anti-aircraft guns, more searchlights, barrage balloons and nightfighters, but German losses never equalled those of the daylight raids during the Battle of Britain.

The second phase of the Blitz started in February 1941. London and western ports were the main targets and casualties reached over 1000 killed on some nights, with massive damage to property. Then in May the raids stopped. (At the time it was thought that the defences had won but in fact the Luftwaffe was being redeployed eastwards for the attack on Russia.) Despite extensive damage to the fabric of Britain, strategic bombing had failed to demoralise the people; the theory that air power alone could win a war had suffered another setback.

Yet even as London was resisting the last raids, so plans were being drawn up to use the RAF to try to demoralise the German people. In May 1941 Churchill was urged to start unrestricted bombing of Germany. Churchill agreed for a number of reasons: there was no other way of hitting back; there was no possibility of reinvading the continent for years; and politically revenge was what the British people wanted. By July the RAF was bombing Germany's industrial heartland in the Ruhr and the surrounding residential areas, but its accuracy was very poor and it had little effect either on morale or industrial output, though Bomber Command suffered huge losses.

Following their success in Holland and Belgium, Hitler had planned to drop a division of paratroops between Folkestone and Dover as part of the invasion of

Air Power at Sea

In June 1940 Mussolini declared war on Britain; the Italian Fleet represented a threat in the Mediterranean from its base at Taranto in the heel of Italy. On 11 November 22 ageing Swordfish biplanes from HMS *Illustrious* attacked with bombs and torpedoes, sinking the new battleship *Littorio*, two older battleships, a cruiser and two destroyers – half Italy's fleet.

Reconnaissance photograph of Taranto taken the following morning

THE LUFTWAFFE'S FLYING TRUCKS

The Ju 52 was the workhorse on all fronts; its vulnerability dropping paratroops at low level was clear during the invasion of Crete (*above*) and it was too small to carry the soldiers' heavy equipment. The Messerschmitt 323 heavy transport (*right*) started life as a glider; engines were added later and they served on the Eastern Front and across the Mediterranean to supply Rommel where they were cut to pieces by Allied fighters.

Britain. In June 1940 Churchill had ordered the establishment of a British parachute force but resources were so stretched that it was given low priority. That changed in May 1941 when Germany invaded Crete entirely from the air. Crete was occupied by the British with the Navy defending the sea approaches. Its air defences were thin, just a handful of Hurricanes. From newly-occupied Greece the Luftwaffe bombed the island's airfields, then on 20 May, with complete surprise, Ju 52s dropped 3000 paratroops on key points. By evening their number had doubled and on the following day, after fierce fighting, they captured the airfield at Maleme, enabling more Ju 52s to land more soldiers and equipment. They were a small but élite force and took enormous casualties in the fighting. Seaborne reinforcements and heavy equipment were repulsed by the Royal Navy which then came under attack by Stukas and Bf 109s carrying bombs: three British cruisers and six destroyers were sunk; thirteen other ships were damaged including, on 26 May, the Navy's only aircraft-carrier in the Mediterranean, HMS *Formidable*, leaving the ships with no air cover. Lacking air support and with the land battle swinging the German way as 22,000 soldiers were landed by air, the British evacuated Crete, still harried by the Luftwaffe.

It was an outstanding military operation by the Germans, based solely on tactical air power, but their losses were very heavy – 170 Ju 52s and 6000 killed and wounded. The loss of so many hand-picked soldiers undermined Hitler's faith in the idea of airborne assault and he never used it on any scale again. Britain, on the other hand, and America drew the opposite conclusion and stepped up training and resources for parachute forces.

The German Navy was a greater threat. Its task was to blockade Britain from the sea. Until mid-1940 it could do little, but with the fall of Norway and France it suddenly had a long Atlantic seaboard from which to attack British merchantmen in the Atlantic approaches to the English Channel. Its main weapon was the submarine and British losses mounted steadily. Britain used convoys for protection, but few warships could be spared for escort duties. Aircraft-carriers had to protect the fleet first and using them as escorts was very costly; within weeks of the start of the war HMS *Courageous* had been lost to a U-boat.

Losses from U-boats were alarming though the trend was in the right direction. They peaked in April 1941 at 644,000 tons, but in return Coastal Command and the Navy had sunk 47 U-boats. Long-range Hudsons, Sunderlands, Catalinas and, later, Liberators from America steadily pushed the U-boats further out into the ocean. By November no merchant ship was sunk within the range of a Coastal Command base.

But the real answer for the convoys was to have air cover which sailed with them. In 1941 Britain built the first auxiliary aircraft-carrier out of a captured German merchant vessel; a 460-foot-long flat deck was put over the entire

*In January 1940 a Sunderland assisted surface vessels in sinking a
German U-boat off Ushant, the first such action; Sunderlands
remained one of the mainstays of Coastal Command throughout the war*

superstructure and six Grumman F4F fighters were put aboard; she was renamed
HMS *Audacity*. On 14 December she was escorting a convoy from Gibraltar to
Britain when it was sighted by Focke-Wulf 200 Kondors, four-engined pre-war
airliners converted to military use, which brought up twelve U-boats. In a hit-
and-run battle lasting from 17 to 21 December the Germans lost four submarines
and two Kondors. One British destroyer and the *Audacity* herself were sunk, but
significantly only two of the merchantmen were lost. It was a triumph for the
idea of 'cheap and cheerful' carriers and they became major contributors to the
safety of convoys in the Atlantic.

The Battle of the Atlantic went on and fortunes fluctuated as new technology
or new tactics gave the U-boat commander or the long-range pilot a brief
advantage in the deadly game of cat and mouse. Merchant seamen remained in
danger from U-boats, but the flow of war supplies across the Atlantic increased.
Aircraft had once again played a vital part in Britain's survival.

Japan resented the dominance of Europe and America in eastern Asia and the Pacific. Like Germany it was looking for a greater place in the world. In 1932 it annexed Manchuria; in 1937 it invaded northern China and the two countries began an undeclared war; in 1940, after the fall of France, it absorbed French Indo-China through its alliance with Germany. In consequence the US and British governments froze all Japanese assets and stopped its trade in oil, causing yet further resentment. After a year of fruitless negotiations the Japanese government decided to invade oil-rich Java in the Dutch East Indies. Holland had been overrun; Britain still had its strategic naval base in Singapore but was preoccupied in Europe; and though the US had bases in the Philippines, her forces there were not strong. Japan's only real fear was that, given warning, she would intervene with her Pacific Fleet from Hawaii. An inescapable prelude to any action in eastern Asia therefore was a pre-emptive strike against her base at Pearl Harbor.

America had six aircraft-carriers though they were not all in the Pacific. The Japanese had an excellent air force, well experienced after years of war in China, but Hawaii was beyond the range of its bombers. The task of hitting Pearl Harbor therefore fell to the Navy; at the heart of the Japanese fleet were six aircraft-carriers. The date for the attack was set for 7 December 1941; it was planned in two waves of torpedo-carrying Nakajima B5Ns and high-level bombers for attacking the ships in port, Aichi D3A dive-bombers, and Mitsubishi A6M Zero fighters to attack the military airfields. The night before the scheduled attack, the commander, Admiral Chuichi Nagumo, received intelligence that none of the American carriers was in port. Although they were the prime targets, he decided to attack nevertheless.

Keeping just a few Zeros to defend the ships, he launched 360 aircraft early the following morning from about 200 miles north of Hawaii. The force had all the advantages of complete surprise: it was a Sunday and the Americans were not at a high state of alert. Radar picked up the attackers well in advance, but there was no alarm because the operator believed they were a flight of B-17 bombers which were expected from the U S mainland. The Japanese plan worked almost like clockwork. Between 7.55 and 8.35 am the first wave of torpedo-bombers made straight for the nine battleships moored in the harbour while fighters and dive-bombers strafed the airfields. Five minutes later the second wave repeated the performance, leaving four battleships, three light cruisers, three destroyers and several smaller vessels sunk, 350 aircraft destroyed, 2403 Americans dead and over 1000 wounded. Japanese losses were 30 aircraft and 55 aircrew. By any account it was a victory for the Japanese, but none of the US Navy's aircraft-carriers was even scratched and it was aircraft-carriers, not battleships, which would fight future battles in the Pacific.

Spearheaded by sea power and attendant air power, Japan unleashed a kind

THE BATTLE OF THE ATLANTIC
The chief threat to the supply
line from America to Britain
came from submarines, but
Germany converted pre-war
airliners, Focke-Wulf
Kondors (*right*), into
maritime reconnaissance
bombers with a 2000-mile
range; they acted as the eyes
of the submarines and
attacked ships themselves.
Britain's answer was to equip
35 merchant vessels with a rail
from which a Hurricane could
be launched with rockets; the
Hurricanes only shot down
five Kondors, but their
presence with the convoys
acted as a deterrent.

After his sortie, the Hurricane pilot had to ditch in the sea or bale out

HMS Biter, *one of the small escort carriers whose attack aircraft and fighters were the ultimate protection for the convoys*

Caught on the surface: the moment the U-boat commander dreaded

The battleships USS West Virginia *and* Tennessee *on fire
in Pearl Harbor, 7 December 1941*

of naval Blitzkreig through eastern Asia. Guam and the Gilbert Islands fell on
10 December as Japanese aircraft attacked US naval units in the Philippines. On
the same day the Royal Navy battleship HMS *Prince of Wales* and the battle-
cruiser HMS *Repulse* were off the Malayan coast. They had no air cover when
84 Japanese aircraft, mainly torpedo-bombers, found them and sank them. Wake
Island, one of Pan American's staging posts in the Pacific, fell on 23 December
with help from Admiral Nagumo's force returning from Pearl Harbor and now
free to support other landings. Hong Kong fell on 25 December and Singapore
on 15 February; four days later Japan invaded Java, their prime objective, which
surrendered on 8 March. Next day Rangoon fell.

Admiral Chester Nimitz took over command of the Pacific Fleet in 1942; he
had to fight with what he had – four aircraft-carriers: *Yorktown, Lexington,
Enterprise* and *Hornet*. They began by probing into the new Japanese Empire
and raiding their island bases. They were pin-pricks at first, but slowly Nagumo
began to regret that he had missed them in Pearl Harbor. Ideally he would have

The end of the USS Lexington: *216 sailors lost their lives; 2730 were rescued and some of her aircraft transferred safely to the* Yorktown

confronted them with his superior force, but the Japanese Army was still carrying out amphibious operations and, with American carriers in the area, he had to provide air cover for them first.

Nimitz had one major advantage: America had broken some of the Japanese codes. On 17 April he heard that the Japanese planned to invade Tulagi Island and Port Moresby in New Guinea. Three carriers – *Shokaku*, *Zuikaku* and *Shoho* – were to give air cover and Nimitz knew that they would be in the Coral Sea in early May; he sent the *Lexington* and *Yorktown* to confront them.

The Battle of the Coral Sea was a sea battle fought by aircraft: the opposing carriers stayed between 70 and 200 miles apart and launched aircraft at each other. The main problem was finding each other. On 7 May both sides sent their scouts up before dawn and a Japanese pilot reported sighting an American carrier. Rear Admiral Takeo Takagi launched a large force of aircraft which found the target but it turned out to be an oil-tanker; they sank it and its escort destroyer. Meanwhile another misidentification resulted in Admiral Frank Fletcher laun-

*Evicting Japan from her Empire: B-25 medium bombers attacking Japanese
shipping and shore installations at Rabaul in New Britain in the South Pacific*

ching strikes of Dauntless dive-bombers, Devastator torpedo-bombers and
Grumman Wildcat fighters against Japanese cruisers rather than carriers. But by
a combination of luck and good lookout the bombers found the *Shoho* themselves,
and though Zeros scrambled to intercept them, the *Shoho* was sunk.

Both sides had scouts up again at dawn on 8 May and they found each other
some 200 miles apart; both commanders launched torpedo- and dive-bombers
protected by fighters. The Americans found the *Shokaku* and damaged her badly
while the *Zuikaku* managed to hide under a rain squall. The American captains
had the advantage of radar: *Lexington* picked up the Japanese bombers and was
able to launch her remaining Wildcat fighters. A fierce battle developed but
enough attackers got through and one bomb pierced the flight deck to explode
deep in the ship. Nakajima torpedo-bombers then launched their weapons from
both sides simultaneously and two hit, followed quickly by strikes by Aichi dive-
bombers. *Lexington* began to list, but managed to stay operational until aviation
fuel started to explode and she had to be abandoned.

On paper it was a Japanese victory: *Lexington* was a fleet carrier, much more
important that the smaller *Shoho*, and the Americans had lost two other ships
and *Yorktown* had also been damaged. But the invasion of Port Moresby was
postponed, never to be resumed, and the Japanese Blitzkrieg, spearheaded by

aircraft, had been brought·to a halt by aircraft. Sinking each other's carriers, to give them air superiority, became the priority for both sides.

Admiral Isoroku Yamamoto, Commander-in-Chief of the Imperial Japanese Navy, now devised an ambitious plan to provoke a battle. First he sent a diversionary force to the Aleutian islands in the Barents Sea, anticipating that Nimitz would send his carriers to intervene. Then he planned to strike at another of Pan American's staging posts, Midway Island, with his flagship, the battleship *Yamato*, six large carriers and three smaller ones, eleven other battleships and an amphibious force supported by some 200 further ships; the carrier element of this force was commanded by Nagumo. Yamamoto believed that he could take Midway, then destroy the American carriers when they returned.

From his intelligence reports Nimitz knew what Yamamoto was up to. But even with *Yorktown* being hastily repaired at Pearl Harbor he still had only three carriers. He was able to give them more fighters: the old Wildcats were swapped for a new version with folding wings which enabled more to be squeezed on board.

On 3 June Yamamoto duly attacked the Aleutians but Nimitz ignored it, leaving his carriers some 200 miles north of Midway. The following day the US carriers sent scouts out but it was a Catalina flying boat from Midway which spotted the Japanese first, 200 miles to the west. Events moved fast: Nagumo had already launched his first air-strike against Midway from where US Marine Corps fighters took off to intercept it. Army and Marine bombers, plus Grumman Avengers which had arrived from Hawaii, set out to attack the Japanese fleet; they had no success. Still working on the assumption that there were no US carriers within striking distance, Nagumo decided on another attack on Midway, but just as his crews were preparing for it, his scouts reported that the US carriers were just 200 miles away and all three had launched their aircraft. Zeros were launched and they had plenty of targets: the Devastators from *Hornet* lost their fighter escort on the way and all fifteen of them were shot down; fourteen more from *Enterprise* came in next, also without fighter protection, and ten were shot down. The Wildcats then joined the battle and drew off some of the Zeros, but only two of the next wave of Devastators from *Yorktown* survived. Not one torpedo found its mark. But the Dauntless dive-bombers which came next were decisive, hitting three large Japanese carriers in quick succession: first the *Kaga*, bombs exploding in the middle of the flight deck while planes were launching, then Nagumo's flagship at Pearl Harbor, the *Akagi*, then the *Soryu*. The Americans returned to their ships in high spirits leaving the opposition blazing and sinking. But when they arrived back *Yorktown* came under attack from all sides. Wildcats swooped on the attackers and her anti-aircraft guns joined in to account for half the force, but enough bombs and torpedoes got

Douglas Dauntless dive-bombers on the USS Ranger; *the perforated dive-brakes were opened in the dive to maintain a steady speed of 270 mph*

through to do severe damage and the captain ordered her abandoned in fear of capsizing.

In the afternoon a US reconnaissance aircraft found a fourth large Japanese carrier, the *Hiryu*. *Enterprise* launched 23 Dauntlesses and they attacked just as her captain had ordered a launch. The *Hiryu* was crippled before she could launch and sank later. The battle of Midway was over. America had won a decisive air battle against superior forces by a margin just as narrow as the Battle of Britain. Victory was based on superior intelligence, the edge which radar gave, highly motivated aircrews fighting in their own backyard, and improved tactics in the air. They were helped by some luck and by the enemy's mistakes, but that took nothing away from the sweetness of victory. The Japanese had lost the core of their naval air power in the Pacific and they had no strategic air force.

The Americans struggled to save the battered *Yorktown*, but days later she was torpedoed and sunk. Meanwhile the *Saratoga* arrived in Pearl Harbor and America's other carrier, *Wasp*, arrived from the Mediterranean. At home new

A massed exercise from the deck of the USS Saratoga *before the war*

aircraft were coming off the production lines; American industrial muscle was gearing up to take the fight back to Japan.

In Britain, Bomber Command was also gearing up to take the offensive. So far there had been little to show for the effort expended; more RAF aircrews had been killed than German civilians. The policy of going for military targets became a strategic attack on the German population simply because Bomber Command could not hit its targets. Only ten per cemt of bombs had fallen within five miles of their target. The problem was navigating at night; electronic devices were being introduced, but Gee, the first system, gave only general assistance in finding the target area and was no good for pin-point bombing. The only target against which night bombing was effective was a whole town.

By November 1941 the bomber offensive had virtually ceased, then early in 1942 two changes had profound effects: new aircraft and a new leader. The force of twin-engined Whitleys and Wellingtons was strengthened by four-engined heavy bombers, the Handley Page Halifax, the Shorts Stirling, and the heaviest so far built, the Avro Lancaster, with four Merlin engines which could carry six or seven tons of bombs over 2000 miles. The new leader was Air Marshal Sir Arthur Harris, who believed fervently in the psychological effect of what he called 'Area Bombing', destroying the will of the German people to go on fighting by bombing whole cities. He told Britain: '. . . the Germans have sown the wind and they will reap the whirlwind.'

Meanwhile Germany had improved her air defences by building an electronic wall which stretched from the Swiss frontier to Denmark and through which the bombers had to fly. It consisted of a series of 'boxes' in the sky, each equipped with two types of radar: a Freya system to give early warning of approaching bombers, backed up by two Würzburg systems, one to track the bomber, the other to guide the German nightfighter pilot into visual contact; each box also had its own radar-guided searchlights and anti-anticraft guns.

Within a fortnight of taking over, Harris ordered a raid on Essen. Over 200 bombers, many of them equipped with Gee, battered their way through the defences; but some bombed other towns, and the great Krupp steelworks was barely touched. To justify Bomber Command and the strategic offensive, Harris needed a success. He chose Lübeck, a small town on the Baltic coast. His reasons were chillingly practical: it was a medieval town, built largely of wood, and would consequently burn well; it was less well defended than industrial centres in the Ruhr; but above all Lübeck, near the mouth of the Trave river, was easy to find using Gee. On 28 March 1942 it was burnt to the ground. Rostock, another small Baltic town with an aircraft factory, was given the same treatment.

Seen against previous efforts the raids were successful, but the war was not

*A bomber crew's first tour was 30 missions, the second 20; if losses rose above 3%,
mathematically there was no chance of survival. The RAF lost 55,000 men,*

going to be won with targets like Lübeck and Rostock. What Harris really needed
was a spectacular success against a prominent industrial target. The heaviest
raids up till then had never been much over 200 aircraft. Using all his reserves,
training aircraft and others borrowed from other duties, Harris could muster just
over 1000 bombers. He conceived the 'thousand bomber raid' to hit a major city
as hard as Lübeck.

Churchill warmed to the idea and the date was set for the end of May. The
weather was poor and Harris waited until the full moon on the 30th; the weather
reports from Germany were not helpful, but at midday he decided to go, choosing
Cologne at the last minute. The plan was to swamp the radar and nightfighters
at a single point by flying in a continuous stream. The leaders were equipped
with Gee and in clear weather they found the target; two-thirds of their loads
were incendiaries. Next came medium bombers who dropped their bombs on
the fires, and lastly came the Halifaxes, Stirlings and Lancasters. The raid
achieved all its immediate objectives: Cologne came to a virtual halt, 500 people
were killed, 45,000 made homeless and 600 acres were devastasted. RAF photo-
reconnaissance aircraft could not see the city the following morning for the huge
pall of smoke. The defences had been saturated: only 39 bombers were shot
down, 3.3 per cent of the total, an acceptable level. It lifted the morale of RAF
crews, lifted morale in Britain, and Harris and Bomber Command had another

The Flying Fortress – the B-17

*The de Havilland Mosquito was built out of plywood, its two Merlin engines
making it extremely fast. It took on all kinds of jobs, and was even used in
civilian colours to fly over Norway to Sweden to collect cargoes of ball-bearings*

powerful argument for resources. But within weeks Cologne was functioning
again, albeit with severe difficulties, and there was little evidence that the raid
had dealt a shattering blow to morale in Germany, any more than the Blitz had
done in Britain in 1940. The Luftwaffe brought back fighters, stripping some of
the protection from the armies in Russia and North Africa. Harris repeated the
formula against Essen and Bremen but both were covered in cloud and the results
were poor; as German nightfighter defences improved, so losses rose again.

Stalin was calling for a second front; Roosevelt and Churchill wanted to
invade Europe, but America, under pressure in the Pacific, also had to provide
for the build-up of her own forces as well as help supply Britain. At the Casablanca
Conference in January 1943 they agreed that, until a full-scale invasion could be
mounted, the bombing offensive would continue as the principal means of hitting
back. It was to be stepped up by greater participation by the USAAF in Europe.
Harris and others believed that they were trying to win the war by air power
alone; the political leaders saw it as paving the way for invasion.

The first units of the US Eighth Army Air Force had arrived in England in the summer of 1942. They believed in precision bombing of specific military targets in daylight, relying on the combined firepower of the machine-guns on their bombers flying in formation to ward off fighter attacks. Their first raid was in August 1942 when twelve B-17s attacked the railway yards at Rouen in France. Nine squadrons of RAF Spitfires were packed around them and they dropped sixteen tons of bombs without loss. But fighter protection could not be mounted over Germany; neither Spitfires nor the Americans' Republic P-47 Thunderbolts had the range. When in 1943 they started bombing Germany, they stuck to their policy of daylight bombing and had notable successes, particularly against the U-boat yards in Bremen. Initially the losses were bearable, but the Luftwaffe brought back more fighters from other fronts, including the Focke-Wulf 190 which was faster than the Bf 109, and gradually began to get the measure of the B-17. The fighter pilots found the weak spots in the 'Flying Fortress's' battery of machine-guns and losses began to mount: of 107 B-17s which attacked Bremen sixteen were lost with 159 aircrew.

Between 24 and 30 July 1943 Bomber Command and the Eighth USAAF cooperated to bomb Hamburg 'round the clock'. The Americans made two daylight raids and the RAF bombed on four consecutive nights using for the first time a new device against the electronic defences – 'Window' – small strips of foil dropped by the thousand which blinded the enemy's radar. It was an outstanding success and losses fell: only twelve out of 741 bombers were shot down on the first night. For Hamburg the worst night came on 27 July when the RAF used a high proportion of incendiaries and started a completely new phenomenon, the firestorm. The fires were so intense that they sucked in air from out of town, creating winds which in turn fanned the flames still further. There were no rescue services, no water, no gas or electricity; thousands of homeless people trekked into the surrounding countryside looking for shelter; 40,0000 people were killed out of a population of two million, and the city and its industry were severely disrupted for months. But the Germans were resilient; they reorganised their defences, using ground observers to plot the bomber stream, then broadcast its route to all the fighters.

On 17 August the Eighth Air Force found out how costly daylight raids could be: 363 B-17s set out to bomb the ball-bearing factory at Schweinfurt and the Messerschmitt factory at Regensburg deep inside Germany; 59 were shot down and 55 damaged beyond repair. The answer was escorts and air force engineers were improvising drop tanks to increase the range of the P-47s. They were ready in September. The first time they went all the way to the target and back was to Emden on the 27th: 262 P-47s, each with two 108-gallon drop tanks, escorted 246 B-17s; only seven B-17s and one P-47 were lost. But Emden was only just

Hamburg after the firestorm, 1943

over 400 miles and when they were ordered to attack Schweinfurt again the crews knew they would have to do without the fighters. Of the 229 B-17s which set out, 60 were shot down, 138 damaged and 594 crew killed, wounded or missing.

Schweinfurt, Regensburg – these raids were intended to damage German arms and aircraft production. Goering had bombed aircraft factories in 1940, but Hitler had his Beaverbrook in the form of Albert Speer, the armaments minister, who dispersed production into small units and with brilliant organisation increased arms production by 50 per cent in 1943. RAF bombing accuracy improved in 1943 through the use of improved electronic aids and by using 617 Squadron and Pathfinders to mark targets with precision at night. But Harris pursued area bombing, turning his attention to Berlin. The Battle of Berlin was the peak of the area campaign; between 18 November 1943 and the end of March 1944 there were sixteen major raids, and many more diversionary ones. But the Germans responded as the British had in the Blitz: civil defences were excellent and only 10,000 people were killed. The air defences also improved: in the same four months, Bomber Command lost over 1000 bombers and Speer again managed to increase armaments production.

Waist-gunners on a B-17

AMERICAN AIR POWER IN EUROPE

America's commitment to the air war in Europe was huge and their policy of daylight raids costly: the three air forces, the Eighth, Ninth and Fifteenth, lost 94,000 men and 8067 four-engined bombers.

B-17s on a raid in 1944

The saviour of the bombers was the long-range fighter:
a flight of the superb P-51 Mustangs over Germany during the war

In late 1943 the Eighth Air Force began to get a new long-range fighter, the P-51 Mustang. It started as an American aircraft built to a British specification, but when it first arrived in Britain with its Allison engine, the RAF found it underpowered. However, with the latest Merlin engine it proved a stunning machine, good in a dogfight and with a range, with drop tanks, of well over 1500 miles, enough to go to Berlin and back. The Eighth Air Force also got a new leader: General 'Jimmy' Doolittle, appointed by General Dwight Eisenhower, the Supreme Allied Commander. In 1944 his objective was the invasion of Europe; like Hitler in 1940, he needed air superiority over the Channel and over his battlefields. He wanted an air general who would support his armies, not try to win the war alone by bombing Germany. He wanted the Luftwaffe swept from the skies of north-west Europe.

Doolittle sent the bombers to attack aircraft factories and ordered the fighter escorts to fight the Luftwaffe for control of the sky. It was what Goering had tried to do in the Battle of Britain. The fighter pilots responded with enthusiasm but the bomber crews did not like it much. Where Goering had Adlertag, Doolittle had 'Big Week': on 20 February he sent out 1800 bombers and fighters, everything he could muster, and in the next six days he mounted five more such raids, all against aircraft factories. It cost him 80 bombers but his men shot down 100 fighters.

After Big Week came Berlin. Doolittle wanted to provoke a battle with the Luftwaffe by attacking Germany's capital in daylight. On 6 March 672 B-17 Flying Fortresses and B-24 Liberators, escorted by 801 long-range fighters including 100 Mustangs, set out. Some 400 German fighters attacked them on the way out and the P-47s went for them, sometimes following them right back to their airfields. They had to turn back before reaching Berlin but the Mustangs were there for Berliners to see, and again two days later. In four months the Luftwaffe lost over 1000 aircraft. Speer replaced many of them with improved versions, but Goering's best pilots were now being lost and they could not be replaced. It was what Dowding had dreaded in the Battle of Britain, the steady draining away of experience, skill and, above all, leadership in the air.

Germany and Japan were on the ebb; strategic bombing was no longer the only way the Allies were hitting back: the Russians were advancing in the east; Rommel's 'Afrika Korps' had been thrown out of Africa; Italy had surrendered and the Allies were occupying it despite continued German resistance; America was grinding down Japan in the Pacific. None of those campaigns could have succeeded without a different kind of air power, the kind first wielded by Germany and Japan – tactical air power. No allied army commander would risk a major operation without it.

The turning-point in the Pacific came just after the Battle of Midway. America needed air bases closer to Japan. On 7 August 1942 19,000 US Marines, backed up by carrier-borne attack aircraft with fighter protection, made an amphibious landing on Japanese-held Guadalcanal in the Solomon Islands. One of their first tasks was to capture the half-built airfield and finish it. Renamed Henderson Field, it was ready by 20 August for Marine Corps Wildcats and Dauntlesses to land. The Wildcats took on the Japanese counter-attacks while the dive-bombers became aerial artillery for the Marines, dropping high-explosive and petrol bombs right into the front line. In November the Japanese tried to reinforce the garrison with 11,000 fresh troops; with their carriers preoccupied with the US carriers and unable to provide air cover, US aircraft from Henderson and the *Enterprise* sank seven of the convoy of eleven troopships. The remainder landed 4000 troops without supplies but they were of little value in the battle. The Japanese finally evacuated the island on 7 February 1943, having lost over 1000 aircraft defending it. Worse still, the US had a firm foothold in the south Pacific from which General Douglas MacArthur and Nimitz planned to move from island to island, each time building an airfield to leapfrog closer to Japan.

In the war against Germany, the turning-point was another land battle supported by tactical aircraft. In 1942 Rommel had pushed the British armies along the north African coast into Egypt. General Sir Bernard Montgomery was planning a counter offensive but he would not move until his forces were strong enough to assure him of victory. The RAF in the Middle East was under Air Marshal Sir Arthur Tedder, a supporter of tactical air forces, who had 96 squadrons, 1500 fighters and medium bombers, against a 350-strong Luftwaffe. Tedder put his superiority to good use, shooting up the Afrika Korps on the ground but more importantly by bombing its extended supply lines, in particular across the Mediterranean. German ships and transport aircraft, the ubiquitous Ju 52 and giant, six-engined Me 323s, which were slow and without fighter escort, were hammered from the air. In September a third of Rommel's supplies never reached him; in October less than half made it, and when the Second Battle of El Alamein started on 23 October his tanks and the vehicles on which he relied to fight his mobile desert war were on very short rations of fuel, restricting his ability to manœuvre.

By August 1943 the Allies had occupied north Africa, invaded Sicily, and followed tha⁺ with amphibious landings on mainland Italy. The pattern of tactical air support was broadly the same in each case: bomb the defences and attack the lines of supply and communications; give close support to ground forces with rockets and medium bombers, and protect the airspace above them with fighters.

That pattern was repeated, but on a much greater scale, in support of the greatest invasion in history, the Allied re-entry into Europe on 6 June 1944. Aircraft had begun to pave the way long before D-Day. Photo-reconnaissance had started as far back as 1942, high-flying Spitfires photographing the coast from Holland to the Spanish frontier and low-flying Mustangs flying along the beaches to get close-ups of the defences. The bomber offensive had drawn fighters back into Germany and Doolittle's 'Big Week' had sapped their strength, forcing Speer to build defensive fighters rather than bombers to attack the allied armies. Tedder had authority to use the strategic bombers and his first priority was German transport. Over such a short distance they could carry heavy loads and with fighter escort they were less vulnerable. Tedder drew up a list of targets and, despite protests from Harris and General Carl Spaatz, commander of all US air forces in Europe, as D-Day approached the French railway system was reduced to chaos and all the bridges over the Seine and the Loire were destroyed, isolating northern France and making movement of German reinforcements difficult. Ground-attack fighters – Fighter Command's Typhoons and Tempests and American P-47s – strafed and rocketed the German airfields and radar stations, and Coastal Command went for the German Navy, clearing the Channel for 4000 ships carrying 175,000 men and their 600 naval escorts.

The first troops across went by air, a night attack to secure key points behind the beaches by three paratroop divisions in DC-3s and gliders. Meanwhile

Construction teams scatter as low-level fighters reconnoitre anti-invasion defences on French beaches prior to the invasion

bombers made their last pulverising raids on the defences, particularly as a diversion in the Pas de Calais. As the troops waded ashore in Normandy early in the morning, fighters patrolled the beaches giving an umbrella of air superiority. By nightfall 156,000 men were ashore and the U-boats and the Luftwaffe had barely put in an appearance.

On 13 June Hitler launched a renewed bombing offensive against London. He was convinced that Britain would sue for peace in the face of his new 'wonder weapons', the unmanned V-1 flying bombs. British reconnaissance had been photographing their launching sites for some time and Bomber Command had been bombing them, but in the face of invasion the Germans built improvised sites and at the height of the offensive were despatching 190 a day aimed at London. They had only a rudimentary guidance system and many fell miles away from their target but 1½ million people were evacuated and over 6000 killed. Gradually the defences got the better of them, particularly the anti-aircraft guns which fired shells with radar proximity fuses. The V-1s flew level like an aeroplane and fighters could shoot them down, or the fastest ones, the Spitfire XIV, the Mustang III and the first British jet fighter, the Gloster Meteor, could fly alongside and tip them over. Some 10,000 were fired before the sites were overrun.

After the invasion the strategic bombing offensive was stepped up again, the

General Dwight Eisenhower bracketed the DC-3 with the jeep, the 2½-ton truck, the amphibious DUKW and the bulldozer as the equipment which brought victory in World War Two

priority target being Germany's oil industry, followed by communications. With air superiority and escorts, the RAF flew in daylight again and in the last three months of 1944 dropped more bombs than in the whole of 1943. The air war over Germany became a battle of attrition with the Allies growing ever stronger while the Luftwaffe grew weaker; German aircraft production declined, but the most acute problem was the shortage of pilots. Germany had the fastest fighter in the world, the jet-powered Me 262, and élite units were equipped with them, one under the Battle of Britain veteran Adolph Galland, but they had only a short range and there were never enough to cope with the numbers of bombers.

Harris's last chance to use area bombing came when the Russians asked for help in the east. He believed that one huge effort, wiping out a whole city, would finally crack German morale and bring them to surrender. Dresden was chosen as the target and on 14 February 1945 it was flattened by wave after wave of heavy bombers. It is impossible to know how many people died because the city was packed with refugees fleeing the advancing Russians, but it was well over 100,000 and possibly as high as 250,000. But it did not crack German morale. Victory only came when armies invading from both sides, supported by their tactical air forces, crushed the Third Reich between them, and it still took a further three months before Admiral Doenitz surrendered on 8 May 1945.

Tactical air support: a Beaufighter attacks German positions in a Yugoslav town

A V-1 about to hit Drury Lane in London. Inset: *A V-1 is tipped over by a Spitfire*

While Allied armies had been advancing across Europe, so American land, sea and air forces had been working their way from island to island in the Pacific. On 6 June 1944 the US Fifth Fleet under Admiral Raymond Spruance put to sea and headed for the Marianas Islands – Saipan, Tinian and Guam. The fleet symbolised US industrial and military muscle: fifteen aircraft-carriers with over 900 aircraft in four carrier groups, supported by seven battleships, 21 cruisers and 69 destroyers. Their task was to provide firepower and protection for the invasion force of 130,000 men who would make the amphibious landings supported by aircraft from another eleven escort carriers. Opposing Spruance was Rear Admiral Jisaburo Ozawa with nine carriers and 450 aircraft, five battleships, twelve cruisers and 27 destroyers. His fleet was smaller, but he suffered from one other crucial difference – like Goering he had lost many of his most experienced pilots and the replacements had been less well trained because of lack of fuel and time. America had plenty of fuel and its new generation of pilots was well trained.

The first task of the US Fleet was to attack the defences on Saipan ahead of the invasion. American pilots destroyed 318 aircraft, mainly on the ground. The invasion went ahead on 15 June: 8000 men ashore in twenty minutes, supported by naval gunfire and rocket-firing fighters.

The two carrier forces fought their battle on 19 June. Ozawa sent four waves of attack aircraft against the US fleet; all were detected some 150 miles out by

After the invasion, strategic bombers were switched to direct support of ground forces;
the first such raid was on 7 July at Caen where the Germans were holding up the
Allied advance; the damage was so great, it held up the Allies once the Germans had gone

radar and the American fighters were launched in plenty of time. It was a
slaughter: 218 were shot down for the loss of 29, in what the American pilots
dubbed 'the Marianas Turkey Shoot'. Two of the Japanese carriers were then
sunk by submarines and Ozawa retreated.

By August the Marianas were in American hands and engineers started to
repair the airfields and enlarge them to take America's latest bomber – the four-
engined Boeing B-29 Superfortress. It was the largest bomber of the war: it could
carry $4\frac{1}{2}$ tons of bombs 3250 miles at 35,000 feet. The first arrived on Saipan in
October and made their first raid on 24 November against an aircraft factory in
Tokyo in daylight. The Japanese air defences were far less effective than the
German and the B-29s kept up their daylight raids for the next three months.
But the results were disappointing: there were a great many mechanical problems,
and flying at great heights they encountered very strong winds over Japan,
making aiming difficult over targets often obscured by cloud. In January General
Curtis LeMay was charged with getting results from the new bomber. He decided
that, since Japan had no nightfighters and high-altitude attacks were not working,

DESPERATION
A Japanese kamikaze pilot
(*right*) just failed to hit his
target on this occasion; the
majority of kamikazes were
destroyed before they could
complete their mission.

they would have to risk flying lower and at night. He also changed from precision to area bombing and, with so many of the Japanese buildings made of wood and bamboo, he used incendiaries. He sent the first raid to Tokyo on 9 March 1945: 330 B-29s, each carrying enough incendiaries to burn sixteen acres. The results were devastating: 185,000 people killed, a quarter of the city, 270,000 buildings, destroyed, and only fourteen B-29s lost. Virtually unopposed, LeMay bombed other cities so heavily that at one point he outstripped the Navy's ability to supply his force with incendiaries.

The Japanese military and their leaders had already shown that they would fight a suicidal battle; as the US Navy came closer and closer, taking Iwo Jima just 400 miles from Japan on 26 March, soldiers had sacrificed themselves in their thousands long after it was clear that defeat was at hand. In the air, in a last-ditch attempt to hit at the US carriers, young, partly-trained pilots – Kamikazes – aimed their explosive-packed aircraft at ships in suicide attacks. The government ordered the civilian population to be ready to meet the invaders on the beaches with whatever weapons they could find. Although there was a peace group within the government, Japan's military leaders wanted a negotiated surrender. The allies would accept nothing less than unconditional surrender, so the bombing campaign went on.

In July a B-29 with a heavily modified bomb bay arrived on Tinian. Its captain was Col. Paul Tibbets, who had been on America's first B-17 raid against Rouen in France. On 6 August he took off escorted by two observation aircraft and flew at high level to Hiroshima, a city so far largely untouched by strategic bombing. He arrived over the city on a clear, sunny morning and at 8.15 am he dropped the world's first operational atomic bomb, diving away to avoid the blast he knew was coming. The bomb exploded above the city, killing 80,000 people and flattening virtually all its buildings. Three days later another B-29 dropped another atomic bomb on Nagasaki. The Japanese leaders were still trying to agree on what form their surrender should take, but the atomic bomb finally led them to unconditional terms.

Hiroshima and Nagasaki took their place alongside Guernica, Warsaw, Rotterdam, London, Coventry, Hamburg, Berlin, Dresden and Tokyo as milestones in the progress of strategic air power. It had come a long way in eight years and with the atomic bomb it succeeded in bringing an end to the war without the invasion of Japan. The raids on Dresden and Tokyo had each killed many more people than both atomic bombs put together but there was a chilling quality to the nature of the atomic bomb itself, its singular destructive power and the after-effects of radiation, which put it in a different class of horrors. With it, air power clearly could win a war on its own, but only against an enemy with no defence against it at the price of obliterating that enemy altogether.

The ruins of Hiroshima. Inset: *Photograph taken at 20,000 feet*

HIROSHIMA

The atomic bomb had been developed in America by a joint team of US, British, Canadian and refugee European scientists, under the codename 'The Manhattan Project'. The first experimental device was exploded on 17 July 1945 after expenditure of $2bn, one of the factors at least which weighed in favour of the decision to drop it.

Col. Paul Tibbets and his crew after the raid

CHAPTER SEVEN

PUSHING THE LIMITS

War had put the spur to technical progress for a second time and Germany had outpaced the field. Even before the surrender expert national teams from the Allies were scouring Germany, competing with each other to plunder her scientific secrets. It was soon evident that they were picking over a very advanced aircraft industry with a huge range of basic research projects: strategic rockets, anti-shipping guided missiles, jet, rocket and ramjet engines, a range of helicopters, swept-wing rocket interceptors, anti-aircraft missiles, jet bombers, jet fighters, and even faster fighters on the drawing-board. For a country at war and, in the last two years, in overall retreat, it was too much: rare skills and scarce production resources had been spread too thinly, over too many projects. What remained of the world's most advanced aircraft industry was crated up and shipped back to Britain, France, Russia and America.

For the foreseeable future the German aircraft industry was dead; as was Japan's and Italy's. The French were starting all over again; Russia's had survived but it was not technically advanced. Britain and America had the only really advanced industries left intact. Now, with victory, each of the Allies was out for itself; their teams, including the French, scrambled to secure whatever they could. The Russians found the complete archive of Germany's primary aeronautical research institute in the ruins of Berlin; it went to Russia. The Americans found the Messerschmitt P.1101, a prototype single-jet fighter with swept-back wings which could be adjusted to research different angles of sweepback for high speeds; the French found microfilm of the development data for the P.1101 but kept it from the Americans, who have not seen it to this day.

Hardware and the back-up papers were the first pickings, but the real prizes were the scientists themselves. The new British Labour government wanted to see the German scientists continue their work in the occupied zones of Germany, with the results pooled. The Russians took a more robust view: they simply took

OPPOSITE: US F-15 Eagle fighters pushing the limits

the scientists they captured. As a consequence many fled to the British and American zones where the Americans had an overwhelming advantage: the biggest aircraft industry in the world with exciting research projects of their own, and above all the money to offer interesting work, good living and good contracts. The bulk of the intellectual spoils of war – dozens of scientists and technicians, including the leading rocket expert, Werner von Braun, Messerschmitt's chief designer, Woldemar Voigt, and the pioneer of swept wings, Adolf Busemann – steadily drifted across the Atlantic.

Another scientist who emigrated to America was Dr Hans-Joachim von Ohain, the German pioneer of jet propulsion. Much later, in 1976, he was followed by his British counterpart, Sir Frank Whittle. The birth of the jet engine was a landmark in the development of aviation second only to the first flights by the Wright Brothers forty years previously. Working completely independently, both Whittle and Ohain had jet engines running before the war. Both men suffered initially from scepticism, and both development programmes were slower than they might have been. In Britain Whittle had patented his engine in 1930 but neither the RAF nor the Air Ministry would back him; they saw the jet engine as a long-term project and gave it a low priority. In March 1936 Whittle formed his own company, Power Jets, and started development work on a shoestring, without proper research facilities and having to fight to get the materials he needed. He was up against companies like Rolls-Royce which had strong vested interests, pride and investment tied up in superb piston engines like the Merlin. Designers in those companies did not relish a young RAF officer effectively telling them that their life's work was about to be overtaken. Whittle had ground-run a jet engine in 1939 and the prospect of war finally stirred British interest: more funds were found to develop the Whittle Unit; the Gloster company was given a contract to build one research aircraft to take a jet engine, and in 1940 they got another to build a prototype twin-engined fighter.

There had also been a lurking scepticism of such a radical engine within the German Air Ministry, but the mood there had been more innovative and Ohain, who started work after Whittle, was the first to see his engine power an aircraft, the He 178, in August 1939. By then jet-engine development had already been taken up by the traditional engine manufacturers, Junkers and BMW, who were working on more powerful models with official support, and Messerschmitt was set against Heinkel to design prototype fighters to take them.

Both teams made their next big steps within a few weeks of each other in the spring of 1941. Heinkel had completed its prototype, the He 280, but neither Junkers nor BMW were ready so two of Ohain's less powerful engines were installed in what was a highly innovative aircraft: it had a tricycle undercarriage (a nose-wheel instead of a tail-wheel), and it was the first aircraft to be fitted with

On the first test run of Frank Whittle's jet engine on 12 April 1937 it ran out of control after fuel collected in puddles inside the combustion chambers. Whittle is on the left

an ejector seat. On 2 April Heinkel's test pilot, Fritz Schafer, made the first flight, a single circuit of Marienehe airfield. On 18 April he made a timed run of 485 mph, to break Fritz Wendel's 469 mph official record, though the result was kept a closely guarded secret. He also gave a demonstration flight; once its speed was seen, support for jet engines grew.

A month later, on the evening of 15 May, Frank Whittle and a few colleagues stood on the airfield at RAF Cranwell in a bitterly cold west wind, watching Gerry Sayer, Gloster's test pilot, taxi the Gloster/Whittle E.28/39 to the take-off point. Sayer opened the throttle slowly, holding her on the brakes until the engine was giving maximum power, then eased them off to roll down the runway. After 600 yards he eased back on the control column and she lifted smoothly off and climbed to 1000 feet, out of sight behind clouds; all the spectators could hear was the distinctive sound of the engine. Seventeen minutes later Sayer reappeared and made a perfect landing. There were no official observers or cameramen, it

BRITAIN'S JET PIONEER

Air Commodore Sir Frank Whittle not only invented the jet engine but foresaw all the major developments in it: after-burners, turboprops and turbofans. He emigrated to America in 1976 where he still works.

Sir Frank Whittle

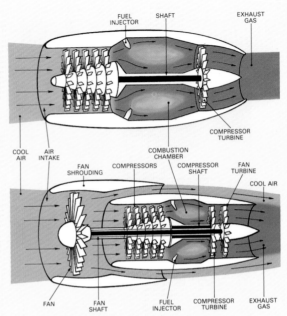

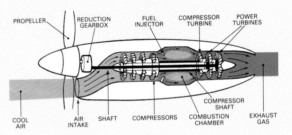

The Whittle W2/700 engine intended for the M.52

TOP: *The Turbojet*
Air is compressed into a combustion chamber where it is mixed with fuel; the hot gases expand and escape through the jetpipe, pushing the aircraft forward and driving a turbine which in turn drives the compressor

MIDDLE: *The Turbofan*
More power can be achieved by using a second turbine in the exhaust to drive a fan, in front of the compressor, which pushes cold air back too, adding to the thrust. Turbofans are more efficient and less noisy

BOTTOM: *The Turboprop*
The same principle is used in a turboprop, the difference being that the additional turbines drive a propeller instead

RIGHT: The Gloster E.28/39

BELOW: Britain's first two jet fighters: the Gloster Meteor (bottom) *and the de Havilland Vampire*

was thought too unimportant an event; but when news reached the Air Ministry that Whittle had actually done it, that the little jet had flown and exceeded its design expectations, like their German counterparts they wanted a demonstration. On 21 May the British aeronautical establishment, headed by Sir Archibald Sinclair, the Secretary of State for Air, watched Sayer take off and make a high-speed run in front of them. The mood in the Ministry changed; an initial production run of 1200 engines and 500 Gloster Meteor fighters was ordered; a contract to develop a single-engined fighter went to de Havilland, who would also build the engines.

The subsequent development of the jet in Britain is a story of establishment intrigue, secrecy, evasiveness and consequent muddle. Whittle wanted a concentrated development effort at Power Jets to get an engine ready for the Meteor as quickly as possible, but much of the development and production work was placed with other companies, notably the Rover car company, and when Whittle protested at the diversification of effort he was politely ignored. Then Rolls-Royce, realising that the jet was the way forward, in a surprising deal about which Whittle was not even consulted exchanged a tank factory for Rover's interest in jet propulsion. This improved production but Power Jets was steadily eased out of the picture and ultimately nationalised. Whittle had to supply other companies with information while still trying to carry out the more advanced development work. The engine's secrets were also given to the Americans as part of the war effort (a move which had Whittle's full support), but that added to the pressure on him too. Scant regard was paid to his workload or the effect it was having on basic research work; he became steadily depressed and in December 1941 he had the first of three nervous breakdowns. In April 1942, when a demonstration flight of the E.28/39 was put on at de Havilland's at Hatfield for Winston Churchill, Whittle was not even invited.

Messerschmitt was ready with its prototype fighter, the Me 262, in 1941. BMW were ready with their engine in November and Messerschmitt installed two, taking the precaution of adding a piston engine for safety. It was a good job they did: both jets failed and Fritz Wendel had to use the piston engine. The Junkers engine, the Jumo 004, was heavier but more powerful; two were installed in July 1942 and Wendel made the first test flight on the 18th. He found a new problem: the Me 262 had a tailwheel; on the ground, with the fuselage sloping back, the jet's exhaust was directed at the runway and interfering with the airflow over the tail. As he raced down the runway, Wendel found that he could not lift the tail to get airborne. In an inspired moment he touched the brakes briefly, tipping the nose forward, the tail stayed up and he took off. He made more test flights in this unorthodox fashion until Messerschmitt adopted a tricycle undercarriage similar to the He 280. The He 280 was the faster of the two, though at high speeds there was a flutter problem with the tailplane. The Me 262 was bigger and, crucially, had a longer endurance and it was Messerschmitt which got the orders. It was two years before they were in the hands of fighter pilots and by then the production versions had a top speed of over 550 mph; on 6 July 1944 a high-speed version flew at 624 mph, the fastest aircraft in the world.

While the Me 262 was making its first test flights, Frank Whittle was in America to see progress with his engine there. General Electric, the company chosen to build it, had far better facilities than existed in Britain but the main difference was the enthusiasm and the pace with which they tackled it. They had received an engine from Britain in October 1941; within six months they had their own running. They soon had more than Britain, and by October 1942 the first American jet aircraft, the Bell XP-59A Airacomet, made its first flight at an obscure Army camp at Muroc in the California desert where Rogers Dry Lake formed a huge natural airfield. The Airacomet was underpowered and would never have made a fighter but it was an impressive performance and showed how Britain, though a long way ahead technically, had hopelessly mismanaged the production phase.

What followed was even more impressive. On 24 June 1943 the Army contracted Lockheed to produce America's first real jet fighter, the P-80 Shooting Star. The contract allowed 180 days for delivery. It was ready in 145 days but the engine, from de Havilland in England, was two months late and it did not fly until 8 January 1944 – even then only eighteen days late.

, Despite mismanagement Britain was still just ahead. On 12 July 1944 the RAF received its first two Meteors, just in time to see limited action against the flying bombs, and the first jets to enter service anywhere in the world. The Meteor was a conservative aircraft and Whittle's engines were reliable, which was just as he had intended, but he never bargained for the delays; it was over three years since the E.28/39 had made its first flight. The Me 262 entered service on 3 October 1944 and saw much more action because Germany was on the defensive. It was faster and more aerodynamically advanced than the Meteor; so were its engines but they had a far shorter life and were very tricky to handle in the air: many valuable pilots were lost in accidents.

After the war honours were showered on Frank Whittle. He was knighted and the government granted him £100,000 for his invention. Ohain acknowledged his lead in the theory of jet propulsion: in his view, had Whittle been properly backed Britain would have had a jet fighter before the war. Instead, the Second World War saw the piston engine developed to its apogee while jet engines played only a small part. Yet of all the technical developments during the war, undoubtedly the one which was to have the most far-reaching consequences afterwards was the jet engine.

The next great landmark in aviation was the successful development of the helicopter. Like the jet, it was a reality before the war and was fully developed during it, but only saw limited wartime service. The idea had attracted a good many pioneering spirits. The principle was simple – a spinning rotor to create lift would support an aircraft and enable it to take off vertically and hover – but the aerodynamic and engineering problems were formidable. A single rotor spinning in one direction tended, through torque, to overturn the machine as it lifted off.

A Spaniard, Juan de Cierva, produced the 'autogyro' with a single rotor to support it. In an autogyro the rotor is not connected to the engine but spins freely, turning like a horizontal windmill as the whole machine is pulled through the air by an engine with a propeller. It needs a short runway to take off but once in the air it can be controlled. Cierva had hinged the blades at the rotor-head, allowing their angle to be changed by a control column so that the pilot could turn, rise and descend. It could not hover but its rotor influenced the next generation of helicopter pioneers.

There were many pieces to the puzzle and it was Heinrich Focke, a World War I German pilot, who succeeded in putting them together to build the first completely successful helicopter. He started out building winged aircraft, but he was critical of the Nazi regime and was eased out of his Focke-Wulf company. He started experimenting again, first with autogyros, then with helicopters. His Fa 61 had two contra-rotating rotors mounted on outriggers on either side of the fuselage; their angles could be altered in flight to control it and the engine was in front. In June 1936 his test pilot, Ewald Rohlfs, tentatively lifted the Fa 61 off the ground for the first time for a flight lasting 28 seconds; by the end of the day he was hovering for up to a quarter of an hour. Later, in 1937, he set several new records: a closed circuit of 76 miles, endurance of 1 hour 20 minutes, altitude of 11,200 feet, and a speed record of 76 mph.

The Fa 61 first attracted popular interest when Hanna Reitsch, a young woman test pilot, gave Charles Lindbergh a demonstration flight. Then in February 1938 she flew it inside a huge exhibition hall, the Deutschlandhalle in Berlin, flying forwards, backwards, sideways, up and down in front of the crowds. The flights were propaganda for the Nazis but they could also see the military potential, and Focke was given a contract to build a much larger machine which could lift a useful load. The Fa 223 Drache (Kite) was ready in 1940: it could carry 8–12 people, lift itself to over 20,000 feet and fly at 115 mph. It was put into limited production but was bombed out of several factories, and by the end of the war it was only in very restricted use in exercises supplying troops in mountainous areas. The British captured one and it was flown to Britain by a German crew in 1945, becoming the first helicopter to cross the Channel.

Igor Sikorsky flying the VS-300 in 1940. INSET: *Hanna Reitsch inside the Deutschlandhalle in 1938*

HELICOPTER PIONEERS
The idea of vertical flight
originated with Leonardo da
Vinci in the 1480s; it took
nearly 500 years to become a
reality.

*Sikorsky and Col. Frank Gregory shake hands in front
of Orville Wright to mark the delivery of the XR-4 to
Wright Field, Dayton, Ohio, in 1943*

But in vertical flight Germany was behind America. By the end of the war the US Army had a much more practical helicopter. Igor Sikorsky had emigrated to America after the Russian Revolution in 1917 and started building aircraft in farm sheds on Long Island, NY, using Russian émigré labour. In the 1930s he had equipped Pan American with its first generation of Clippers, the S40 and S42 flying boats. His company was taken over by United Aircraft and in 1938, when Juan Trippe turned to Boeing for its flying boats, United closed it down. In 1931 Sikorsky had patented his own design for a helicopter: a single rotor on top and a small vertical rotor at the rear of the fuselage. With the closure, he turned once more to helicopters.

By 1939 Sikorsky had built an experimental flying machine, the VS-300. It was purely for research and to develop his theories and he was his own test pilot. On 14 September 1939 he strapped himself into the VS-300; it was tethered by four ropes tied to stakes in the ground in case it became uncontrollable. When he started the engine it shook violently, but he pulled the pitch lever up and increased the angle of the blades and felt it rise; once all the wheels were clear of the ground he quickly throttled back and reduced the pitch and put it back on the ground again. He repeated the performance several times, conferring with his colleagues after each little hop. Over the next seven months they tried different configurations of tail rotor, each time trying out the effect with tethered test flights. Finally, on 13 May 1940, he made the first free flight. More changes followed, but by June 1941 the VS-300 was flying more smoothly and under better control and Sikorsky was showing it off in public. He loved amusing the crowd: regularly flying in a fedora hat which became his trademark, he would hover as an assistant placed a package in a basket or changed a wheel. On 6 May 1941 he broke the endurance record set by Rohlfs in the Fa 61, staying up for 1 hour 32 minutes and 26 seconds.

Among the enthusiasts who had gravitated towards Sikorsky and his experimental helicopter was a USAAF colonel, Frank Gregory. He and Sikorsky discussed building a light two-seater observation machine for the Army, to be known as the XR-4. It would be bigger and more powerful than the VS-300, which would be modified again to embody everything that Sikorsky had learnt and then act as a training machine for Gregory and other Army test pilots. On 8 December 1941, the day after Japan attacked Pearl Harbor, the VS-300 was flown in its final configuration for the first time, and by the end of the year it was flying perfectly. On 13 May 1942, two years to the day since the first free flight of the VS-300, the first US Army XR-4 took off from the Sikorsky plant at Stratford, Conn., for the 760-mile flight to the Army's Test Flight Center at Wright Field, Dayton, Ohio. The US Army and Navy ordered the production model, the R-4, and it saw limited service in Burma and on Iwo Jima.

In the post-war years, however, it was speed rather than hovering which absorbed the most effort in experimental aviation. On 7 November 1945 a Meteor of the re-formed RAF High Speed Flight streaked along a measured 3-km course off the south coast of England. It was a highly modified aircraft: the guns and other unnecessary weight had been removed, the gunports covered; the wing-tips had been clipped and it had two Rolls-Royce Derwent jet engines boosted beyond their normal power. It was the first attempt on the official air-speed record since the war and the first jet aircraft to try for it. Gp Capt. H. J. Wilson averaged 606 mph, well above Fritz Wendel's 469-mph official record of 1939. On 7 September 1946 Gp Capt. E. M. Donaldson in another Meteor raised the record to 615 mph.

But British tenure of the title lasted less than a year as national rivalry in the quest for speed re-emerged with a challenge from the USAAF. It spent $35,000 modifying a P-80 Shooting Star, clipping its wings and giving it a tiny cockpit and a glossy paint finish. On 19 June 1947 Col. Albert Boyd, Chief of the Flight Test Center, averaged 623 mph over a 3-km course at Muroc.

Stripped to their essentials, the British and American jets were flying at speeds comparable with those reached in secret by the Me 262 three years earlier. The difference lay not in the engines – the British engines were more powerful than the Jumo 004s – but in the aerodynamics, where the Germans were far ahead. The Me 262 was altogether a sleeker design and among the features which made it faster were its swept wings. In the Me 262 the sweepback was almost accidental, but in Germany's next generation of fighters, which were on the drawing-boards, it was far more pronounced and it was quite deliberate. The Messerschmitt P.1101 the Americans found, which was designed as an inter-ceptor, had marked sweepback; all the evidence from the German high-speed wind-tunnels suggested that sweepback was fundamental to reaching the next great landmark in the quest for speed – the speed of sound.

During the war, fighters on both sides had been pushed faster and faster and pilots reported that in very high-speed dives, close to and over 500 mph, they encountered heavy buffeting. Others had not lived to report what had happened as their aircraft broke up in mid-air. As an aircraft flies it disturbs the air around it, sending out pressure waves; the faster it flies, the more the pressure waves pile up in front of it. At the speed of sound, the waves build up in front to form a shock wave. The air passing over the wings moves faster than the aircraft itself, thus creating lift, so the shock wave in front of the wing builds up earlier than in front of the aircraft as a whole. The Germans discovered that, by sweeping the wings back, the onset of the shock wave was delayed to a higher speed.

Foremost amongst the researchers into sweepback was Adolf Busemann, who had presented a paper on the subject as early as 1935, but he had been largely

On 2 November 1947 Hughes flew the Spruce Goose for just over a mile.
INSET: *Howard Hughes at the controls just before its one and only flight*

THE BIGGEST AEROPLANE IN THE WORLD

The industrialist Henry Kaiser conceived the idea of giant flying boats in 1942 to ferry supplies and troops to Europe. He joined forces with Howard Hughes who eventually took over the project. Hughes was a perfectionist and the H-4 cost far more than planned and the war was over before it was finished. Built largely out of wood, it was known as the 'Spruce Goose'; with a wingspan of 320 feet it would have carried 700 troops.

After Hughes's death in 1976 the Spruce Goose was installed in a special hangar in Los Angeles alongside the Queen Mary

ignored except in Germany. Producing a fighter which could operate at or above the speed of sound was clearly the goal. With the P.1101 Busemann was close to producing a very high-speed fighter but it was not ready to fly when it was captured. But it showed what the fighters of all countries would look like only a few years after the war.

America got Busemann, and its industry was quickest off the mark in absorbing the importance of his work. Two aircraft on the drawing-board were completely redesigned: North American Aviation's new fighter, the P-86, was to have straight wings, but as early as May 1945 the USAAF agreed to have them swept back; the result when it flew for the first time on 1 October 1947 was one of the classic early jet fighters, the North American Aviation F-86 Sabre (see p. 254). Boeing's first jet bomber, the B-47, was also redesigned with swept-back wings.

Britain reacted more slowly and in something of a muddle. In October 1945 the Ministry of Supply ordered a swept-wing, tailless research aircraft from de Havilland's, the DH 108. A few months later it cancelled another high-speed project, the Miles M.52. This extremely ambitious plan, to build an aircraft which would fly at 1000 mph, had been started in October 1943. By late 1945 the designs were almost complete and the mock-up had been built. It was expected to fly the following year but instead in February 1946 it was cancelled and the design teams began to break up. The same month Whittle resigned from Power Jets, giving his reasons as disagreements on policy.

In the same month there was another setback. Hardly had the M.52 dust settled than disaster struck the swept-wing DH 108. The first prototype had not been designed to fly faster than sound; it was flown for the first time at Woodbridge in Suffolk on 15 May 1946 by Geoffrey de Havilland Jr, the son of the pioneer. The second prototype was designed for higher speeds and flew first on 23 August. In September it appeared in public at the Radlett Air Display, where it gave an aerobatic display. Then on 27 September, on a test flight over the Thames estuary, the DH 108 broke up in the air; Geoffrey de Havilland was killed. Examination of the wreckage showed that the structure had failed under the very heavy loads imposed on it as it approached the speed of sound.

Just two weeks earlier, a small research aircraft dropped out of the bomb-bay of a B-29 flying high over Muroc. It was the Bell X-1, America's supersonic research aircraft and, like the M.52, bullet-shaped with straight wings (see p. 248). It had been dropped before for gliding experiments but this time the pilot, Chalmers 'Slick' Goodlin, was going to try out his rocket motors for the first time. They worked well and once the fuel was spent he glided down to land. On 8 January 1947 he reached 540 mph or Mach 0.8 – 80 per cent of the speed of sound – where he began to feel the onset of the buffeting associated with high-speed flight. (The speed of sound decreases the lower the air temperature. At ground level it is 760 mph, falling to 660 mph at 36,000 feet, the height above which the temperature no longer falls but remains constant.)

The X-1 had been given the official go-ahead on 16 March 1945 solely to look into the characteristics of flying close to and beyond the speed of sound. The early flight tests were carried out by company test pilots, but as they approached the speed of sound the USAAF decided to take over. Col. Boyd, Chief of the Flight Test Center, chose a 24-year-old, recently-graduated test pilot. Capt. Charles 'Chuck' Yeager, an ex-Mustang pilot who had served over Germany and shot down thirteen enemy aircraft, was a natural. Though he had no formal engineering training, he instinctively understood engineering problems and possessed the special combination of courage and caution needed for research flying.

Yeager made his first glide flight in the X-1 on 6 August and his first powered flight on the 29th. He had been briefed to stay below Mach 0.8 but something of the quality which Boyd had recognised took over and he went to Mach 0.85. Over the next month he steadily pushed up the speed and on his seventh flight reached 0.94. There he encountered a new problem: in addition to the buffeting, he found that he was losing the effectiveness of the elevator. When he pulled back on the control column nothing happened; at that speed the shock wave was making them ineffective. The tailplane of the X-1 was adjustable and Yeager believed that by moving it in flight he could regain elevator control. On the next flight he flew to 0.94, moved the tailplane and it worked; later analysis of the data from on-board instruments indicated that he had reached Mach 0.997.

On 14 October 1947 he went out to fly even faster. Around 10 am a B-29 mothership rolled down the runway at Muroc with Yeager sitting just behind the two pilots. As it passed through 10,000 feet, the height at which it was safe to drop the X-1 in an emergency, he went back into the bomb-bay where the X-1 was shackled like a bomb. It was painted bright orange for high visibility and round its middle was a band of white frost where the liquid-oxygen tank had cooled the skin. To get in he had to squeeze between the X-1 and the side of the open bomb-bay, then into the cockpit through a side door. Two minutes before the drop he pressurised the fuel system and waited; the B-29 captain counted the seconds, then the shackles opened and down he went, the cockpit suddenly bathed in sunlight. Close by were two P-80 Shooting Star chase planes to observe the flight. He switched on the four rocket motors and left them behind, accelerating into the familiar buffet, then into elevator ineffectiveness which he corrected with the movable tailplane. Now he was going into the unknown. With the Machmeter showing 0.96 he actually began to get back some elevator effectiveness. Then, quite suddenly, the Machmeter went to 1.05 – 700 mph. The buffeting stopped and the X-1 was easier to control. Far below, a crack like thunder was heard as the shock wave reached the ground.

THE SHAPE OF THINGS TO COME

In the beginning aircraft were built out of wood, wire and fabric; now they are mostly aluminium. In the future they will increasingly be made out of 'composites', highly developed glass fibres and carbon fibre, which is stronger and lighter than metal. Burt Rutan in California has pioneered their use in light aircraft but bigger ones will use them soon.

ABOVE: The Rutan Defiant first flew in 1978; it can fly for 15 hours without refuelling; plans are available for pilots to build their own
OPPOSITE TOP: The Predator: a prototype composite agricultural aircraft
MAIN PICTURE: Beechcraft 2000 Starship: a corporate aircraft built with 'composites' and with accommodation for 7 passengers and a range of over 3000 miles

There was great excitement at Muroc but Boyd put a clampdown on publicity: the Air Force (it had been separated from the Army as an autonomous body in September 1947) wanted to get more information about high subsonic and supersonic flight first. On 26 March 1948 Yeager reached Mach 1.45; other pilots flew the X-1 too and the information they gleaned was fed to the designers of the F-86 Sabre to give America the first of the new generation of 'transonic' jet fighters which could operate around Mach 1 and just beyond. On 25 April a prototype F-86 flew beyond Mach 1 for the first time in a dive, the first combat aircraft to do so. In June the USAF announced that it had 'broken the sound barrier'.

Meanwhile the official speed record had been snatched from the Air Force by the US Navy in August 1947 with its experimental Douglas Skystreak D-558-I, with runs of 640 and 650 mph. On 15 September 1948 Maj. Richard Johnson USAF, in a standard F-86A, complete with guns, raised it to 670 mph. America now had an indisputable lead in transonic fighters. The Russians were not far behind: with their German scientists and Rolls-Royce jet engines, given to them by the post-war British government, the MiG-15 flew for the first time in December 1947. A resurgent France was next with the Dassault Mystère; Britain, inevitably, was last in the field with the Supermarine Swift and Hawker Hunter in 1954. In the interval the RAF was equipped with the F-86; Britain had paid a high price for dithering over high-speed research.

John Cunningham, the night-fighter ace, had replaced Geoffrey de Havilland as Chief Test Pilot at de Havilland. On 27 February 1948 he flew a Vampire to 59,492 feet, setting a new world altitude record for aircraft. He was accompanied up to 58,000 feet by John Derry in a DH 108. Derry was steadily pushing the DH 108 closer and closer to the speed of sound in a series of high-speed dives. On 6 September 1948, after climbing to 45,000 feet, he nosed down into a 30° dive. As the speed rose above Mach 0.9 the nose began to feel heavy, which he had experienced before; at 0.94 it started pitching up and down but he pressed on; at 0.96 there was a pronounced nose-down move and the DH 108 began to feel unstable. Instead of pulling out, Derry pushed the nose further down to increase speed and as he passed through 38,000 feet he went into the vertical and out of control. He managed to recover and pull out of the dive and at 23,500 feet the Machmeter went past Mach 1. John Derry was the first pilot in Britain to fly faster than sound.

In the US Muroc was becoming the Mecca for American experimental aviation. The Flight Test Center and the Air Force Test Pilot School were moved there from Wright Field in Ohio. On 8 December 1949 it was renamed Edwards Air Force Base after Capt. Glen Edwards who was killed in the crash of a giant experimental bomber, the YB-49 Northrop Flying Wing. The ramshackle col-

JOHN DERRY

After flying faster than sound, Derry continued to work as a test pilot at de Haviland; he also flew the company's aircraft at flying displays. Sonic booms became a feature of the Farnborough Air Shows and in 1952 Derry was scheduled to make one in a prototype swept-wing naval fighter, the DH 110. It broke up in mid-air, killing Derry and his observer; 28 spectators died and 60 more were injured.

TOP: VW120, the record-breaking DH 108. Only three were built and all crashed killing their pilots: the first prototype went to Farnborough and crashed in 1950; Geoffrey de Havilland was killed in the second; and VW120 suffered the same fate as the first
CENTRE: John Derry with VW120
BOTTOM: The fatal crash of the DH 110

lection of sheds and tents of the 1940s mushroomed into the heart of a huge experimental aircraft programme as America surged ahead of Europe in aeronautical research, as the USAF grew in size and sophistication, and as America became the dominant military and economic world power. On 25 May 1953 the first of a completely new generation of American jet fighters, the North American Aviation F-100 Super Sabre, made its first flight at Edwards. On 9 October the second prototype, flown by Lt-Col. Frank Everest, took the speed record from Britain's Neville Duke, who had recorded 727 mph the previous year in a prototype Hawker Hunter, and above the speed of sound for the first time, with 755 mph. (Up to 1954 world speed-record flights were made at low level; in that year the rules were changed to allow modern high-speed aircraft to break the record. Most flights took place at 36,000 feet.)

That was the official record. Unofficially there was as much rivalry between the USAF and the Navy for the absolute record set by their research aircraft. The Navy's Douglas D-558-II Skyrocket was air-launched like the Air Force's X-1. In 1951 it had set a staggering pace, overtaking Yeager's Mach 1.45 in May and pushing it up to Mach 1.88 by August. Then on 20 November 1953 Scott Crossfield, a civilian test pilot working for the National Advisory Committee on Aeronautics (NACA), flew the D-558-II past Mach 2, the first man to fly at twice the speed of sound.

Air Force pride was dented, especially since 17 December would be the fiftieth anniversary of the Wright Brothers' first flights and the whole nation would be celebrating that event with Scott Crossfield's milestone. The Air Force had a new research aircraft which was theoretically capable of flying at Mach 2.4 and Chuck Yeager decided that he would beat Crossfield's record before the anniversary. On 12 December he was launched from a B-50 bomber; the Bell X-1A was much more powerful than the X-1 and, with all rocket chambers burning, he shot up to level off at 80,000 feet, in a dark sky where the stars shone in the middle of the day. Controlling an aircraft in the rarefied atmosphere of the stratosphere was tricky; he reached Mach 2, then pushed the nose down into a dive and watched the Machmeter move to 2.2 then 2.3, over 1600 mph. At Mach 2.4 the X-1A began to yaw to the left and the right wing started to come up. Yeager corrected but in the thin air he was too late and in seconds the aircraft was tumbling out of the sky, throwing him around inside the cockpit. By instinct and coolness he managed to put the X-1A into a real spin from which he recovered at 25,000 feet, severely shaken but, by the time he glided into Edwards, back to his normal self. At midnight on 16 December he took off in a P-80 Shooting Star and landed at dawn on the 17th at Andrews AFB, Washington DC, where, just as the nation was paying its tributes to Orville and Wilbur Wright, the Secretary of the Air Force was able to present him as the Air Force pilot who

WINGED SPACECRAFT
America's reusable spacecraft, the Shuttle, made its first flight on 12 April 1981; nearly five years later the fourth Shuttle blew up on take-off and the remainder were grounded.

ABOVE: Take-off
LEFT: Landing
INSET: Kitty Hawk on the barrier beaches of North Carolina: the Wrights' historic site from 568 miles above the Earth's surface

THE QUEST FOR SPEED
Between 14 October 1947 and
3 October 1967 the speed of
aircraft went up nearly sixfold.
The X-1 flew at mach 1.06
(700.66 mph); the X-15
reached Mach 6.72 (4534 mph).

*ABOVE: The Bell X-1, named
Glamorous Glennis after Yeager's
wife*

*Charles 'Chuck' Yeager with the X-1A in which he
upstaged NACA in 1953 by flying at nearly Mach 2.5*

had beaten the Navy and NACA and flown at nearly two and a half times the speed
of sound.

The X programme spawned a whole series of research aircraft: the Bell X-5,
very reminiscent of the Messerschmitt P.1101, to investigate variable sweepback;
the Ryan X-13, an experimental vertical-take-off jet which sat on its tail; the
swept-wing Bell X-2 which flew beyond Mach 3 on 26 September 1956, killing
the pilot, Mel Apt, in the process. One project followed another and many ran
in parallel; the pulse at Edwards AFB scarcely missed a beat. On 8 June 1959
Scott Crossfield made the first glide flight in the North American X-15, an
aircraft conceived in 1952 to fly in excess of Mach 6.5 at heights above 250,000
feet, on the verge of space.

The two decades following the Second World War had been a period of
extraordinary advance in aircraft technology. In the Soviet Union the pace of
research was no less, and possibly even more, frantic. Its aircraft industry caught
up with America and even overtook it in some aspects of space flight. In response,

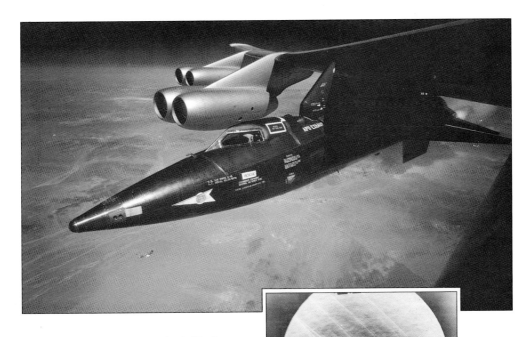

*The North American X-15 also holds the
world's altitude record for an aircraft:
354,200 feet (67 miles)*
*RIGHT: Shock waves: a scale model of the
X-15 undergoing tests at Mach 1.4 in a
supersonic wind-tunnel*

and whether wisely or not is still a matter of debate, by the early 1960s winged
aircraft had given way to manned rockets as a means of pushing further away
from the Earth. Britain lacked both the resources and the will to catch up; as she
readjusted to a much smaller role in the world and the RAF withdrew from its
imperial role and shrank, so research project after research project was cancelled.

Rivalry in space was strictly between the superpowers. In the Soviet Union
virtually everything went on in secret; in America it almost invariably went on
in public. The spectacle of aviation had not dimmed since Pilâtre de Rozier
ascended over Paris. When America came to launch the world's first winged, and
therefore reusable, spacecraft, the Space Shuttle, in 1981 over a million people
made the pilgrimage to Florida to watch and hundreds of millions more watched
on television. It went up like a rocket and came back to Earth like an aeroplane,
and when John Young and Bob Crippen landed at Edwards, a quarter of a million
people trekked out into the wilderness to see them while the rest of the world
watched on television.

CHAPTER EIGHT

COLD WAR WARRIORS

On 16 July 1945 the victorious Allied leaders – Churchill, Stalin and Truman – met at Potsdam outside Berlin to discuss the occupation of Germany. Four Zones were created to be occupied by the Big Three plus France and each was to control a sector of Berlin which was itself deep inside the Soviet zone. Road, rail and air links from Berlin to the other zones were also agreed. But when it came to the political systems in countries liberated by the Soviet Union there was no agreement; Stalin simply imposed a communist system in the east while America and Britain eventually installed elected governments in the west. Europe was divided. In the Far East, Japanese-held Korea was split at the 38th Parallel: Russian troops to the north and Americans to the south; each side imposed its political system. At Fulton, Missouri, on 5 March 1946 Churchill spoke for the first time of 'an iron curtain' which had descended across Europe, a barrier to freedom of movement and thought. In 1947 Bernard Baruch, a presidential adviser since the First World War and a friend of Churchill's, coined a new phrase to describe the hostility implied by the divided world: the Cold War.

In the early years America had a major advantage in the Cold War: it was the only country in the world with the atomic bomb and the long-range bombers to deliver it. It was the answer to the air-power theorists' dreams: an independent air force capable of deterring an aggressor from waging war against the US or her allies by the threat of retribution at least on the scale of Hiroshima. On 21 March 1946 a new force was created to carry out the new task: Strategic Air Command (SAC). To start with it was equipped mainly with conventional bombs; in 1946 there were only nine atomic weapons and only one unit capable of delivering them.

In 1948 the Western Powers began to return the government of Germany to its own politicians. A new currency was introduced, the Deutschmark, and it was to be valid in the three western sectors of Berlin. The Russians objected, seeing

OPPOSITE: Northrop F-20 Tigershark: US export fighter

it as a means of linking West Berlin with West Germany. In protest, on the day it was introduced the Soviet Army halted road and rail links between Berlin and West Germany. President Truman and Prime Minister Attlee decided to break the blockade, but rather than risk confrontation on the ground, on 26 June they ordered an airlift to supply the needs of West Berlin's $2\frac{1}{2}$ million people.

The first Cold War warriors were USAF and RAF pilots and commercial operators under contract. Day after day heavily-laden aircraft took off from West Germany and funnelled into the air corridors (policed by Soviet fighters). In fifteen months 277,264 flights ferried a total of 2,343,000 tons of supplies from coal to toothpaste; at its peak, one aircraft was landing in Berlin every 63 seconds. In 1949 the Soviets began looking for a way out and began talks and the blockade was finally lifted on 12 May.

Cold War tensions were at a peak during the Berlin Airlift and in that atmosphere SAC got a new commander. Lt-Gen. Curtis LeMay was a no-nonsense Cold War warrior, a firm believer in the concept of air power. Just around the corner were two new bombers: Boeing's 600-mph B-47 was America's first jet bomber, and the six-engined B-36, which had been designed during the war in case America needed to bomb Germany from across the Atlantic, became the world's first intercontinental bomber. To give them more range LeMay had Boeing KC-97 in-flight refuelling tankers.

Russia had no strategic bombers during the war; the Soviet Air Force, like the Luftwaffe, was dedicated to supporting the Army. In 1944 three B-29s force-landed near Vladivostok after a raid on Japan; they were handed over to the Russian designer Tupolev to copy and the result was the Tu-4, the Soviet Union's first heavy bomber, with a range of 1500 miles. It made its first public appearance over Moscow on 1 May 1947; on the same day the first Soviet jet fighters made their appearance. Then in 1949 the Soviet Union detonated its first atomic device.

On 25 June 1950 the North Korean Army invaded South Korea in a surprise attack. The United Nations Security Council debated the invasion the same day but the Soviet Union boycotted the session and so could not veto the decision to send a UN force, which was principally American, to support the South. SAC was not of any great value in such a war and for LeMay it was a sideshow: atomic weapons were out; there were few strategic targets; and his B-29s were used for the despised role of supporting ground troops. However, there was always a worry that the assault on Korea was really a diversion by the Soviet Union which might attack elsewhere; SAC was kept on full alert.

The main North Korean Air Force (NKAF) base was at Pyonyang and the UN force mounted a carrier-borne assault of piston-powered attack aircraft protected by fighters, including Grumman Panthers, US Navy jets from the USS *Valley Forge*. In a series of such raids the NKAF was reduced to a handful of aircraft. The UN had convincingly established air superiority. The North Korean troops in the South, without any air cover, were within range of P-80 Shooting Stars and veteran Mustangs from Japan. Massed troops were excellent targets for UN fighter-bombers with anti-personnel fragmentation bombs, napalm (jellied petrol) and machine-guns, and they gave vital support in checking the North Korean advance and forcing them to make any movements at night. On 15 September the UN commander, General MacArthur, made an amphibious landing, supported by carriers, at Inchon near the 38th Parallel. As the North Koreans retreated the Mustangs and Shooting Stars were merciless, attacking columns of undefended men and vehicles. Seoul was liberated on 26 September and by the end of the month the North Korean Army had been pushed back to its own half of the country.

But MacArthur did not stop at the 38th Parallel. He wanted the whole of Korea and he pushed north towards the Yalu River, the border between Korea and China. China warned that they would intervene and they sent an army of 180,000, supported by the Chinese Air Force, which launched an offensive on 25 November. Meanwhile on 8 November a force of B-29s escorted by Shooting Stars had set out to bomb two bridges across the Yalu. As they approached they were attacked by Chinese MiG-15s, the first Russian jet fighters. Faster than the Shooting Stars, they should have got the better of them, but the American pilots turned to meet the MiGs head on, splitting them up in disarray; one made the mistake of diving away from the battle and was shot down. On later raids the MiG pilots found a way through the Shooting Stars to shoot down four of the bombers.

In response the USAF committed its swept-wing transonic fighter, the F-86 Sabre, to the battle. The first Sabre–MiG dogfight took place on 17 December, Col. Bruce Hinton, leading a patrol of four, scoring the first victory. On the 22nd one Sabre was lost but at the cost of six MiGs, and that was the pattern of things to come. There was little to choose between the two aircraft; the difference lay in the pilots: the USAF had a high proportion of World War II veterans training and leading their new pilots, whereas the Chinese had little experience of jets and less of air fighting.

The Chinese army pushed the UN forces back, capturing Seoul again in early 1951. UN forces recaptured it in March and the line stabilised around the 38th Parallel. Negotiations for an armistice started in November, dragging on until 1953 when President Eisenhower was elected with a pledge to end the war. In the air the UN never lost the initiative or their prowess: 811 MiGs were shot down, 792 of them to Sabres, for the loss of 78.

*The F-84 Thunderjet was too slow to take on the MiG-15s but performed superbly in the
ground-attack role. INSET: The USAF accepted 6353 Sabres; they remained in service
until the early 1960s; large numbers were used by allied air forces*

The Korean War added new momentum to development of US military aircraft
and the defence budget continued to rise. America, and on a far smaller scale
Britain, concentrated on strategic air power; at its heart were new bombers, a
new generation of nuclear bombs and interceptor fighters. On 15 April 1952
'Tex' Johnston of Boeing flew the biggest bomber yet for the first time. The B-
52 Stratofortress had eight jet engines giving it a speed of over 600 mph, a ceiling

of over 50,000 feet and a range of 3000 miles; later versions would have ranges up to 10,000 miles. Then on 1 November America carried out a test explosion for a hydrogen bomb. The following year, on 12 August, the Soviet Union exploded its first hydrogen bomb in Siberia, and on 1 March 1954 America exploded its first full-sized hydrogen bomb, 750 times the size of the atomic bomb dropped on Hiroshima. The Soviet Union was also building long-range bombers: the Tu-16 made its first public appearance on 1 May 1954; the Tu-95, a giant turboprop with a range of around 7000 miles, flew in 1955.

The USAF was also getting a new generation of supersonic fighters for air defence: they were known as the 'Century Series'. The North American F-100 Super Sabre, the first fighter capable of exceeding Mach 1 in level flight, first flew in 1953; the McDonnell F-101 Voodoo with longer range was designed to escort bombers; the Convair F-102 Dagger was an experimental delta-winged interceptor which later became the F-106 Dart; the Lockheed F-104 Starfighter

The B-52 Stratofortress is still the backbone of SAC after three decades in service. Today its weapons are delivered by cruise missiles which are launched hundreds of miles from the target

was the utimate lightweight interceptor, capable of Mach 2 and of climbing to 40,000 feet in a minute; the Republic F-105 Thunderchief was designed for the interdiction role, hitting targets behind enemy lines with nuclear bombs. The Soviet Union had its new generation of fighters too: the supersonic MiG-19 and the Mach 1.6 Sukhoi Su-7 followed by the Mach 2 MiG-21 interceptor which flew for the first time in 1956.

The basic concept was a strategic bomber force equipped with hydrogen bombs, with supersonic interceptors to defend against a similar attack. SAC reached its peak in 1959: 51 bases circling Russia, over 3000 aircraft, of which 1854 were B-47s and B-52s dedicated to the nuclear role. But the race for faster bombers went on: in 1960 SAC got the B-58 Hustler, a complex Mach 2 high-altitude bomber, equipped solely to carry nuclear weapons. In 1961 the Soviet Union showed off its Mach 1.4 Tu-22 bomber.

However, before these two aircraft came into service, it appeared to many that the manned bomber would soon be obsolescent. On 1 May 1960 an American U-2 ultra-high-altitude reconnaissance aircraft took off from a US base at Peshawar in Pakistan on a CIA mission to fly across the Soviet Union at 80,000 feet at speeds approaching Mach 1, taking photographs well above the reach of fighters, and then land in Norway. The pilot was Gary F. Powers. Such flights had been going on in great secrecy for four years and though the Russians could see the U-2s on radar, until 1960 there was nothing they could do. Over Sverdlovsk, 1000 miles inside the Soviet Union, Powers saw a guided missile snaking towards him; in seconds he was hit; he baled out and was captured.

It was a graphic demonstration of the threat which missiles posed to all military aircraft. The threat was not new: missiles had been amongst the most valuable booty taken from Germany in 1945; both sides had been installing anti-aircraft missiles since the mid 1950s; and in 1957 Russia had launched the world's first orbiting satellite into space on top of a huge rocket. It was these larger rockets, which America had too, which threatened not only America but the very concept of the manned bomber; nuclear warheads could be delivered by intercontinental ballistic missiles instead.

In August 1962 a U-2 flying over Cuba brought back photographs showing crated components of missiles and military aircraft being unloaded. When President Kennedy saw the evidence he reacted decisively: SAC was put on high alert, with B-52s and B-47s armed and flying round the clock with in-flight refuelling. The Navy was ordered to quarantine Cuba and the Soviet Union was ordered to remove the missiles. On 27 October a U-2 was shot down by an anti-aircraft missile, but the following day more reconnaissance photos showed that the Russians were dismantling the sites. The crisis was over.

From the early 1960s the high-altitude manned bomber was in decline.

America's 'Minuteman' land-based ballistic missiles were put under the control of SAC, and at the same time submarine-launched ballistic missiles came into service with the US Navy, giving delivery systems for nuclear warheads from land, sea and air.

On 2 August 1964 North Vietnamese patrol boats attacked the destroyer USS *Maddox* in the Gulf of Tonkin off North Vietnam. In response President Lyndon Johnson authorised the US Navy to carry out air strikes against the patrol boat's base. On 7 August Congress gave the President the power to increase support to South Vietnam, which was facing infiltration from its communist neighbour in the North. The Gulf of Tonkin Incident had sparked off America's longest war.

America could have obliterated North Vietnam and there were calls from within the Air Force to mount a strategic attack against the North rather than commit more ground forces. Johnson and his Defense Secretary, Robert McNamara, decided on a graduated response, sending over ever-increasing numbers of ground forces in the hope of wearing down the guerilla opposition. Far from intimidating them, once America started committing combat troops in numbers, the North Vietnamese regular army escalated too, by moving south. Early in 1965 the USAF and Navy combined to mount 'Operation Rolling Thunder', a campaign against the North's supply network – its road, rail and military installations and the Ho Chi Minh Trail, a network of jungle tracks through Vietnam and neighbouring Laos. The plan was to start at a low level and gradually increase bombing, with the intention of bringing North Vietnam to the conference table. For political reasons, the pilots had to operate under severe restrictions.

The brunt of Rolling Thunder was borne by Navy attack aircraft and Air Force fighter-bombers. The Century Series fighters had not been designed to support the army, let alone in a counter-insurgency war; they were high-speed, high-altitude interceptors: they had to change tactics. The Mach 2 F-105 Thunderchief nuclear-strike aircraft became the medium bomber of the Vietnam War: instead of flying at high level at Mach 2, they flew low at under Mach 1, with high-explosive bombs and air-to-ground missiles. The F-100 Super Sabres escorted them to the North, and carried bombs, napalm and rockets themselves in the South. The Navy was better prepared: the carriers steamed 100 miles off the coast; Douglas A-4 Skyhawk lightweight attack aircraft could carry a good load over the short distances to the target; Grumman A-6 Intruders, highly sophisticated two-seaters with all-weather and night capability, did much of the precision work. There was also the new two-seater Mach 2 McDonnell-Douglas F-4 Phantom.

In April 1965 photo-reconnaissance over North Vietnam brought back evidence of SA-2 anti-aircraft missile sites being prepared. The Air Force and Navy

**WORKHORSES OF THE
VIETNAM WAR**
The Bell UH-1 'Huey' (*left*).
The flying truck of the
Vietnam War, on any one day
as many as 2000 would be
flying; 12,000 were built.
The Douglas A-1 Skyraider
(*top*) was 20 years old when
the Vietnam War started.
The McDonnell-Douglas F-4
Phantom (*above*) was used by
the US Air Force, Navy and
Marines as a fighter, a bomber,
for reconnaissance and for
close support.

proposed knocking them out before they became operational but Washington said no and soon flying over the North became deadly. On 24 July, when an SA-2 shot down a Phantom, the ban was lifted and the first raids on SAM sites came three days later. Electronics began to play an ever-increasing part in the air battle: US aircraft were fitted with a device which detected when an enemy missile had locked on and sounded an alarm in the pilot's headphones; the SA-2 was the size of a telegraph pole and once the pilot knew it was on its way he could look for it, and then dodge it by violent manoeuvres at the last second. US fighter-bombers already had 'Bullpup' air-to-ground missiles for hitting targets, but a more advanced missile, the 'Wild Weasel', came into service which locked on to the radar of the SA-2, homed in on the transmitter and blew up the site. The North Vietnamese learned to switch on their radars to draw the Wild Weasels, then switch them off.

In the South Navy and Air Force fighters and bombers could operate with much greater safety and they were always on hand to give fire support to soldiers on the ground. The problem was finding the enemy: there was no front line and guerillas hit their targets, then disappeared. Jets were often too fast for pin-point bombing, and early in the war propeller-driven Douglas A-1 Skyraiders of pre-Korean War vintage were brought out of retirement for really close work.

But the greatest direct assistance which aircraft gave soldiers on the ground in Vietnam came from helicopters. They were ideally suited to the type of war being fought: they could carry soldiers into action and evacuate casualties straight from the battlefield to hospital. When helicopter-borne operations were mounted the troops flew in transport machines while helicopter gunships flew alongside to spray the landing-ground with fire. By far the most numerous helicopter was the UH-1, the 'Huey'. The Boeing Chinook could lift as many as 44 combat troops or more supplies than a DC-3. Sikorsky HH-53 'Jolly Green Giants' had a particular mission which was to rescue pilots who had been shot down before they were captured; the first pick-up they made was just twenty miles from Hanoi. Mini battles were fought over downed pilots with colleagues shooting up the countryside while the helicopters flew in to lift them out.

On 31 January 1968, Buddhist New Year, the communists launched their 'Tet' offensive, simultaneously attacking most of South Vietnam's provincial capitals and 25 airfields. The offensive achieved some early successes, but for once the communists were out in the open and pilots had something to shoot at and bomb. Nowhere did the mistake of presenting themselves as targets for tactical air power show so clearly as at Khe Sanh, a US Marine outpost in the north-west of South Vietnam. Wave upon wave of North Vietnamese rushed the perimeter wire to be repulsed by the Marines. Holding Khe Sanh became an article of faith for the Americans, and it was only possible with massive use of tactical air power. On any given day there would be literally hundreds of aircraft involved, waiting for a call to bomb the attackers: Skyraiders, Skyhawks and Phantoms with bombs, rockets and napalm were directed on to troop concentrations by light observation aircraft flying lower over the battlefield; whatever the weather, above them B-52s would arrive after a six-hour flight from Guam to drop up to 30 tons of bombs each on a tiny area with radar-directed accuracy. Hercules transports and Chinook helicopters became Khe Sanh's lifeline, bringing in ammunition, food and reinforcements and carrying out the wounded, often under fire. The siege lasted 77 days before the attackers gave in and disappeared on 6 April. Khe Sanh was won and the Tet offensive as a whole was turned by the use of tactical air power.

US forces could lay waste paddyfields and defoliate jungle by the acre and destroy bridges and railways, but it seemed to Americans at home that it was an impossible war to win, however much firepower was used; after the Tet offensive there was little stomach left for the war and American involvement began to decline. Bombing of the North was restricted again and in October, shortly before America went to the polls to elect Richard Nixon on a promise to get America out of the war, it ceased altogether. American troops started to go home.

The C-130 Hercules provided a supply lifeline in Vietnam; it is operated by 57 air forces

By 1972 North Vietnam had rebuilt its ground forces, and on 2 April 120,000 troops launched a new offensive. It was election year in America again, but Nixon decided that a show of strength was needed. He authorised Operation Linebacker, a new bombing offensive against the North, this time without many of the restrictions which had been placed on pilots seven years earlier; it included industrial targets, oil depots, railyards and, crucially, airfields. On 9 May US Navy A-6 Intruders laid thousands of mines in Haiphong harbour to deny it to Russian ships. Linebacker lasted six months and left North Vietnamese communications in tatters, but it failed to break the people or the government.

They promised progress in the peace talks in Paris if the bombing stopped. Nixon stopped it on 23 October, shortly before the election. But the North Vietnamese stalled, and once he was back in office Nixon decided on another

Over 5000 Phantoms (left) *have been built, many of them for export to America's allies. US Navy A-7 Corsair attack aircraft* (below) *about to launch from USS* Independence

attempt to 'bomb them to the conference table'. This time he brought in SAC with a vengeance. Up to that point about 50 B-52s from Guam had been used, but never against the North. The number was increased to 200 and on 18 December they started Linebacker 2, a concerted attack on military targets in the Hanoi and Haiphong area. Ten airfields were put out of action and oil depots in the towns were set ablaze in virtually continuous bombardment. By the end of January a cease-fire had been signed and American involvement in the war was over. B-52s had flown over 700 missions and lost seventeen aircraft to SAM missiles; the MiG-21 fighters proved less successful, losing two to B-52 gunners without shooting down any.

As many had suspected, the cease-fire was really a way to get America out of the war once and for all. Two years later, in March 1975, the North attacked in force again, and without American air support the South crumbled. America had dropped over six million tons of bombs, more than was dropped by all sides in World War II, and lost 2700 aircraft and 4900 helicopters; it had won the battles, but it lost the war.

While the Vietnam War was at its height, the long-standing tensions between Israel and her Arab neighbours in the Middle East boiled over. Egypt was a client state of Russia and, like North Korea and North Vietnam, its armed forces were Soviet-equipped. By 1967 the Egyptian Air Force (EAF) was equipped with MiG-19 fighters, Su-7 fighter-bombers, the latest MiG-21 interceptors, and two squadrons of Tu-16 bombers. Chel Ha'avir, the Israeli Air Force, was equipped by France: Dassault Ouragon fighter-bombers, Mystère swept-wing transonic fighters, Mach 1 plus Super Mystères, and Mach 2 Mirage III interceptors equipped with cannon and American Sidewinder air-to-air missiles. In 1967 it had 300 jet aircraft but only the Mirage III had the very latest technology.

On 15 May President Nasser of Egypt began moving 100,000 troops into the Sinai Desert; on 18 May he ordered the UN peace-keeping force out. In Jordan and Syria armies were on the move preparing for an attack. On 22 May Nasser closed the Gulf of Aqaba to shipping heading for the Israeli port of Eilat.

Israel was surrounded. The Arab Air Forces had up to 850 aircraft including the Tu-16 bombers which could reach Tel Aviv; if the initiative was left to the Arab countries, then those air forces might be unleashed. The only way to avoid that was to establish air superiority as quickly as possible. Early in the morning of 5 June virtually the entire fighter and fighter-bomber strength of the Chel Ha'avir took off and flew, literally at roof-top level, under the Egyptian radar to attack airfields in the Sinai and the Nile Delta. The Egyptians had SA-2 missiles but they were useless at such low level; by mid-morning over 300 of the EAF's 350 aircraft had been destroyed, including the Tu-16s. In the afternoon the Chel Ha'avir turned its attention to Syria, Jordan and Iraq, adding another 120 aircraft to the tally. It was a textbook example of how air power is best used; by the end of the second day Israel had complete air superiority, and for the next four days the Chel Ha'avir was able to concentrate almost exclusively on direct support of the army. By 10 June the war was over and Israel had won.

The defeat in the Six Day War was a severe blow to Arab morale and to the prestige of the Soviet Union which had supplied the weapons. New supplies were sent quickly. Air defence was a high priority and SA-2 and SA-3 missile sites began springing up along the Suez Canal which divided the two armies. They were followed by heat-seeking SA-6 missiles on mobile launchers and SA-7s which were fired from the shoulder. By 1969 the EAF had 600 aircraft. Nasser died in 1970 and was succeeded by Anwar Sadat; he wanted Sinai back but for

ISRAELI AIR SUPERIORITY

After the 1967 war France stopped supplying aircraft to Israel; America stepped into the breach with Phantoms and A-4 Skyhawks. The Chel Ha'avir turned Israel into a local superpower, able to extend air power beyond her borders to retaliate against the Palestine Liberation Organisation for terrorist attacks; in 1981 F-15s escorted F-16s to Baghdad to bomb Iraq's nuclear reactor.

Egyptian MiG-21s destroyed on the ground

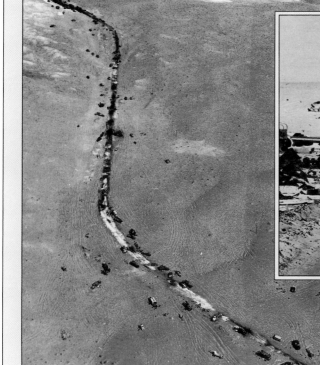

Roads in the Sinai after the Chel Ha'avir caught the unprotected Egyptian army in the open

the next three years, while Russia poured in resources, he planned joint action with Syria.

On 6 October 1973 250 EAF fighters and fighter-bombers streaked over the Canal to bomb Israeli positions; Israel was caught completely by surprise and the Egyptian Army was quickly across the Canal and advancing into the Sinai, taking its mobile SAM missiles with it. At the same time Syria launched an armoured offensive in the Golan Heights and pushed the Israelis back almost to the pre-1967 border. Israel was fighting a war on two fronts and the Chel Ha'avir was needed on both. When it attacked EAF airfields or the Egyptian army in the Sinai, it met a barrage of missiles for which it was unprepared; it was the same over the Golan Heights. In the first day the Chel Ha'avir lost 41 aircraft, around one in ten of its fighters, nearly all to missiles. To avoid the SA-2s and SA-3s around 2000 feet the Israelis flew low, where they ran into the heat-seeking SA-6s and SA-7s and anti-aircraft fire from Russian ZSU-23 guns. To establish air superiority over the Sinai they had to go for the missile sites and their pilots carried out near-suicidal attacks, diving vertically down on them; but the Egyptians had so many that they then ran the risk of being hit from another battery. The pilots worked out new tactics and Israel quickly developed new electronic countermeasures and, coupled with sheer courage, they eventually turned the tide in the air war and were able to go to the help of the hard-pressed army.

Both sides used up enormous amounts of military hardware, especially missiles (Egyptian soldiers fired 5000 SA-7s), and looked to their superpower patrons for help. Both superpowers started massive airlifts to resupply their clients. The Egyptian position looked grave and Secretary Brezhnev let President Nixon know that he was considering intervening directly. US intelligence confirmed that Soviet airborne divisions were being prepared for movement. Nixon decided that a shock was needed: he placed the whole of the US military machine, including SAC, on the highest state of alert short of shooting, and moved the US Sixth Fleet with its aircraft-carriers into the eastern Mediterranean, a clear threat to the stream of Russian transports. The superpowers leant heavily on their clients, and a cease-fire was established by 28 October.

America is still the world's leading country in military aviation. After the Century series came a new family of jets: the Grumman F-14 Tomcat, the McDonnell-Douglas F-15 Eagle interceptor, which can climb vertically to 60,000 feet in two minutes, the General Dynamics F-16 Falcon multi-role fighter, also flown by the Israelis, and the McDonnell-Douglas F-18 Hornet. The speeds of these aircraft have risen above Mach 2, but speed is no longer the only hallmark of a fighter: its electronic systems are the key to combat both offensively and defensively, and that is where America continues to lead the world.

BRITAIN'S HARRIER

Aircraft on airfields are highly vulnerable to attack. The British Aerospace Harrier does away with the need for a runway and can operate from farmyards, forests or roads (*below*). Britain leads the world in vertical-take-off technology and the Harrier is manufactured as the AV-8B in America. In the Falklands conflict Harriers played a central and decisive role, operating from ships.

CHAPTER NINE

THE JET AGE

On 25 August 1944 there was a lunch in London to celebrate the 25th anniversary of the first daily international air service, between London and Paris. Proposing the toast, 'The pioneers of British civil air transport', Sir Archibald Sinclair, the Secretary of State for Air, said that Britain, having been first, 'would never accept a secondary role in civil aviation'. Lord Brabazon of Tara, pioneer pilot, former Minister of Aircraft Production and lately chairman of a government Committee to look into Britain's post-war civil aviation needs, replied. He suggested that the Secretary of State visit America to see for himself their lead in military transport aircraft which would be suitable for civil use. He ended: 'If you are looking for a fall you are going the right way about it. That is all I have to say to you, Mr Secretary of State.'

Aircraft manufacture had become one of the largest industries in Britain during the war, producing 125,000 aircraft. But they were almost exclusively fighters and bombers. In the House of Lords in October 1944, Lord Brabazon repeated his concern that Britain would have nothing suitable for conversion to civil use after the war; he pointed again to America, where air transport was seen as part of the war effort. Scale of production had been one of the hallmarks of the Allied victory, and to meet the demand America mass-produced 300,000 aircraft of all types in under four years. Alone among the Allies she used her resources and her expertise to build transport aircraft on a grand scale. Up to Pearl Harbor Douglas had built 800 DC-3s for the civil market; by August 1945 they had turned out 11,000; at its peak the production line was producing one DC-3 every five hours. In 1945 America had a virtual monopoly in building transport aircraft.

With victory, transport aircraft were suddenly cheap. In 1935 a 24-seat DC-3 cost the airlines $110,000; in 1945 a demobbed pilot could buy one for around

OPPOSITE: Jet airliners have shrunk the world for millions of people. A Lockheed TriStar on approach to Hong Kong's international airport

Lockheed built 850 Constellations; they reduced the US coast-to-coast time to 10–11 hours. The bar and lounge in the Boeing Stratocruiser (inset) *was all part of turning long-distance flying from an adventure into a comfortable routine*

$1000, probably with some spare engines thrown in. If he could raise $10,000 he could buy the next size up in the Douglas family, a four-engined DC-4 with room for 60 passengers. Many ex-Air Force pilots did just that, setting up small airlines operating charter and freight services; many of them, in love with the idea rather than with the business of flying, also went bust. They were competing with well-established airlines, and in America where, far from declining, passenger traffic had risen during the war from four million in 1941 to over six million in 1945. In 1946 it surged to twelve million.

America had a new generation of piston-engined military aircraft which were eminently suitable to meet the demand. They were big, reliable, long-range, and pressurised to fly at 25–30,000 feet, high above rough weather. First came the Lockheed Constellation, which had actually been designed as a long-range airliner before the war. Under the dynamic leadership of Howard Hughes, TWA won the race to introduce it coast to coast, starting between New York and Los Angeles on 15 February 1946. United and American followed within a month, but with slower unpressurised DC-4s. In 1946 it was the Constellation which appealed to passengers but its supremacy was short-lived: on the same day it first flew the route, Douglas's answer, the pressurised DC-6, flew for the first time.

The crews of the great piston-engined airliners included two pilots, a navigator, flight engineer and radio operator. Electronics have simplified the systems to the point where two pilots can do all the jobs in many modern jets

It was a beefed up DC-4 with accommodation for up to 100 passengers in high-density seating; it was introduced on transcontinental routes in May 1947.

The principal asset of these two thoroughbred airliners was range: they could fly from New York to the capitals of Europe. Pan American and BOAC had operated flying boats across the Atlantic for military purposes throughout the war, but it was clear that the days of the gentle giants were numbered: people wanted to fly from city to city and in landplanes they could. When Pan American restarted passenger services to Britain in January 1946, it wanted to use Constellations. On 31 May 1946 the RAF station at Heathrow was opened to them; it had no buildings, let alone passenger facilities, and when the first Americans arrived at London's new international airport they found the immigration officials housed in ex-Army tents. Pan American had the route to themselves for a short time but it was no longer the 'chosen instrument' it had been in the 1930s; the buccaneering Juan Trippe had met a match in Howard Hughes of TWA, who started transatlantic services on 6 February 1946 with a New York–Paris flight, again using Constellations.

The North Atlantic was clearly the premier air route and European airlines were anxious to compete; what they lacked was the right aircraft. BOAC had a motley collection: the ubiquitous DC-3, ex-Luftwaffe Ju 52s, wartime flying boats, Avro Yorks, and Lancastrians, converted Lancaster bombers which carried mail and nine passengers in considerable discomfort to Australia. The Europeans were short of dollars but to compete with Pan American and TWA they would have to buy American aircraft; BOAC did buy eight 'Connies' and started a twice-weekly service between London and New York on 1 July 1946. Air France and KLM also ordered Connies.

In 1949 another luxurious American airliner came into service on the North Atlantic, the Boeing Stratocruiser. Britain still had nothing to compare with these long-range aircraft; Lord Brabazon's worst fears were becoming reality. Virtually all airliners operating in the western world were American. Their manufacturers had to compete for orders from airlines, who in turn were competing for passengers. Competition led to constant improvement of the products and that is how the manufacturers saw them: as products for a market.

In Britain the approach was different: discussion replaced competition, and under the Labour government there was no question of anything but a state-controlled airline. The policy was to buy British but there were few British aircraft to buy. In 1946 the long-haul and short-haul parts of BOAC were split, creating British European Airways. In Europe the premier route was London–Paris and to start with many of BEA's aircraft were American, mainly DC-3s, while Air France used DC-4s. But it was in short-haul operations that British aircraft first began to make their mark: in 1946 BEA ordered a total of 49 Vickers Vikings, a derivative of the Wellington bomber.

Britain still lacked new long-haul airliners because ordering new aircraft was a bureaucratic process involving government committees, a nationalised airline, numerous small manufacturers, the Treasury, and the Ministry of Supply which was actually responsible for ordering a prototype. Civil servants had only vague notions of aircraft as industrial products, or aviation as a competitive international transport industry. Cost, and with it the economic operation of aircraft, were not high priorities; prestige was. When the Brabazon Committee drew up proposals for post-war civil aircraft in 1943, its priorities were imperial, its framework was essentially monopolistic, and it simply took the benefits of technical progress and applied them to pre-war thinking. Air travel was still seen as the preserve of the very rich or government and colonial officials used to luxury and high standards of service; aircraft were designed accordingly. They were bold in embracing new technologies such as the jet engine, but the jet, they suggested, was purely for mail, a wholly pre-war concept.

Nothing symbolised British thinking better than the aircraft which was given the highest priority in 1945, the giant which carried the name of the Committee chairman, the Brabazon I. The specification called for a range of 5000 miles,

COMET – A FALSE START
TO THE JET AGE
The first Comet into
commercial service was the
ill-fated G-ALYP (*below*).
Left: The first substantial
section of 'YP' to be recovered
from the Mediterranean.
Inset: The wreckage
reassembled for the
investigation at the Royal
Aircraft Establishment at
Farnborough.

The prototype 707. INSET: *Photograph taken upside down over Lake Washington by the flight engineer*

BOEING – MASTER
AIRLINER BUILDERS
The Boeing 707 was one of the milestones in the progress of aviation. On one demonstration flight (*inset*) Tex Johnston, the 707 test pilot, rolled the aircraft for the benefit of airline customers. *Right:* Bill Allen greets Tex Johnston after he had set a new transcontinental record from Washington DC to Seattle of 3 hours 58 minutes in the 707. *Opposite:* The 747 Jumbo will be the principal long-haul airliner well into the next century.

Tex Johnston and Bill Allen

enough to fly from London to New York in a single hop at 35,000 feet pressurised to 8000 feet. The wingspan was 230 feet, twice that of the DC-6, yet its planned passenger load varied between 25 and 70. Bristol built a gigantic assembly hall at Filton and the runway had to be lengthened to 8250 feet which involved rerouting a major road and demolishing part of a village. The maiden flight on 4 September 1949 was an astounding spectacle; nothing like it had flown before and only days later the test pilot, Bill Pegg, took it to Farnborough to give thousands a treat with a low fly-past.

By 1950 Sir Miles Thomas, the man charged with turning BOAC into a paying proposition, had reduced its operating deficit from £7.75 million to £4.5 million by using more efficient aircraft. In 1951 he was heading for a surplus for the first time and the last thing he wanted was an expensive status symbol. But work on the Brabazon continued: a second prototype was ordered, this time a turboprop, jet engines driving propellers, but still there were no orders. Work continued until 1953 when the government announced its demise, giving the reason that neither airlines nor the RAF could foresee any use for it. Britain still had nothing with which to compete with America on the Atlantic; the Brabazon would have been wholly uneconomic against Constellations.

But 1952 and 1953 were watershed years for the British aircraft industry. Two jet aircraft made the world sit up and take notice: the turboprop Vickers Viscount and the turbojet de Havilland Comet promised to make Britain an international force in aircraft manufacture again. The Viscount had flown for the first time on 16 April 1948 and the prototype Comet on 27 July 1949. On 2 May 1952 the first-ever scheduled service in a jet-powered aircraft started from Heathrow when a Comet 1 flew to Johannesburg with 36 passengers, covering 6725 miles in stages in 23 hours 34 minutes. A year later, on 16 April, BEA introduced the Viscount to its routes for the first time. Both aircraft had enormous passenger appeal: they were smooth and quiet, and there was a certain cachet to jet travel – no other country had jet airliners of any description. Airline presidents from Europe and America beat a path to Vickers and de Havilland. Air France ordered twelve Viscounts; other airlines followed suit and in Europe the Viscount established Britain as a leader in air transport. Both BEA and Vickers benefited: European airlines which had to compete with BEA had to have the Viscount and between 1953 and 1957 430 aircraft were sold to sixteen airlines.

The Comet started commercial life with an even more promising future. As the Comet 1 ushered in jet travel, so Comets 2 and 3 were already being built for different airlines' needs and orders came from far and wide. But the breakthrough came when Juan Trippe placed a pilot order for three of the even longer-range Comet 3 which was aimed at the North Atlantic; Air India and BOAC ordered it too. A family of Comets was in the making and the possibilities seemed limitless; Geoffrey de Havilland, the old pioneer who had gambled on new technologies and leapt ahead of the opposition, seemed about to recoup huge dividends.

On 2 May 1953 a BOAC Comet was lost in a tropical storm near Calcutta; it was unexplained but it barely dented confidence in the aircraft. Then on 10 January 1954 Yoke Peter, the first Comet to go into service, took off from Rome bound for London; as it passed through 26,000 feet radio contact was lost in mid-sentence and minutes later fishermen saw it plunge into the sea off Elba. Sir Miles Thomas grounded all his Comets and they were subjected to minute examination; nothing untoward was found and they went back into service. Meanwhile the Royal Navy searched for wreckage. Just two weeks later an SAA Comet disappeared off Sicily and they were grounded again. The Navy then found and managed to lift most of Yoke Peter to the surface. Gradually the story was pieced together and the final, irrefutable evidence came when a whole fuselage was submerged in water and pressurised and depressurised over and over again to simulate operation. After the equivalent of some 10,000 hours' flying time, the fuselage burst, leaving a jagged gash eight feet long starting from the corner of a square navigation window. The combination of square windows, the thickness of the skin, the high speed at which the Comet reached its cruising altitude of 40,000 feet and the repeated pressurisation of the cabin had combined to cause the aircraft literally to blow up in flight.

None of the Comets on order saw commercial service. The Jet Age had made a brief and magnificent false start and during the interregnum the piston-engined stalwarts, the DC-6, its derivative, the DC-7, and a new generation of Super Constellations went on flying, went on selling and went on earning. But their days were numbered: within a few weeks of the grounding of the Comets, on 15 July 1954, Tex Johnston, chief test pilot at Boeing, made the maiden flight of their 367–80, better known as 'the Dash 80', a prototype jet military transport and in-flight refuelling tanker for the USAF. It was also a potential airliner.

Boeing's chairman, William Allen, had been at the Farnborough Air Show in 1950 and seen John Cunningham give a matchless display in the prototype Comet. There were a great many sceptics about the future of jet travel at the time, but Allen saw the future in the Comet and back in Seattle he set his designers a new task: a large jet aircraft suitable as a military transport, a tanker and a civil airliner to replace the C-97 and Stratocruiser. It would take time to develop the Dash 80 into an operational aircraft, so when the Boeing board met on 22 April 1952 he proposed that the company start work without orders, putting $16 million behind the project, a quarter of the value of the whole company. The board agreed and work started on what eventually became the Boeing 707.

CONCORDE

The supersonic airliner incorporates many technical innovations: the droop nose enables pilots to see on landing and take-off; the fuel is used to cool the cabin and it is pumped round the fuselage to maintain equilibrium in flight; the air is slowed down to subsonic speed at the intakes before it reaches the engines; the fuselage heats up in flight due to friction with the air and has to expand.

If Boeing took a gamble with its investment, it took no risks with the design and construction. The skin was over four times thicker than the Comet's and titanium 'tear stoppers' were placed at intervals to stop a crack developing. In March 1955 the USAF ordered 29 KC-135 tankers based on the Dash 80. But Boeing was no longer the only company with a big jet in the field. Donald Douglas, who had been in the forefront of civil aircraft since the DC-1 in 1931, had an even bigger one on the drawing-board, the DC-8. Juan Trippe of Pan American, who had cancelled his order for Comets, was instrumental in persuading Douglas to get into jets because he felt that it might be unhealthy for the airlines if Boeing had no competition. On 13 October 1955 Trippe ordered twenty 707s and 25 DC-8s; other airlines ordered DC-8s. Allen was forced into another gamble: he had the 707 redesigned, making it wider and longer and giving it the more powerful JT4 engine and the range to fly the Atlantic. Trippe increased his order and other airlines, both US and foreign, followed his lead. Soon Boeing was back on top with orders for its Intercontinental 707.

In the mid-1950s, after the success of the Viscount and the unfulfilled promise of the Comet, Britain once again lapsed into muddle. To fill the gap left by the Comets, BOAC used Constellations and DC-7s. Bristol was developing the Britannia, a four-engined, long-range turboprop which could cross the Atlantic in a single stage; but it was slow coming into service – there were teething troubles with the engines. De Havilland's Comet 4 had a speed of 500 mph and incorporated all the lessons of the crashes. Once the prototype was ready, John Cunningham, like Tex Johnston with the 707, was off flying the routes, appearing at displays and letting the airlines get the feel for it.

In 1955 the prototype of the Vickers V.1000 was also nearing completion. Unlike the Britannia and Comet 4, it promised to be a match for the big American jets in size, speed and range. It had been ordered by the Ministry of Supply for the RAF and BOAC, but neither would commit themselves: the RAF was being pressed to buy Britannias because it meant that jobs would be saved in Belfast where they would be built; and BOAC was adamant that supporting two British projects with orders was quite enough. At a press conference on 11 November 1955 the Minister, Reginald Maudling, announced the V.1000 had been cancelled. The prototype was 80 per cent complete; it should have flown the following year and could have been in service alongside the long-range versions of the 707. In response to a question in the House of Commons Maudling stated that 'BOAC is satisfied that it can hold its own commercially on the North Atlantic routes well into the 1960s with the Comet and the Britannia'.

Less than a year later BOAC realised that it needed the capacity of the 707 and asked the government for £44 million to buy fifteen of them: 'since no British aircraft would be available' they were needed to 'bridge the gap'. There was no gap, it was a precipice; it was too late to restart the V.1000, the jigs and tools had been destroyed. BOAC got 707s and Britain took another step backwards.

On 4 October 1958 two BOAC Comet 4s flew in opposite directions between London and New York. On 26 October Pan American responded with flights to London and Paris with 707s carrying over 100 passengers; it was still little more than a flag-waving exercise since they were not the aircraft intended for the route and it was a full year before the Intercontinental 707s entered service. But if the Comet won the race, it lost the battle for orders: on the ten major world air routes, only BOAC and Aerolineas Argentinas used Comets. On 27 May 1960 BOAC flew its first 707 service across the Atlantic; on 16 October it flew its last Comet service. Comet 4s were adapted for short-haul operations and used by BEA, some minor airlines and the RAF, but only 63 were built. The 707 did for the airlines of the world what the DC-3 had done in the 1930s; by the time the production line closed down in the 1980s, over 800 had been built and it had fathered a family of jet transports, giving America a second era of dominance.

Boeing and Douglas had both introduced smaller jets, the 727 and DC-9, to replace the ageing piston-engined aircraft on short-haul routes inside America; they were highly successful. Britain had produced similar short-haul jets in the Hawker Siddeley Trident and the BAC 1-11, and France had produced its first commercial jet in the Sud Aviation Caravelle.

Despite years of growth, in 1960–61 airlines round the world started losing money. Fares on scheduled routes were regulated and many airlines owned by governments were cushioned from the rigours of the market-place by subsidy. As a result there was little competition on ticket price; competition meant offering more lavish surroundings and higher standards of service to passengers. As the flag-carriers replaced their older aircraft with more and more jets, so many older machines were bought by charter operators, small airlines which offered cheaper fares to groups who block-booked and could therefore fill their aircraft at well below the scheduled prices. The scheduled carriers blamed the charter operators for pinching their business, but the majority of charter passengers were a new market, those who could not afford the scheduled fares anyway.

The scheduled carriers found that, as they reduced prices, so they filled more seats and improved profitability; it followed that if a bigger aircraft could be filled then the airline business would be even more profitable. As long-haul traffic began to grow again, the manufacturers looked to ways of enlarging the 707 and DC-8. The DC-8 was stretched to accommodate over 250 passengers. In Europe the thinking went in the opposite direction. It clung to regulated fares and the belief that there was a market for an exclusive service. Jet airliners were already flying not far below the speed of sound: rather than build a bigger airliner which would bring down fares for the masses, Britain and France had both been studying the possibility of building one exclusively for the first-class market which would halve the time across the Atlantic to 3–4 hours by flying at twice the speed of sound.

On 29 November 1962 Britain and France signed a Treaty jointly to build a supersonic airliner; the estimated development costs of £150–170 million would be split between the two countries; Concorde had been born. BOAC and Air France were practically captive customers but in June 1963 Juan Trippe, ever in the forefront of technical advance, bought options on eight Concordes. Hardly by coincidence, the very next day President Kennedy announced that America would build one too; America may have been piqued at the thought of Europe building the world's first supersonic transport (SST), but more importantly, Russia was doing the same. The American SST would be bigger and faster than Concorde or the Tu-144 and the US government would pay 75 per cent of the estimated $1.5 billion development costs.

But while America joined others in an international, government-backed race into the supersonic age of civil air transport, Boeing decided to build the biggest airliner in the world as a private venture. In April 1966 Bill Allen gave the go-ahead for the biggest-ever aeronautical project: a 490-seat airliner with a second deck underneath for cargo, which would fly at 600 mph. Boeing proceeded to construct the largest building in the world, 200 million cubic feet, alongside its factory in Seattle, and then set itself what looked like an impossible timetable – a first flight $2\frac{1}{2}$ years later on 17 December 1968, the 65th anniversary of the Wright Brothers' first flight. It got off to a good start when Juan Trippe ordered 25 747s at a total of $525 million. In December 1966 Allen heard that Boeing had also won the SST contract.

Building a supersonic airliner was a big step. Supersonic fighters were commonplace in the air forces of advanced countries, but even they only flew supersonically in short bursts on short flights. Concorde would have to fly at Mach 2 or over for hours at a time, with standards of safety at least as high as for subsonic airliners. Work on the two prototypes started in 1965. On top of the technical difficulties, work on the engine and airframe was going on in several factories in two countries and in two languages, which demanded a lot of goodwill on both sides of the Channel. Costs rose inexorably but the two governments continued to come up with the cash since they were bound by Treaty. The final development costs topped £1000 million.

In America the technical innovations for Boeing's 747 were different but no less daunting. They were able to make considerable use of the work done on the 707, and they had done a design study for a large military transport. In many ways the 747 was a scaled-up 707. The JT9 engines which were the key to its success were a pioneering task in themselves for Pratt & Whitney: $4\frac{1}{2}$ tons of high

AIRBUS

American companies have dominated the international market for airliners since the war. In the wake of Concorde, European aerospace companies formed a consortium with their governments' support to compete with America.

The main Airbus components are built in France, Germany and Britain and assembled at Toulouse. To ferry the pieces round Europe Airbus uses Super Guppies, gigantic freighters with a 39,000-cubic-foot hold, converted out of Boeing Stratocruisers in the 1960s to do the same job for the US space programme.

Airbus A310 (top left), *Airbus A320* (top right), *and Super Guppy* (above)

technology and new metallurgy inside an 8- by 12-foot tube. Production was a race against time and a battle against weight. The programme drew heavily on Boeing's and Pratt & Whitney's cash reserves but the first 747 was rolled out of the new factory on 30 September 1968, though it failed to make the anniversary maiden flight. On 9 February 1969 the world's press gathered at Seattle for the first flight of the 747; the weather was marginal but the test pilot, Jack Waddell, decided to go. The flight was planned to be over three hours and the take-off was uneventful, but a fault in the flaps caused him to come back early.

A month later, on 2 February, Henri Turcat of Aerospatiale, the French half of the Concorde partnership, took the prototype 001 out on to the runway at Toulouse for its maiden flight. Once again the world's press was in attendance and the world watched live as he took off for a low-speed 42-minute flight. Britain's prototype, 002, took off on 9 April.

Within the space of a month, the world had seen the biggest and the fastest airliners fly. The next stage for both was certification by the world's aviation authorities and getting them into service to start earning back some of the investment. Pan American was committed to the 747 and held options on Concorde, as did many other world airlines. Concorde, breaking many new technological barriers, would take several years, but Boeing hoped to get the 747 into service before the end of the year, although the test programme was beset by a range of problems, especially with the engines. The 747 finally received its passenger-carrying certificate on 30 December and Pan American made its inaugural flight to London on 22 January 1970. By then 190 had been ordered by 28 airlines. It remains the biggest airliner today and one of the most financially successful. Douglas and Lockheed brought out smaller wide-bodied jets, the DC-10 and the TriStar, with three engines each, but both ceased production leaving the 747 to dominate long-distance travel in the western world.

Boeing was less successful with its SST. After spending over $1 billion there was nothing to show but a mock-up; the technical problems of flying with passengers at close to Mach 3 turned out to be greater than expected. The SST was also attracting opponents in America: Senator William Proxmire believed that it was completely wrong to invest public money in civil aircraft and campaigned for such projects to be left to the market; more vocally, an environmental lobby believed that aircraft flying supersonically at 60,000 feet would do irreversible damage to the Earth's atmosphere by diminishing the ozone layer which protects us from the sun's radiation. In May 1971 President Nixon referred the project to the Senate, which looked at the books and, deciding that some $3 billion would be spent before a prototype would fly, cancelled it. The mock-up was auctioned and fetched $31,000 as a tourist attraction.

Concorde's test programme progressed steadily in the early 1970s, and it did well on the publicity circuit: wherever it went few could help being impressed by its speed, its technical excellence or simply its beauty. But the airlines wanted to see it in service first and not one turned its options into orders until 1972, when BOAC ordered five and Air France four. What was needed was a sale in the US, the imprimatur of Juan Trippe, who had been promoting and backing advances in technology for nearly half a century; but he had retired. Good or bad, Concorde was seldom out of the headlines: the environmental lobby, fresh from what it claimed was its victory over the American SST, promised that same reception for Concorde; economists probed the mounting development costs for some sign that it could still be profitable to operate, especially after the price of fuel shot up in 1973 after OPEC's crude-oil price increases. But Britain and France went on with the test programme, meeting opposition with argument and a barrage of publicity.

When Concorde was certified to carry passengers, nearly six years after the first prototype flight, it was still barred from the US. Instead British Airways (BOAC and BEA recombined again in 1972) and Air France opened supersonic services to Bahrain and Buenos Aires simultaneously on 21 January 1976 (BA had to fly subsonic over land for part of the way). In America the environmentalists focused on the noise of Concorde's engines which were louder than most airliners, but underneath the debate were two undercurrents: a protest at what was clearly a rich man's preserve – the price of tickets was well beyond everybody except the super rich – and the US aircraft industry was quietly hostile to Concorde because it had not produced an SST.

Concorde came to symbolise European technical progress like nothing else could. After protests came the hearings which established that it must be allowed into America and a trial service was authorised to Washington on 24 May 1976 and to New York on 22 November 1977. In both cases British and French solidarity was symbolised by simultaneous arrivals, Air France and British Airways Concordes taxying, droop nose to droop nose, in front of the airport buildings.

Economically Concorde is absurd. The production lines in France and Britain, if they can be called that, were shut down in 1979 after producing a total of sixteen aircraft. The two governments not only bore the cost of development but also poured millions of pounds into getting it into service. But they paid the bills, and unsurprisingly the chief benefits of Concorde's 'success' are political. Its most significant plus is that it revitalised European civil aviation and showed that on a technical level Europe was still in the van of progress. It also showed that two European countries could co-operate in a complex venture, which was vital since neither could have afforded to go ahead alone and the only way that Europe could meet the Americans on level terms was by co-operation.

In four decades jet aircraft have changed the world. By 1977 63 per cent of all Americans had flown inside the previous twelve months, and America's status as a superpower is derived in part from its dominant position in civil aviation. Jet travel is now commonplace for many people outside America. The biggest effect of the Jet Age has been to shrink the world for the tourist, and to open up previously inaccessible parts of the world for a few weeks' relaxation. The effect on the people in the new resorts thus created is dramatic, bringing them into contact with a culture quite alien to their own and sharpening the divisions between rich and poor. It has had an equally dramatic effect on business, creating and servicing new economic zones. A national airline remains a potent symbol of a country and in consequence a target for that country's enemies. The overall environmental effect of all these factors – crowded skies, hijacking, saturation of holiday resorts, air and noise pollution, land needed for airports, litigation after crashes and cultural imperialism – are steadily growing issues which will not go away. The airline and aircraft industry will need all the technical ingenuity it has shown so far and other skills to address them.

The Airbus A320 cockpit: the control column has now given way to a small side stick which operates the computer-driven 'fly-by-wire' control system; traditional instruments have been replaced by cathode-ray tubes with integrated displays of flight information

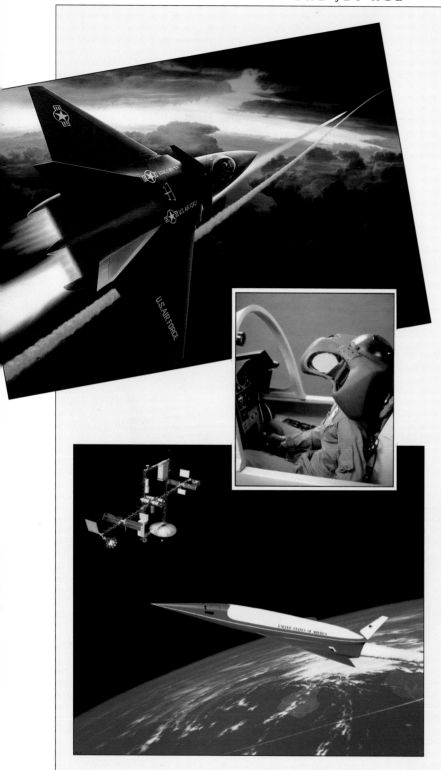

A GLIMPSE OF THE FUTURE
Left: The Advanced Tactical Fighter. The next generation of fighters will not be all that much faster than existing ones, but in design and systems they will be very much more advanced: composite materials and a shape designed to give a very low radar signature, and a highly automated cockpit to give the pilot beyond-visual-range capability while remaining agile enough to fight at close quarters.

Inset: The fighter pilot of the future may fight in a helmet like this experimental version; it gives the pilot all-round electronic vision and delivers information about his aircraft, the terrain he is flying over, enemy threats and targets and navigation straight into the eye-pieces and headphones. One day, such helmets may even read the electric impulses from the pilot's brain.

Bottom: America's National Aero Space Plane. Work has already started on the next great leap for aviation – into space. NASP has some similarities with the Shuttle except that it will take off and land on a runway; its first applications will be military, but sometime in the first half of the next century derivatives could be carrying passengers through space.

INDEX

Italic figures refer to
illustrations and
captions